A DEFENSE OF JUDGMENT

A Defense of
Judgment

MICHAEL W. CLUNE

The University of Chicago Press CHICAGO AND LONDON

The University of Chicago Press, Chicago 60637
The University of Chicago Press, Ltd., London
© 2021 by The University of Chicago
Published 2021
Printed in the United States of America

29 28 27 26 25 24 23 22 21 20   1 2 3 4 5

ISBN-13: 978-0-226-65396-9 (cloth)
ISBN-13: 978-0-226-77015-4 (paper)
ISBN-13: 978-0-226-77029-1 (e-book)
DOI: https://doi.org/10.7208/chicago/9780226770291.001.0001

Library of Congress Cataloging-in-Publication Data

Names: Clune, Michael W., author.
Title: A defense of judgment / Michael W. Clune.
Description: Chicago : University of Chicago Press, 2021. |
Includes bibliographical references and index.
Identifiers: LCCN 2020047074 | ISBN 9780226653969 (cloth) |
ISBN 9780226770154 (paperback) | ISBN 9780226770291 (ebook)
Subjects: LCSH: Judgment (Aesthetics) | Criticism.
Classification: LCC PN81 .C684 2021 | DDC 801/.95—dc23
LC record available at https://lccn.loc.gov/2020047074

♾ This paper meets the requirements of ANSI/NISO Z39.48-1992
(Permanence of Paper).

And the bull's head I took from mighty meats and bone
And stuck beside the wall.
Above the world I shook it, like a soldier of the truth:
Behold, here it is!
Here is that curly brow which once inflamed the crowds!
And horrified
I understood that I was seen by none:
That one must sow the eyes,
That the eye-sower must go!

VELEMIR KHLEBNIKOV,
"The Lone Performer," trans. Gary Kern

CONTENTS

Introduction

Professors of literature make judgments about value. Literary scholars—like art historians, musicologists, and classicists—say to our students: These works are powerful, beautiful, surprising, strange, insightful. They are more worth your time and attention than others. Such claims are implicit in choosing what to include on a syllabus. And yet for several decades now, professors have felt unable to defend these claims. So we pretend we're not making them. We bend over backward to disguise our syllabi, articles, and books as value neutral, as simply means for students to gain cultural or political or historical knowledge.

But this stance is incoherent. It's impossible to cordon off judgments about literary value from the practices of interpretation and analysis that constitute any viable model of literary expertise. If I judge that a certain poem contains a historical insight that can't be captured by a history textbook, or that a particular novel knows something about political dynamics that a student can't get from a work of political theory, then I'm making a literary judgment. I'm saying that it has value, not just for me but for everyone. This belief is what justifies my requiring students to read it. If I think students can get the same insights from a history or economics or sociology or philosophy course, then why should students bother with my class at all? Even a project as ostensibly value neutral as a study of the material composition of the paper that makes up a Shakespeare folio is indirectly dependent on our sense of the value and interest of Shakespeare's writing.[1] The absence of a defense of judgment paralyzes our capacity to defend our discipline at a time when it is threatened on many fronts.

Powerful barriers to acknowledging the central role of judgment in our professional practice have arisen over the past half century. They include the following widely shared, related but distinct, implicit and explicit claims:

- All judgments of artistic value are equal.
- Judgments of artistic value are subjective.
- Educated artistic judgment is primarily an expression of social status.
- Artistic judgment, expressing opinion rather than knowledge, is not a suitable subject of academic expertise.
- The artistic judgments of experts don't have a claim on those of nonexperts.
- The artistic judgments of experts necessarily codify racial and sexual prejudices.
- Expert judgments of art focus only on a narrow set of features—such as form—and are thus unable to capture much of the social interest of art.
- In an ideal world, expert aesthetic judgment may be a valuable professional practice; but more urgent problems face our society and our profession, so now is not the time to prioritize judgment.

This book proceeds by exploring each of these objections, challenging them, and reversing them in a positive account of literary studies as an institution of aesthetic education and literature professors as experts in literary judgment. At the outset, I want to highlight something about these objections that may not be obvious. They present as exemplifying the modern, rational skepticism of traditional practices. But in fact, each of these objections to expert artistic judgment depends on a concealed alternative vision. To reject the claims or possibility of expert judgment is not to believe there's no way to decide on the value of artworks. It is to endorse a historically specific system of value judgment, a system in which all values are determined by consumer preference and coordinated by the market. As I will show, the skepticism about judgment arises with market culture, and it is enthroned as an intellectually dominating position only with the late nineteenth-century transition from classical to neoclassical economics. The idea that the value of artworks is entirely a matter of subjective opinion, without any public standard, is so counterintuitive that even after a century it has succeeded not in repressing aesthetic education but merely in forcing it to wear the mask of hypocrisy.

Yet this mask is disabling enough. Beneath it, the judgments made every day in every classroom by every literature professor are largely cut off from meaningful critique by peers, and they run the risk of decaying into authoritarianism. Professors inherit a rigid and largely static canon, the residue of a time when aesthetic judgments were still part of the public work of the profession. Thus, a writer like John Guillory can, in his spirited defense of literary education, come up with no value term more substantial than *important*.[2] The "importance" of the classic works that still largely compose our syllabi is parasitic on a past regime of artistic judgment which we have no means of contesting on artistic grounds.

Among the losses inflicted by judgment's retreat is the profession's current blindness to its political possibilities. The fact that the resistance to judgment is historically and conceptually bound up with commercial culture endows the defense of judgment with an unprecedented political salience. The key feature of commercial culture in this context is its erection of consumer preference as the sole standard of value. Here it is useful to distinguish between two kinds of evaluative skepticism. Commercial culture, by declaring all preferences equal, gives me no reason to be skeptical about my own values. Aesthetic education, by denying that all preferences are equal, gives me reason to be skeptical about my existing values. The perspective developed by aesthetic education discourages me from identifying with the preferences generated by the commercial environment. It shows that it is possible to evaluate my existing values and to acquire new ones. By smothering this possibility under the aegis of a false egalitarianism, commercial culture prevents us from seeing aesthetic enrichment as a basic human need, which has the practical effect of restricting access to the wealthy. By hobbling aesthetic education, commercial culture restricts the creation and dissemination of alternative concepts, perceptions, and experiences.

That which has disabled judgment for so long has also transformed its meaning. To defend judgment today is not to express nostalgia for a regime before the consolidation of commercial culture. By carving out a space beyond the reach of market valuation, by defining a practice of valuing distinct from that of the market transaction, aesthetic education sets up a material barrier to market totalitarianism. We teach students to transcend preference by cultivating judgment. We foster and disseminate forms of life, thought, and perception repressed by commercial culture.

Accordingly, the first two chapters of the first part of this book, "The Theory of Judgment," analyze the resistance to artistic judgment as the most characteristic expression of the dogmatic equality of commercial culture. The third and fourth chapters then develop a positive model of expert judgment. What is expert judgment? What prevents aesthetic education from decaying into the dogma of expertise? What criteria can our students and publics use to test our judgments? In answering these questions, I describe actual, if often tacit, concealed, or even disavowed, practices in current literature departments.

These departments are under threat from the very market forces that have already succeeded in eviscerating their capacity to defend their social function. Yet we still possess, in the thousands of such departments across the nation and the world, an extraordinary institutional base, a large and increasingly diverse corps of teachers and students, and venues of dissemination ranging from academic journals and presses to the new venues of the internet. My defense of judgment is designed to liberate this existing community, with its skills, traditions, and protean valuing capacities. But the descriptive dimension of my project is linked to a normative dimension. The educational and political efficacy of our existing practices are severely hampered by the systematic misrecognition of their nature.

The second part of this book, "The Practice of Judgment," contains examples drawn from the ordinary work of the discipline. In part, this section is intended to supplement the necessarily abstract quality of the theoretical section with illustrations of exactly how professional judgment discloses new forms of thought, life, and politics. But to put its intention this way is to get the relation of the two sections backward. Each of the three chapters in part 2 originates in an experience of classroom teaching and predates my work on the theoretical section of the book. Far from being written to exemplify a theory of judgment, that theory is in fact derived from practice. Two of the three chapters were originally published in peer-reviewed academic journals. I take this to demonstrate the extent to which my argument doesn't call for a radical transformation of what we do in our ordinary professional practices, nor does it advocate a mode of criticism incapable of flourishing under existing modes of professional exchange. Through reflection on what we already do, I derive a model intended to defend, coordinate, and enhance that practice.

In each of the final three chapters, then, I show how a literary work sets up a new mode of perception, which constitutes an enrichment or expansion of our ordinary experience of the world. I then show how reflection on this mode of perception furnishes us with new ideas, the significance of which is established through engagement with extradisciplinary knowledge. Finally, this knowledge suggests a new moral or political application. The perceptual, cognitive, and political levels are imbricated; the practice of judgment is the practice of disclosing these dimensions. Aesthetic education isn't the process of getting students to like the same objects they formerly disliked. It is the practice of enabling them to see what had been concealed.

The writers I study—Emily Dickinson, John Keats, Gwendolyn Brooks, Samuel Beckett, and Thomas Bernhard—come from a range of historical and national backgrounds. Part of my understanding of judgment is that it doesn't necessarily involve the application of existing criteria to a work. I am interested in exploring the capacity of professional judgment to discover a new criterion for itself in the process of engaging with its object. If there is a single theme that links all these examples, it is their conceptual originality. Here I confess to a bias. The legacy of Kant's aesthetics has been nowhere more baleful than in the idea that aesthetic judgment must restrict itself to formal concerns rather than concepts. To correct this, my practical judgments lean in the opposite direction. It is from my encounter with the astonishing conceptual dynamism of literature that my account of ideas in literature, found in the theoretical part of the book, has its origin.

A note on terms. In the broadest sense, as will become evident, my theory of judgment represents a development and revision of David Hume's "Of the Standard of Taste." For reasons I will detail, this skeptical, empirical, and materialist model of judgment as the consensus of those best educated in the arts represents a viable model for aesthetic education in the way that later models—from Kant to Adorno—do not. But the historical distance between this Enlightenment theory of judgment and our modern professional practice means that I must subject key aspects of Hume's thought to something more like transformation than revision. Many of his terms fit awkwardly.

To take just one example: Hume formed his sense of the judgment of "the best critics" as the standard of taste at a time before the development of the university literature department. Thus, the modern concept of expertise—crucial for my argument—has no clear analogue in his writing. The term *judgment* itself presents perhaps a worse problem. In Hume's writing, in the writing of his eighteenth- and nineteenth-century successors, and in the connotations it has acquired in our own time, *judgment* often has the sense of a decision, explicitly pronounced, that is at odds with the processual, often tacit attentional qualities I seek to disclose. I ultimately decided to retain the term due to its strong association with valuing, an association not as forceful in such alternatives as *discernment*. I trust I make my understanding of the term sufficiently clear by the end of the first part of the book. But the reader should be warned at the outset that I intend to develop a sense for *judgment* that differs in some respects from the common understanding.

Similar problems attach to terms for the objects of judgment. As will become clear, I reject the narrowly formalist sense of *aesthetic* that is one legacy of Kantian thought, as well as the idea that *aesthetic* names a particular mental faculty. I variously qualify *judgment*—which I intend throughout to refer to the judgment of artworks—with the terms *aesthetic, artistic,* or *literary,* partly for their shades of meaning in different contexts. But my main reason for mixing the more usual *aesthetic* with these other terms is to signal that judgment is a process that attains its definition not from a prior decision about the subjective faculties or criteria that will be engaged but from features of the work itself. In expert judgment, as I will show, the subjectivity involved is in a meaningful but subtle sense a property of the object.

PART 1

The Theory of Judgment

✳ 1 ✳

Judgment and Equality

Among the most exciting critical developments of recent years has been the restoration of the aesthetic to a central position in the study of the arts. Critics have made diverse claims on its behalf, among which we might discern two widely shared themes. First, aesthetic education does not constitute a retreat from politics but rather a means of contesting the neoliberal hegemony of the market. Second, the critics' emphasis on the aesthetic's political potential is matched by an unprecedented refusal of aesthetic judgment.

On the surface, these two tendencies appear complementary: the internal refusal of a hierarchy of aesthetic value matches the external refusal of market value. And it is true that for our political imagination, animated by the master value of equality, aesthetic hierarchy has become indefensible.[1] I will argue, however, that the elision of judgment—which I understand minimally as the claim that a given work has value not just for me but for everyone—disables aesthetic education's political potential.[2]

When Fox News pundits rail against the elitism of artistic hierarchies while implicitly defending grotesque economic inequality, they register a logic that our field has yet to reckon with. Capitalist democracy is founded on the formal equality of individual choice, such that every effort to set up a positive value system counter to that of the market is vulnerable to the charge of elitism. As conservative populists know, the elimination of aesthetic judgment leaves market valuation the undisputed master of the cultural field. Critics' abdication of aesthetic judgment submits to this logic, making any strong distinction—let alone contest—between the realm of the aesthetic and the realm of the market impossible.[3]

The first section of this chapter will detail the double bind that paralyzes the advocates of a new aesthetic education. The second section will show how the commitment to equality undermines two strong recent attempts to save aesthetic judgment, by Sianne Ngai and Richard Moran. The following chapter will then suggest a way out of this dilemma. Marx's image, in "Critique of the Gotha Program," of a progressive politics freed from the strictures of dogmatic equality provides a framework for rehabilitating judgment. By loosening equality's hold on our political imagination, we free aesthetic education to erect a new world within the old.

*

Jacques Rancière is perhaps the most influential recent champion of "aesthetic education," and his work illustrates the challenge this project faces.[4] Shaped by the attack on the "aesthetic ideology" of the 1980s and 1990s, a generation of critics came to believe that tackling urgent social and political problems through art required bracketing or dismissing purely aesthetic considerations. In the face of this consensus, in *Aesthetics and Its Discontents* Rancière declares "there is no conflict between the purity of art and its politicization" (32). Art creates a "suspension [of] the ordinary forms of sensory experience" (23). Its political agency derives less from explicit commentary on social injustice than from a capacity to create a space in which the "relations of domination" are "suspended" (36). If our ordinary social world is corroded by many forms of linked domination, the space opened by the artwork is "the site of an unprecedented equality" (13).

Rancière's vision of a contest between an equal world of art and a dominated social world confronts a problem. Where exactly is the boundary between these two worlds? The problem becomes acute in deciding art's relation to the market. In capitalist society, art is entangled in the nets of the market—through distribution, advertising, the various forms of attentional manipulation associated with new technologies, and so on. If the market is the space of domination and the aesthetic the space of equality, at what point does one stop and the other begin? Rancière describes the effort to create a boundary as "the struggle to preserve the material difference of art apart from all the worldly affairs that compromise it" (42). But "this denunciation" of worldly affairs, he warns, "can easily be incorporated into political attitudes that demand to reestablish republican-style education to counter the democratic dissolution of forms of knowledge, behaviors, and values" (43). In an echo of his earlier work on education, Rancière here contrasts a "republican" effort to erect aesthetic hierarchies with a "democratic" commitment to equality.[5] Rancière also is expressing the paradox on which the effort to rescue the aesthetic for progressive politics founders. Aesthetic judgment is necessary to detach art from a dominated social world, but judgment entails a suspension of democracy. For example, the millions of people who made *The Apprentice* a massively popular work will want to know why some other work—*Madame Bovary*, perhaps, to take one of Rancière's examples—is better, freer, more truly art. To answer this question is to set one community's judgment—that of professors of literature, say—above the judgment of ordinary people. It is to say that *this* work, which you may not know or may not presently like, is worth knowing, is worth trying to like, is a more rewarding object of attention than *that* one. The kind of people who buy Rancière's books of course do not need to be convinced that *Madame Bovary* is better than *The Apprentice*. But if aesthetic education is to reach anyone not already in possession of it, this question must be answered. Yet Rancière refuses.

His awareness of the struggle to distinguish art from the market is trumped by his awareness that any strong distinction must violate the principle of equality. The claim that *Madame Bovary* is better— more worthy of attention—than *The Apprentice* must set itself against "the democratic dissolution of forms of knowledge, behaviors, and values." For most of his book, Rancière can avoid this unpleasant dilemma. If his few examples suggest a vague hierarchy of aesthetic value, one he can safely assume to be implicitly accepted by most of his readers, it is nevertheless the case that at no point is he called on to say that this judgment amounts to anything more than private opinion.

But in the passage I've quoted, he's brought to a halt before the problem. Faced with the struggle between art and the market, Rancière has two options. He can decide that it isn't important to establish a barrier between the market and the aesthetic. But this would violate his justified belief that in contemporary society, (1) the market is a realm of domination, and (2) aesthetic experience is thoroughly entangled with, and dominated by, market dynamics. His other option is to say that it *is* important to establish a barrier between the market and the aesthetic. But this would violate his commitment to equality, since it would involve placing aesthetic values in conflict with the empirical preferences registered, and shaped, by the market. This would in effect mean saying to someone: You should devote your attention to *these* works rather than *those*. You should attend like *this* rather than like *that*.

Rancière registers the necessity of distinguishing aesthetic value from market value. He warns of the danger of an education that would confront people with an aesthetic hierarchy. But he doesn't choose. The cost to his program is severe. The desire to open an alternative to a neoliberal world ruled by the market is neutralized by a rigorous commitment to equality. If no one can tell people why the works Rancière has in mind for democratic aesthetic education are better than the works they already know and enjoy, the transformation he imagines will simply fail to materialize. His impassioned advocacy of the aesthetic can amount to no more than an empty imperative: keep doing what you do.[6]

Rancière's perception of the conflict between the claims of judgment and those of equality distinguishes his work from what otherwise remains the most cogent analysis of art's effort to define itself with respect to its capitalist context: John Guillory's *Cultural Capital*. Revisiting Guillory's book will remind us of the stakes of aesthetic distinction, even as the distance of twenty-five years reveals the limits of his argument.

Guillory attacks the postmodern tendency to collapse the aesthetic and the economic. He responds in particular to Barbara Herrnstein Smith's influential argument that aesthetic value is simply a mask for subjective choice, and that aesthetic choices are no different from any other private consumer choice.[7] Guillory argues that aesthetic judgment, far from being identical to market value, is historically a "privileged site for reimagining the relation between the cultural and economic in social life" (xiv). Aesthetic value evolves in distinction to economic value. Traditionally, the aesthetic has been fastened to the process of class stratification through the dynamic analyzed by Bourdieu, in which the wealthy pursue cultural distinction through aesthetic education. The fact that aesthetic distinction is not equivalent to wealth is precisely what enables it to serve the interests of wealthy people seeking a noneconomic justification for their social status.

Bourdieu suggests that the progressive response to the traditional ties between class and aesthetic judgment is to forswear the latter. Guillory argues that this would deprive us of a potent means of carving out a space distinct from an increasingly omnipresent market. Aesthetic judgment is imbricated with social stratification, but this doesn't mean that it's simply an ideological illusion. Guillory warns us against the temptation to "deny" the "reality" of aesthetic experience due to the "revelation of its impurity" (336). Rather, we should seek to eliminate the barriers restricting those from certain class, racial, and ethnic backgrounds from access to the schools where aesthetic education flourishes. "A total democratization of access to cultural products would disarticulate the formation of cultural capital from the class structure" (337).

Some recent accounts of the aesthetic appear to have forgotten Guillory's insight, dismissing aesthetic judgment by simply identifying judgment with market value. Kristin Ross, in her study showing the potential of the Paris Commune for our current situation, makes this identification. The body set up by the commune to administer art "exhibited no concern whatsoever . . . over any aesthetic criteria." "They did not presume to act as judge or evaluator from an artistic point of view. . . . This is particularly important since it shifts value away from any market evaluation."[8] But as Guillory shows, to eliminate aesthetic judgment is in fact to rob art of its most enduring bulwark against total reduction to market value.

Rancière, however, in his reference to the "struggle" of art to free itself from "commerce," recognizes that aesthetic criteria can function as resistance to market valuation, much along the lines Guillory elaborated.[9] But he recognizes something else, something that eluded Guillory in 1994 and has made *Cultural Capital*, with its stirring and carefully argued defense of aesthetic judgment, among the best-known and least-influential works of modern theory.

Guillory sees the chief source of resistance to the distinctive social role of judgment in arguments, like Herrnstein Smith's, that collapse the aesthetic into the economic. But he seems also to sense some other source of resistance. "The strangest consequence of the canon debate has surely been the discrediting of judgment, as though human beings could ever refrain from judging the things they make."[10] The resistance to judgment seems to him like a baffling disciplinary failure, a sign of the immaturity of the field. "If literary critics are not yet in a position to recognize the inevitability of the social practice of judgment, that is a measure of how far the critique of the canon still is from developing a sociology of judgment."[11]

Rancière acutely perceives that the commitment to equality is the fundamental source of the objection to aesthetic judgment. Because Guillory doesn't fully grasp the nature of this problem, his book— despite its contribution to our understanding of the social role of aesthetic judgment—has failed to persuade many critics to recognize judgment's "inevitability" in our educational practice. But if Rancière understands the impasse, he offers no way out. The project of aesthetic education remains paralyzed by the conflict between judgment and equality.

Faced with this conflict, some critics opt to give up on the idea of aesthetic education as a means of transformation. Instead of seeing artistic experience as constituting an alternative to neoliberalism, they bend the aesthetic toward more traditional scholarly ends and see it as a way of generating knowledge about capitalism. This tendency has played a key role in shaping the recent reception of Adorno, the modern thinker who most forcefully conjoins the commitment to judgment with progressive politics. For Robert Kaufman, Adorno's "key idea is that significant facets of society remain to be discovered and that such discovery is unlikely to occur through use of society's own extant concepts for understanding itself."[12] The encounter with aesthetic form offers us the opportunity to generate a new, critical understanding of capitalism. "Criticism finally must work to enunciate . . . the contributions toward conceptuality that art, that mimesis, has nondiscursively offered."[13]

As Robert Hullot-Kentor observes, Adorno's commitment to aesthetic hierarchy as such has not been generally influential. Invoking Tocqueville, Hullot-Kentor suggests that the resistance to seeing some artworks as superior to others is "the fate of the mind most exclusively shaped by the pressure of equality."[14] Kaufman, for example, describes the value of a poet like John Keats in terms of the work's capacity to generate social knowledge. In this he follows not the Adorno who assails popular taste in "The Culture Industry" but the Adorno of *Aesthetic Theory*, who expresses the superiority of Kafka in terms of the level of critical insight his work offers. "Kafka, in whose work monopoly capitalism appears only distantly, codifies . . . what becomes of people under the total social spell more faithfully and powerfully than do any novels about corrupt industrial trusts."[15]

It isn't difficult to see why contemporary critics might want to convert aesthetic judgment into an epistemological claim. Canon formation has in the past been the scene of the exclusion of women and nonwhites. The correlation is sufficiently robust to suggest a problem with the very structure of judgment. That problem lies in judgment's incorrigibly subjective nature. Judgment claims a quasi-objective, universal dimension, but this is an illusion. Judgment is opinion. Aesthetic judgment will transmit without friction whatever biases exist in the persons who perform it. Objectivity is a pernicious illusion because any given judge—accused of bias—can simply retreat behind the mask of objectivity and pronounce his judgment—however interested it may appear to us—as purely aesthetic.

The kind of knowledge produced by the academic analysis of artworks, on the other hand, has a genuinely objective quality less prone to distortion by ideology, prejudice, or passing fancy. The opposition between knowledge and opinion is among the most durable of educational values, and it is unsurprising to see this distinction mobilized by judgment's critics. Thus Sam Rose, in his survey of recent work in aesthetics, describes a consensus among critics and philosophers against the "authoritarian effects" of aesthetic judgment.[16] The "elitist" character of judgment motivates a turn from evaluation to a vision of aesthetics as "epistemology."[17]

This turn from judgment toward knowledge production has come to define academic criticism. The entry "Evaluation" in *The Princeton Encyclopedia of Poetry and Poetics* reads: "Evaluation was once considered a central task of criticism but its place in criticism is now contested, having been supplanted to a large degree by interpretation."[18] When and why did this displacement occur? Northrop Frye's celebrated "Polemical Introduction" to *The Anatomy of Criticism* is often taken to be a watershed in the transformation of criticism from a dilettantish concern with the ranking of various authors to a serious academic discipline. Before returning to the contemporary opposition between judgment and knowledge, it might be worth examining this foundational text a little more closely.

Evaluation, Frye writes, "cannot be part of any systematic study, for a systematic study can only progress."[19] "In the history of taste . . . there are no facts" (18). Pronouncements like these appear, at a crucial moment in the modern discipline's consolidation, to consign judgment to an extra-academic, amateur practice. In this narrative, the subjectivity of judgment is what damns it, and later critics' awareness of judgment's anti-egalitarian tendencies only heaps more dirt on its coffin.

But if we read Frye carefully, a different picture emerges. Far from marking a retreat from aesthetic judgment, the "Polemical Introduction" is saturated with it. At the outset, in describing his critical "science," he refers to "its materials, the masterpieces of literature" (15). He contrasts "the profound masterpiece" with lesser works (19). He excludes from criticism a "sociology of literature" where "Horatio Alger . . . may well be more important than Hawthorne" (19).

How do we square Frye's disavowal of evaluation with such statements as these? Perhaps we have mistaken his attacks on debates about the relative rank of various authors for something they aren't. In key passages of the introduction, it turns out that Frye is contesting not judgment itself but the location of judgment in relation to the critical enterprise as a whole. "Although [criticism] takes certain literary values for granted, as fully established by critical experience, it is not directly concerned with value judgments" (20). "Comparative estimates of value are really inferences, most valid when silent ones, from critical practice, not expressed principles guiding that practice. The critic will find, soon and constantly, that Milton is a more rewarding and suggestive poet to work with than Blackmore" (25).

For Frye, aesthetic judgment represents a consensus that emerges from the work of critics, their daily practices of writing and teaching. This experience is the basis of the distinction between the "masterpiece" and the "lesser work." Explicit arguments about the relative merit of one poem over the other are doomed to irrelevance, simply because the evidence undergirding valid judgments is of a tacit nature. A work's value will be tested and proved only in the work of education—and this is a communal endeavor. The regime of evaluation which Frye confronts imagines that an individual's argument in an essay or lecture will convince people that poem x is greater than poem y. But such arguments can only be spurious, since the enterprise of aesthetic education itself constitutes the mechanism through which values are confirmed or rejected. A professor or student is convinced of the power of Milton or Gwendolyn Brooks not through argument but through the experience of working with the text, the experience of the space it opens, of the possibilities and insights it affords.

It turns out that Frye's criteria for aesthetic judgment—the consensus of the critical community—cannot be contrasted in any easy way with the criteria for knowledge advanced by another discipline-defining midcentury theorist. In judging the validity of a scientific proposition, Thomas Kuhn writes, "there is no higher standard than the assent of the relevant community."[20] The methods and practices of expert engagement with the material furnish the means of legitimizing judgment—means not always fully explicable to those outside that engagement. Or, to put the point differently: to show someone the grounds of a given judgment is to educate that person in the field's characteristic practices.

To say this is not to assimilate critical practice to scientific practice but simply to note that how judgment emerges from expert practice is identical for Frye and Kuhn. If this method isn't objective in a way that would render its verdicts unassailable by an observer, neither is it in any easy sense subjective.[21] Of course communities of knowledge producers, just like communities of critics, can and do manifest bias and thus serve as sites of oppression. The correction of biases requires a broad range of measures—from ensuring genuinely democratic access to contesting harassment in the lab or classroom. My point is simply that the model of institutional aesthetic judgment Frye proposes isn't necessarily more open to distortion than the institutional model of knowledge production often opposed to it in critiques of judgment.[22]

Frye's opposition between judgment and opinion isn't outside the mainstream of aesthetic theory in this respect. That history is dominated by accounts of judgment that fuse subjective and objective qualities, with Kant's "subjective universalism" the most influential example. Unfortunately, these accounts have often concealed or denied the role of learning and expertise in judgment, a tendency ultimately disabling for the project of aesthetic education. In her study of the aspirations for "aesthetic democracy," Linda Dowling traces a lineage from Shaftesbury's eighteenth-century aesthetics through Ruskin, Pater, and Wilde. She argues that Shaftesbury sets an unfortunate pattern by projecting his own aristocratic sense as a *sensus communis* held by all.[23] The later writers tend to understand aesthetic perception as characterized by "spontaneity, decisiveness, and unanimity of judgment."[24] The nineteenth- and early twentieth-century project of aesthetic democracy thus proceeds under the conviction that deep down, everyone possesses the same aesthetic sense as highly educated members of the upper class. This conviction gives way to revulsion at the discovery that the masses actually prefer shoddy culture industry products.

The tension between judgment and equality that Dowling discovers in this history represents a dead end. In assuming that the aesthetic sense is natural rather than a product of education, those who seek to widen the circle of aesthetic participation beyond the upper classes have no practical means of doing so. As Bourdieu shows regarding the analogous French legacy of Kant's aesthetics, the concealment of the basis of taste in education condemns expert judgment to the social role of signaling upper-class status.[25]

The moral of this story is not that the project of aesthetic democracy should be abandoned, but that we should recognize that aesthetic judgment must be shaped through education. David Hume's empiricist, skeptical aesthetics represents a model for such education. He begins "Of the Standard of Taste" by noticing a problem. Philosophers, attempting through reason to discover a universal rule of beauty, fail, and they take their failure to signal "the impossibility of ever attaining any standard of taste."[26] Yet as soon as it comes to actual comparisons between poets, between Milton and Ogilby in Hume's example, "the principle of the natural equality of tastes is then totally forgot . . . it appears an extravagant paradox" (136).

Hume argues that the philosophers are correct that we can never discover rules that will enable us to measure the quality of artworks. But this doesn't mean there is no standard of value, no public means of ascertaining artistic quality. He searches for this standard in the sources of the widespread assent to such judgments as that elevating Milton over Ogilby. Skillful critics, he argues, can discover qualities in artworks that will be endorsed by others. Judgment isn't an innate capacity so much as a skill to be cultivated. One might begin with a certain talent, a certain sensitivity to aesthetic distinctions, but "nothing tends further to increase and improve this talent, than *practice* in a particular art, and the frequent survey or contemplation of a particular species of beauty" (143). "Strong sense, united to delicate sentiment, improved by practice, perfected by comparison, and cleared of all prejudice, can alone entitle critics to this valuable character; and the joint verdict of such, wherever they are to be found, is the true standard of taste and beauty" (147).

Hume's aesthetics rests on an epistemological stance, developed in his wider philosophy, that is skeptical of our capacity to ground our values in claims about the nature of either the world or the mind. We find the ground for our practices not in fundamental principles or rules but in experience. Both Hume and his successor Kant argue that we cannot discover aesthetic qualities with reference to objective properties. Judgment expresses a cognitive and an emotional reaction. Yet for Hume, these reactions can be honed, educated. You can be better or worse at aesthetic judgment, just as you can be better or worse at playing the piano; the way you become an expert is through practice.

But why should we take the consensus of these cultivated critics for our standard of taste? The superiority of Milton to Ogilby is not, as Hume himself acknowledges, subject to a proof of the kind that demonstrates that one rectangle is larger than another. In a crucial passage, he suggests an empirical criterion for assessing the validity of the claim critics make on us. "Many men, when left to themselves, have but a faint and dubious perception of beauty, who are yet capable of relishing any fine stroke which is pointed out to them" (149). We accept those most knowledgeable and experienced in the arts as our guides because they can show us features of the work we're currently unable to see. And once we see those features, we will tend to assent to the critics' qualitative judgment. As we will see, Hume's test represents the ultimate ground of the aesthetic expert's claim to superior judgment.

A "fine stroke" isn't an objective quality. No one can create a set of rules for identifying a brilliant, surprising, or memorable passage of description in a novel, say, or color in a landscape painting.[27] Analogizing to other skilled behaviors can clarify some aspects of Hume's understanding of the critic's situation. A skilled jazz pianist improvising on a tune doesn't perceive the keys before her the same way I—a deeply unskilled pianist—would. I might see a set of keys whose alternating black and white colors are associated with a scale of notes while I hear the beat of the drum and the notes picked out by the bass. The pianist, however, might perceive a certain pathway among the keys. In a fusion of spatial and temporal perception, she notices an illuminated route, darting between dark patches on the piano and the pattern beat out by the drum.

After she performs the lick, I can see it, I can hear it. I have a glimmer of what it is like to perceive the piano keyboard as she does, to grasp the possibilities in the keys, in the accompaniment, as she grasps them. She has pointed the "fine stroke" out to me. What am I perceiving as I begin to grasp what she saw in the musical situation of the jazz standard? It wouldn't be quite right to call it an object. It might be better described as a mental state—the perception of the keyboard from a certain perspective—a perspective from which forms of beauty previously concealed from me become tangible.

The situation alters slightly, but preserves its key features, if we now imagine the scenario in terms of a jazz critic trying to show the pianist's "fine stroke" to a beginning listener. Perhaps the critic begins by playing a variety of performances of the jazz standard. Perhaps she points out certain differences in the improvisations. At first, I the novice hear only noise.[28] Gradually, the noise resolves into definite shapes. At last, there's a pulse of excitement as I hear *something* in a certain sequence of notes. I couldn't say exactly what it is. I might not be able to show it to someone else yet. But there's a glimmer—I am perceiving the notes from a perspective from which their beauty is evident.

And this is Hume's test of the claim of the expert critic—that she can enable others to see what she sees. Like Frye, Hume doesn't imagine that judgment consists of an argument about value. Note that what's involved is not taking an object, which at first the novice feels indifferent to, and causing him to react positively to it. The object itself changes. Before, there is no "fine stroke" anywhere in the object; afterward, it's there. The novice can see and hear it. He can almost put his finger on it—except "it" isn't a thing—it's not an object at all but a curious fusion of subject and object: a situation, viewed from a certain angle, from the background of certain knowledge.

As Peter Jones writes, for Hume "a critic's task includes the determination of the spectator's viewpoint, and he justifies his verdicts by bringing others to perceive and think of the work in the way he has."[29] Hume thus offers us both a description of the qualities and training of an aesthetic expert and a means of testing that expert's claim on us. "Hume hopes to show that criticism is a factually based, rational, social activity, capable of being integrated into the rest of intelligible human discourse."[30] Here I want to highlight something not often emphasized in accounts of Hume's aesthetics. Value for Hume is tacit, bound up in the recognition of the relevant features. The modern fact/value distinction weakens in Hume's account of judgment. The fineness of the stroke is disclosed along with its salient features. The fineness isn't something added to it, a "value" placed on top of a form. To perceive the form is also to perceive its value.

Here Hume is in some ways close to Kant, whom he influenced. But two salient differences between the thinkers account for Hume's superiority as a model for modern aesthetic education. First, Hume is more explicitly focused on the experiential, educational basis on which the capacity to discern the relevant features of aesthetic objects is grounded. For both, the standard of judgment lies in a viewer who perceives the object adequately. But where Kant emphasizes disinterest, a stripping away of the subject's experiential ties to the object, Hume emphasizes education, the adequate background of knowledge, practice, and experience possessed by "the best critics." This leads to a second crucial difference. For Kant, the aesthetic names a mental faculty, the capacity to perceive forms that please "without a concept."[31] Thus, he uses natural and artificial objects as examples indifferently. For Hume, on the other hand, taste is defined by its objects, the kinds of artifacts critics learn about to sharpen their judgment. This distinction has important implications for aesthetic education. Kantian aesthetics will be hobbled by the insistence that ideas aren't part of a properly aesthetic judgment, and they will remain shackled to a restrictive set of criteria. In addition, by focusing on the innateness of the aesthetic sense, Kantian aesthetics will remain vulnerable to the kinds of interpretations Dowling describes among nineteenth-century advocates of aesthetic democracy. Hume's empiricism, on the other hand, doesn't involve circumscribing the aesthetic in advance but encourages a view of critical expertise as the ongoing process of the discovery of new criteria adequate to new kinds of artworks.

I will return to the structure of Humean judgment in my third chapter—with particular emphasis on the conceptual work needed to bridge the gap between the eighteenth-century critic and the twenty-first-century academic expert. But for now, we can see how Frye's discussion of judgment in terms of a consensus of professors follows Hume's account of the standard of taste as the consensus of "the best critics." Similarly, a broadly Humean model underlies the fusion of subjective and objective in Frye's practice of tacit judgment, in his claim that criticism consists in the disclosure of features of a work that tacitly establish its value. A closer example comes from Frances Ferguson's account of the practice of the New Criticism. This criticism is "objective not because it claimed to produce impartial accounts of what poems really meant, but because it identified the literary work's existence with the evaluation of it, and essentially claimed that seeing a literary work is impossible without seeing that it is good ('that it works')."[32] The New Critics for Ferguson literally incorporate judgment into the object of aesthetic education. She shows us, more explicitly than Frye, how judgment becomes a tacit component of expert practice.[33] By the mid-twentieth century, then, we find a robust tradition of aesthetic education in which the standard of value lies in the consensus of appropriately educated experts, and in which the aim is to endow students with the capacity to ascertain the validity of those judgments in their own experience.

This survey, preliminary as it is, should be enough to demonstrate that reducing aesthetic judgment to subjective opinion distorts the history of aesthetic education. Judgment increasingly looks to us like mere opinion because art increasingly looks to us like a consumer good. As Guillory showed in his critique of Herrnstein Smith, to insist on the merely subjective dimension of judgment is to assimilate the aesthetic to the economic, by making judgment indistinguishable from consumer choice. But as my brief discussion of Frye and Ferguson suggests, the tradition offers us a range of alternatives to assimilation.

Yet every effort to reclaim the tradition of aesthetic education shatters against our commitment to equality. Joseph North's 2017 book *Literary Criticism* throws this paradox into stark relief. "The aesthetic that lies at the root of the discipline, and continues to mark its central practice of 'close reading,' is properly understood as part of a longer history of resistance to the economic, political, and cultural systems that prevent us from cultivating deeper modes of life."[34] Aesthetic education represents both a politically meaningful break with neoliberal education and a means of access to "the deepest and richest forms of human life," forms increasingly denied students by capitalism (76). The task for the Left consists "not just of taking reckonings in the service of some longed-for victory in the future, but of taking action in the present: of fighting to develop for ourselves and others lives at least minimally rich in capabilities and sensitivities" (19).

North argues that today, we face "the problem of creating a true paradigm for criticism—the problem of how to build an institution that would cultivate new, deeper forms of subjectivity and collectivity in a rigorous and repeatable way" (127).

The bulk of his book is devoted to exploring how, in the modern history of literary studies, a "scholarly" antipathy toward aesthetic education won out over the "critical" cultivation of sensibility. "Over the last three decades, departments of literature have indeed exchanged the project of evaluative criticism . . . for the very different project of 'cultural analysis'" (10–11). North acutely diagnoses the practical politics of the resistance to aesthetic education, writing that "attacks on 'elite' taste [are] the very stuff of right-liberal discourse" (85) and pointing out that neoliberalism operates as a "democratic leveler of aesthetic distinctions" (86). He exposes the notion that "challenging the aesthetic privileging of literary texts over nonliterary texts, and of some literary texts over others, somehow amounted to a challenge to 'privilege' itself" (93). "The discipline needs to justify its [literary] objects of study, not just its method for studying it" (108). He refers sarcastically to the "democratic, enlightened, free market view" animating the resistance to aesthetic value within academia (86).

Yet even as he describes the complicity of egalitarian attacks on aesthetic distinction with neoliberalism, North finds himself compelled to repeat these attacks. This is most notable in his account of his book's central figure, I. A. Richards, the critic he takes as a model for the kind of aesthetic education we need. He points to the American New Critics' reception of Richards as the moment of criticism's abandonment of a vital, politically effective pedagogy. The New Critics' cardinal sin was their commitment to aesthetic judgment. Richards's practical criticism was "redirected so that the emphasis lay not on cultivating the aesthetic capabilities of readers, but on the cultivation of aesthetic judgment" (15). North assails Cleanth Brooks and William Wimsatt's "enthusiastic embrace of the idea of a hierarchy" (46) as "profoundly antidemocratic" (53) and contrasts it with Richards's suspicion of hierarchies (46).

Even a passing acquaintance with Richards's work will show the absurdity of imagining him to be an opponent of hierarchy. *Principles of Literary Criticism* is saturated with judgment; the erosion of aesthetic standards motivates the book. "The problem presented by the gulf between what is preferred by the majority and what is accepted as excellent by the most qualified opinion has become infinitely more serious. . . . For many reasons standards are much more in need of defense than they used to be."[35] In the same passage, Richards refers to "a collapse of values, a transvaluation by which popular taste replaces trained discrimination" due to "commercialism" (31). His judgment moves beyond aesthetic works to target the kinds of experiences that works afford. "Criticism, as I understand it, is the endeavor to discriminate between experiences and evaluate them" (viii). The arts "record the most important judgments we possess as to the values of experience" (27). "The arts, if rightly approached, supply the best data available for deciding what experiences are more valuable than others" (28).

North makes several awkward attempts to square Richards's pronouncements with his own desire to see Richards as the avatar of a mode of aesthetic education in which aesthetic judgment is minimized. "The whole thrust of [Richards's] project . . . is to try to find a way to assess works of art on the basis of the potential value of the experiences they could make available to their audiences. At times, it is true, this had even led him to make blanket statements about the superiority of some forms or modes over others." But North adds that "the majority of the time," Richards emphasizes the "provisionality of any kind of aesthetic judgment" (*Literary Criticism*, 44). In another passage, he quotes Richards's statement that "to set up as a critic is to set up as a judge of values" and disavows it, writing that "this emphasis is not typical of Richards at his best" and is "irredeemably elitist" (*Literary Criticism*, 47–48). Sometimes North tries to separate Richards's efforts to judge experiences from the effort to judge artworks, focusing on Richards's dictum: "it is less important to like good poetry and dislike bad, than to be able to use them both as a means of ordering our minds" (*Literary Criticism*, 46). Yet Richards's constant distinction between good and bad poetry, while valued primarily for the project of enabling students to discriminate between better and worse forms of life, provides this project with its structure and its practice.

We must ask why so careful a critic as North—who has powerfully made the case for aesthetic education, who is acutely aware of the links between neoliberalism and the rejection of judgment—should struggle painfully when presenting his book's model for aesthetic education. Why must he bend over backward to deny the obvious—that aesthetic hierarchy and aesthetic judgment are central to Richards's practical criticism, that such criticism is inconceivable without them?[36] I believe that the solution to this puzzle can be found in North's conception of politics. He describes the kind of politically attuned criticism he finds in Richards as holding great promise for "the left proper: those whose commitment to equality runs beyond the boundaries set by the liberal consensus" (*Literary Criticism,* 8). There is an irony here. Because he defines the Left as being more committed to equality than liberals, it becomes impossible for him not to succumb to the attacks on "elite taste"—attacks that he elsewhere describes as "the very stuff of right-liberal discourse" (*Literary Criticism,* 85). And to make common cause with the "free market levellers" of aesthetic distinction is—as Richards saw—to make it impossible to challenge the market's values with those of the aesthetic (*Literary Criticism,* 86).

In a passage from *Principles of Literary Criticism,* Richards himself provides us with the clearest possible expression of the tension between equality and judgment:

The expert in matters of taste is in an awkward position when he differs from the majority. He is forced to say in effect "I am better than you. My taste is more refined, my nature more cultured, you will do well to become more like me than you are." It is not his fault that he has to be so arrogant. He may, and usually does, disguise the fact as far as possible, but his claim to be heard as an expert depends upon the truth of these assumptions. (*Principles,* 31)

The expertise of the aesthetic educator offends egalitarian values. Richards describes his development of a psychological theory of value as a means to "defend accepted [expert] standards" against egalitarian attacks (*Principles,* 31). North sees this theory as a "materialist" alternative to aesthetic judgment, when in fact Richards intends it as a means of justifying judgment, a way of replying to judgment's critics. Richards attempts to show why the experiences provided by the works picked out by expert aesthetic judgment are psychologi-

cally superior to those associated with inferior works. Whether the
defense provided by such a theory, even when buttressed by contemporary neuropsychology, can ameliorate the egalitarian objection is
an open question. My own work with neuroscientists suggests that
we are very far from having useful scientific means of describing the
kind of complex, higher-order psychological states associated with
different aesthetic experiences.[37] But for our present purposes, the
significance of Richards's turn to psychology is that it represents a
weapon in a struggle between judgment and equality which aesthetic
education cannot avoid.

*

Two recent efforts to defend judgment evidence a growing awareness
that aesthetic education is untenable without an underlying commitment to the superiority of some works over others. Examining
Sianne Ngai's and Richard Moran's arguments will reveal the depth
of the challenge faced by those who wish to reconcile the claims of
judgment and equality. If, as we have seen, epistemological concerns
have tended to eclipse evaluation, Ngai analyzes the "interesting"
as a form of aesthetic judgment that meditates between "criticism
as appreciation and criticism as knowledge."[38] Following Stanley
Cavell, she wants to use "nonaesthetic, concept-based judgments to
support feeling-based aesthetic judgments" (118). In tracking the use
of the term *interesting* from the Romantics through the present, Ngai
notices how "the epistemological intensification of the interesting . . .
seems accompanied by a noticeable dropping off of its affective tem-
perature" (141). This leads Michael Fried and others to diagnose an
apparent "relinquishing of value judgments," an abdication of "critics'
role in the creation of new art-consuming publics and the shaping of
public taste" (156).

But Ngai thinks the interesting's evasion of judgment is only apparent. "Judgments of value . . . and acts of communicating information
[are not] mutually exclusive" (163). Critics like Fried mistake claims
about artworks as "merely interesting" for an abandonment of value
for two reasons. The first involves the affective weakness of the judgment. Ngai describes the interesting as "the blandest or most non-
committal form of praise" (117). It is associated with "ambivalence,
coolness, or neutrality" (135). Contrasting it with wonder, she notes
"there is a sense in which the interesting simply means surprising—

but not that surprising" (133). The interesting is "common and mild," not rare and intense.

And yet Ngai argues that the interesting "keeps the possibility alive that a critic might actively continue the task of influencing public judgment, if only in the modest way of suggesting that some texts are more worth paying attention to than others" (171). To call a work interesting, after all, is to claim that it rewards attention, that it is a superior use of scarce attentional resources. "The interesting thus shows a way out of the deadlock between the old idea that the task of criticism is to produce verdicts of artistic greatness or mediocrity . . . and the more generally accepted idea that criticism should try to purge itself of aesthetic evaluation entirely" (171).

This brings her to the second reason why the subtle aesthetic dimension of interesting—as opposed to its obvious conceptual dimension—has been overlooked. Ngai argues that the interesting "subordinates the moment of judgment" to the "presentation of evidence on its behalf" (167). "We tell people we find works interesting when we want an opportunity to show them our evidence or to present support for our claims of value in a way capable of convincing them of their rightness" (170).

This account of the interesting brilliantly answers the egalitarian objection to judgment in several ways. First, the mildness of the claim—"surprising but not too surprising"—conceals the invidious aspect of judgment when compared with claims that a work is "powerful," "important," "beautiful," or "sublime." One of the major accomplishments of Ngai's work—exemplified here by her analysis of the interesting—is to discern value claims even in aesthetic judgments that seem to eschew them. Thus, she shows how "interesting," rather than being descriptive and value neutral, constitutes a minimal value claim—that this work is "more worth paying attention to than others" (171). The mildness of its claim assuages the egalitarian objection, even as it implies a hierarchy of works worth attending to.

Second, and more significantly, the idea that aesthetic judgment can be justified through explicit reasons neutralizes the strongest egalitarian objection. If I say that Ralph Ellison's *Invisible Man* is more worth your attention than *Gone with the Wind*, I am saying, as Richards put it, "I am better than you. My taste is more refined, my nature more cultured." But if I go on to tell you exactly why reading Ellison is a better use of your time, then I have made the reasoning behind my judgment transparent and accessible. If you accept my judgment, you are in the position of agreeing with my reasoning rather than submitting to my authority. If the interesting does in fact work this way, then the claims of equality and judgment, knowledge and appreciation, have been reconciled.

But does it? Ngai's account invites two objections. To see the first, lesser objection, consider the claim that a given text is more worth paying attention to than others is not in fact "modest" (171). Imagine a student, possibly incurring debt in order to attend college, trying to choose from an array of course offerings. The choice of a literature class involves a significant investment of time and effort. This course is unlikely to fare well against the rival claims of biology or economics if it advocates for its objects of study as "surprising, but not too surprising," or as providing a "mild and common" pleasure. To the extent that the mildness of the professor's judgment assuages the egalitarian objection, it also risks failing to motivate the attentional investment it solicits.

A deeper objection concerns the second part of Ngai's argument—that the expert can supply reasons for her judgment to nonexperts "in a way capable of convincing them of their rightness" (170). To begin to see the problem here, consider that Ngai's examples of the interesting are works by Philip Glass, Henry James, Sol LeWitt, and Ed Ruscha. Imagine trying to provide reasons to a nonexpert for why one of these artists is interesting. Any explicit reason for James's interest, for example, will involve establishing his relevance in a relatively esoteric context of which the interest is implicitly assumed. Ngai tells us that *Portrait of a Lady* is interesting because it matches the "stylistic indeterminacy" of the novel form with a compulsively interested female heroine (137). Because this reason assumes familiarity with and interest in the history of the novel form, it will have force only with those who have been educated in literary studies, people who, precisely by virtue of that fact, don't need to be persuaded that Henry James is an interesting novelist.

At stake here is the question of expertise. Expertise isn't generally compatible with the capacity to quickly show just anyone the evidence for our judgment in a manner capable of convincing them. The opposite is more often the case. This is why writers like Frye and Kuhn point to the consensus of the community of experts as the standard for assessing the value of a given work, study, or claim. The fact that 97 percent of climate scientists agree that climate change is both real and human caused is far more powerful than the description of particular scientific findings. Even if those findings are described in terms superficially accessible to laypeople, we understand that the expert assessment of their value depends on a variety of background knowledges, practices, and norms that are concealed from us.

Yet the historian Jerry Z. Muller argues that the nature of expert knowledge regularly arouses "the populist, egalitarian suspicion of authority."[39] He describes one powerful contemporary expression of this suspicion in the "metrics fixation" afflicting the managers of many of our institutions. University administrators, for example, have fallen victim to the egalitarian fantasy that we can make the grounds of expert judgment accessible to just anyone. The workings of a discipline should be instantly discernible by managers, taxpayers, and legislators through easy-to-grasp measures of productivity and impact.

The egalitarianism of what Muller calls "metrics fixation" conceals a struggle between administrators and a "professional ethos based on mastery of a body of specialized knowledge acquired through an extended process of education and training" (9). The special knowledge of many fields is simply not susceptible to easy encapsulation in a chart or graph anyone can understand. Muller identifies many contexts—from health care to education—in which decisions based on metrics led to disastrous outcomes. He describes how the proponents of metrics understand professional judgment "as personal, subjective, and self-interested" (6). Yet the poor record of metrics as a replacement for expert judgment leads him to see a source of its appeal beyond the egalitarian ideology espoused by its proponents. "Metrics fixation leads to a diversion of resources . . . towards managers, administrators, and those who gather and manipulate data" (8).[40]

Certainly, experts must be accountable to the publics they serve. But we should be suspicious of any program of accountability that involves demanding simple, measurable justifications for expert practices. As Kuhn writes, experts' attempts to give reasons for their positions ultimately become "circular": scientists who operate under the reigning paradigm think x is of interest because features of the reigning scientific paradigm mark x out as interesting.[41] This is not to say that scientists don't have good reasons for their judgment; it's just that these reasons are often derived from the background assumptions grounding their practice, and this background itself isn't defensible through logical argument. A similar insight underlies Frye's Humean argument that providing an audience with the explicit reasons for Milton's superiority to Blackmore will inevitably fail, not because such reasons don't exist, but because they are embedded in the engaged practice of the critic, operating against the horizon of various background assumptions and norms.

Ngai admits that the interesting starts as the judgment of "those in the know," but that this judgment aims at "enfranchising" outsiders by displaying its evidence (*Categories*, 172). Yet if enfranchisement depends on showing the reasons for judgment, and if those reasons require a background familiarity with the knowledges, norms, and practices of the relevant field, then to show someone your reasons for why Sol LeWitt or Henry James is interesting becomes equivalent to giving that person an aesthetic education. And the significant investment of time and energy that this education requires—both at its outset and for a long time afterward—is channeled in submission to the expert's judgment that *these* works are particularly rewarding objects of attention. The syllabi of an English department's curriculum, for example, codify this submission. Hume's test—the students' assent or dissent with respect to expert judgments—comes after an educational process, not, as Ngai imagines, before.

"Interesting" can operate as Ngai imagines it only within a community sharing at least some degree of aesthetic expertise. Most readers of her book, an academic monograph published by a university press, will find her reasons for the interest of Ed Ruscha's work if not convincing then at least of a kind capable of convincing. But should the expertise of judge and audience differ to any marked degree, the egalitarian objection is likely to arise. If I have been denied the benefits of an aesthetic education, then I am likely to experience the claim that Sol LeWitt, Henry James, or Philip Glass is more worth attending to than the reality TV shows I enjoy as the critic's declaration: "My taste is more refined . . . you will do well to become more like me than you are." For me to be convinced by the critic's aesthetic judgment that Henry James is interesting will mean not that I have evaluated the reasons for that judgment, but that I've decided to undertake an education that promises to endow me with her cultural capacities. By fusing appreciation and knowledge, the interesting may sometimes conceal the contradiction between equality and judgment, but it cannot resolve it.

If Ngai's account of the interesting attempts to save a public role for the critic, Moran takes a more radical approach, concluding that judgment can only be saved by surrendering its claim on anyone other than the individual judge. Kant's celebrated definition of the judgment of beauty "involves the claim that the object in question *merits* this response, *deserves* one's attention, and that everyone attending to it properly *ought* to respond with pleasure and admiration."[42] Moran then asks, "What could it be that places this person [the one who has made the aesthetic judgment] in a position to issue such a demand?" (67). He concludes that no reasons can justify this expectation of universal assent to one's judgment, which renders the Kantian aesthetic subject simply an "overbearing person" (77).

Yet Moran, unlike such earlier critics of Kantian judgment as Herrnstein Smith, recognizes that aesthetic judgment is something more than personal preference. Kant's belief in the "subjective universality" of judgment responds to a real feature of the aesthetic encounter—the sense that the object in question makes a claim on me. "Something we are prepared to call beautiful is not measured purely by its ability to satisfy our given desires, but is rather something to which our pleasures or desires themselves may be answerable, may need to conform themselves to, or be instructed by" (78). Here Moran, guided by Proust's depiction of encounters with beauty, articulates the transformative quality of the aesthetic. His championing of "the idea of a demand on the subject that is independent of one's current likes or dislikes" is crucial for any meaningful concept of aesthetic *education* (81).

But Moran insists that the aesthetic object can place a demand only on *me*, that this demand is incorrigibly personal, tending to isolate the individual rather than draw her into communion with others. In some ways, Moran is responding to a real weakness of Kant's account. Without Hume's empiricist emphasis on the kind of education necessary to disclose the relevant properties of the artwork, Kant's expectation of universal assent can indeed seem unreasonable. But in attacking Kant's idea that an aesthetic judgment expects universal assent, Moran doesn't argue that no grounds for aesthetic agreement are possible. He doesn't, in other words, argue that judgments can never have collective force. Were he to make such an argument, one could simply reference intersubjective models of judgment like those described by Hume, Frye, or Ferguson. Instead, Moran turns to John

Rawls, the great liberal philosopher of justice, to argue that it isn't *important* to agree on aesthetic judgment. "The reasons that make such an agreement necessary in questions of justice do not obtain for judgments of value" (85). He cites Rawls: "It is, in general, a good thing that individuals' conceptions of their good should differ in significant ways, whereas this is not so for conceptions of right" (85).

A classic liberal structure—in which values are coordinated by markets, while equal rights are enshrined in law—undergirds Moran's approach to the aesthetic.[43] I will shortly take up the relation of equality to markets in greater depth. But for now, we can see an important consequence of Moran's critique of the trans-subjective character of aesthetic judgment. If one feels the need for a system of values *outside* the market's, then it becomes "necessary" to find a way of endowing aesthetic judgment with trans-subjective weight. Moran's argument assimilates aesthetic value to economic value—differences abolished in the singular reference to "value"—which differs for different individuals and is coordinated at the collective level by various market or market-like structures.

This assimilation happens at a relatively abstract level. Moran's analysis of the internal dynamics of aesthetic judgment, as we have seen, strongly distinguishes them from consumer preference. But the assimilation has the effect of quashing the kind of consensus about aesthetic judgment that would make aesthetic education a collective space resistant to neoliberal domination. Aesthetic value for Moran is an instance of the kind of value that doesn't require intentional coordination but that may safely be left to the private sphere of free exchange. It would be as inappropriate—as unnecessary, as "overbearing"—for me to urge your attention to a particular book that captivates me as it would be for me to demand that you buy the same brand of dishwasher I use. Moran understands—and beautifully expresses—the transformative qualities that make aesthetic objects different from dishwashers. But this transformation, like the value of a consumer good, is to be felt and enjoyed by isolated individuals.

If I've been emphasizing how Moran's reasoning neutralizes the aesthetic's capacity to serve as a strong counter to the market, I don't mean to imply that this is a problem for Moran. Indeed, from the liberal perspective he adopts, even so mild an imposition on equality as the judgment that Proust *deserves* your attention is a greater evil than the inability of the aesthetic to resist market valuation. The liberal tradition supports the effort to correct egregious market inequities through policies that leave the market itself intact. The significance of Moran's essay for our purposes lies in its careful demonstration of how the rejection of trans-subjective judgment is equivalent to the rejection of a boundary between aesthetic and economic value. This presents a problem for anyone who hopes aesthetic education might serve as a space resistant to the colonization of experience by the market.

Ngai's attempt to save aesthetic judgment from "the generally accepted idea that criticism should try to purge itself of aesthetic evaluation entirely" depends on a form of justification that, as we have seen, reconciles equality and judgment only when performed between equals in aesthetic expertise. Moran, by contrast, produces an account that reconciles the claims of equality and judgment at the cost of abandoning judgment's claim on others, thus undermining its educational role and destroying its potential to offer an alternative form of value. The failure of these efforts to break the deadlock between judgment and equality in aesthetic education suggests that this deadlock is at least as acute now as in Richards's time. Perhaps it is time to change the terms of the problem.

❊ 2 ❊

Judgment and Commercial Culture

Is there a way of reframing our commitment to equality such that it ceases to block the creation of a sphere of value free from the market? The identification of progressive politics with the commitment to equality is today so absolute that we must return to the nineteenth century to recover a sense of the possibilities for revision. Tocqueville, in *Democracy in America*, famously declares that "for equality . . . [Americans] feel an ardent, insatiable, eternal, invincible passion."[1] He suggests a gap between our reasoned commitment to eliminate inequity and a structure of feeling that in certain circumstances distorts that commitment.

Several recent scholars have drawn attention to Tocqueville's sense of some consequences of this "passion" germane to our topic. Matthew Maguire writes that in *Democracy in America*, "modern equality and democracy [are] in tension with the energies of the proud imagination, and thus with a vital dimension of human freedom."[2] Aaron Kunin suggests an intractable opposition between equality and art-making itself. "The knowledge of how to write a good poem depends on gifts that are personal and circumstantial. . . . Hard work counts for something, but, in the end, the art of poetry may be a truly unworkable inequality. It's unfair."[3] Kerry Larson finds in Tocqueville a premonition of I. A. Richards's belief that a democratic suspicion of expertise hobbles the project of aesthetic education. "Americans are continually brought back to their own judgment as the most apparent and accessible test of truth"; the passion for equality resents the pretensions of intellectuals.[4]

Tocqueville perceives some of the symptoms of the association of equality with commercial culture, which lies at the heart of the contemporary paralysis of progressive aesthetic education. Maguire quotes Tocqueville's belief that "equality . . . does not destroy the imagination; but it limits it and only allows it to fly while skimming the earth."[5] In the context of *Democracy in America*, to be earthbound is to have one's imagination circumscribed by a thoroughly commercial social order. As Arthur Kaledin renders the insight in *Tocqueville and His America*, "In the democratic society it is the taste of the marketplace that dominates and shapes literature."[6]

But Tocqueville, for all his awareness of equality's imbrication with social dynamics that militate against human cultivation, doesn't see those ties as disabling equality's benign influence. We must turn to Marx for a more uncompromising account of the logic equating the domination of the marketplace with the principle of equality. This account has not been easy for even some Marxists to accept. But the contemporary crisis of aesthetics—involving the very possibility of a form of value beyond market determination—makes a reckoning with Marx's analysis of equality inevitable. Equality—so crucial to the ongoing liberal struggle against discrimination—is not, for Marx, a weapon that can be turned against capitalism itself. A politics is radical, as Marx says in his "most detailed pronouncement on programmatic matters," precisely insofar as it is willing to abandon equality.[7]

In the letter subsequently published as "The Critique of the Gotha Program," Marx quotes from the proposed program of the German Social Democratic Party: "The proceeds of labour belong undiminished with equal right to all members of society."[8] He attacks this recourse to the principle of equal rights. The very idea of equality—of different values, objects, and persons being reducible to a single level—is an artifact of capitalist exchange. As Marx argues in *Capital*, the sphere of market exchange, "within whose boundaries the sale and purchase of labor power goes on, is in fact a very Eden of the innate rights of man. It is the exclusive realm of freedom, equality, and property."[9] In his assessment of the Gotha Program, he extends this analysis to suggest that the commitment to equality smuggles capitalist dynamics even into an ostensibly radical movement. "Equal right here is still, in principle, bourgeois right."[10]

The commensurability of all goods and persons is a fiction of the market. "Equal right is still constantly stigmatized by a bourgeois limitation." "Unequal individuals (and they would not be different individuals if they were not unequal) are measurable only by an equal standard insofar as they are brought under an equal point of view, are taken from one definite side only" (530). Market valuation reflects a process of equalization, a reduction of diverse forms of life and activity to the universal solvent of money. While the demand for equal distribution of the products of labor represents an "advance" for social welfare, the forms of social and individual life would still suffer the flattening and abstraction intrinsic to bourgeois existence (530).

What political consequences follow from the imbrication of equality with the inner logic of capital? Marx approaches his ultimate conclusion hesitantly. At one point, he implies that we can only dispense with all reference to equality, and embrace the slogan "From each according to his ability, to each according to his needs," once the vestiges of bourgeois society have been swept away (531). But on the other hand, he consistently demands the removal of all reference to equality from the party's current program. He has devoted so much space to the question of "equal right" only "in order to show what a crime it is . . . to force upon our party again, as dogmas, ideas which in a certain period had some meaning but have now become obsolete verbal rubbish" (531). Marx's suggestion that the principle of equality can be strategically useful in the struggle against capitalist oppression is ultimately swallowed by his condemnation of equality as a "dogma" that will undermine and disable the struggle.

While Marx's opposition to equality has been obscured in recent decades, through the 1970s it was well understood. Such eminent scholars of Marx as Robert Tucker and Allen Wood, for example, point to a fundamental discontinuity between liberal commitments to equality and the struggle against capitalism.[11] But starting in the late 1970s, scholars like G. A. Cohen sought to align Marx with liberal values. Cohen sees the struggle against capitalism as an extension and intensification of the commitment to equality. He argues that Marx is committed to equality "but mistakenly thought" he wasn't.[12] R. G. Peffer notes that many want to square Marx's thought with the commitment to equality that broadly unites the contemporary Left. "The problem with this move, of course, is that Marx explicitly rejects it."[13] The egalitarian Marx comports with what Tocqueville called the American "passion for equality," and flatters our intuition that progressive politics is identical to an unquestioning commitment to equality. As we have seen, the contemporary anti-neoliberal humanities tends to define itself, in Joseph North's words, as sharing "a commitment to equality that runs beyond the boundaries set by the liberal consensus."[14]

But if we want to push the project of human liberation beyond the boundaries of the market, we require recourse to a sphere of value not subject to market determination. The double bind of contemporary aesthetics shows that the commitment to equality paralyzes our capacity to develop richer forms of life. The claim that reading Henry James is better than watching *The Apprentice* is the outcome of an aesthetic education that discovers values through critics' engaged practice. The capitalist logic of equality is incompatible with the recognition of expert judgment among forms of life and objects of attention. All consumers occupy an equal plane, free from the imposition of others' values. All values pass through the process of equalization and emerge as market values. This is why best-seller lists can appear egalitarian in a way that literature syllabi do not. The former purports simply to register how many individuals "voted" to buy a certain book, whereas the latter encode a valuation without reference to such "votes."[15]

As symptoms of the limits of equality have grown stronger, scholars from a variety of disciplines have contested the liberal interpretation of Marx as a thinker concerned with eliminating inequality. As the sociologist Daniel Zamora put it in a recent *Jacobin* essay, "As surprising as it may seem, the term 'inequality' *per se* was never a crucial category for Marx."[16] The philosopher Brian Leiter, in his recent critique of Cohen's position, writes, "At one point [Cohen] equates 'marxist equality' with the famous slogan from the *Communist Manifesto*: 'from each according to his ability, to each according to his needs.' But the latter seems a slogan that contemplates vast amounts of inequality, making the exact content of the (alleged) marxist commitment to equality even more puzzling."[17] Leiter continues:

> Marx is committed to equality only in what is now the banal sense accepted by all post-enlightenment thinkers: namely, that in moral deliberations, everyone's interest (well-being, dignity, autonomy etc.) counts equally. . . . At this level, however, equality as a doctrine does not do much to discriminate among possible positions. . . . It seems to me that, in fact, equality is not a marxian value at all—

except in the banal sense just noted—whereas well-being (human flourishing) is the central marxian evaluative concept.[18]

Even during the period of the ascendance of the liberal interpretation of Marx, a number of important studies emphasized his distance from egalitarian ideals. Michel Henry's phenomenological interpretation analyzed Marx's dissent from the objectifying and abstracting processes associated with equality.[19] And Moishe Postone, in his influential *Time, Labor, and Social Domination*, argued that for Marx, "equality has a double-sided character. On the one hand, it is universal: it establishes commonality among people, but it does so in a form abstracted from the qualitative specificity of particular individuals or groups."[20] Rather than embracing an egalitarian posture, Marx explored "the possibility of another form of universalism, one not based upon an abstraction from all concrete specificity."[21]

Scholars from Henry to Zamora have pointed to the lack of textual evidence for Marx's supposed commitment to equality. But such an approach fails to attack the root of the liberal interpretation of Marx. Cohen, after all, never imagines that Marx endorses equality in his writings; he insists rather that Marx was an egalitarian "but mistakenly thought" he wasn't. This incapacity to understand a nonegalitarian-Left commitment to human cultivation indicates equality's success in displacing alternative progressive values. Therefore, when such different writers as Tucker, Henry, and Postone establish the depth of Marx's hostility to liberal egalitarianism, another question arises. Why should we care what Marx thought about equality? As Mike Beggs has argued, only a dogmatic insistence on the literal truth of Marx's word could lead us to retain those aspects of his writings that aren't useful to our current needs—ranging from his commitment to the labor theory of value in some of his economic analyses, to the anti-Semitism expressed in some of his letters and essays.[22]

Is Marx's opposition to the principle of equality simply another artifact of his time and place, rather than a feature of his work that can illuminate our present situation? To understand his position today, we need to decouple two things that have been fused in our minds. Certainly, Marx believed the inequality underlying the ostensible equality of capitalist society to be an evil. But his insight—perhaps his primary, though until recently neglected, contribution to politics—is that the struggle against capitalist inequality cannot be advanced through adherence to the principle of equality. The distinction between substantive and formal equality tends in practice to evaporate. And, as the paralysis of aesthetic education shows especially vividly, the principle inexorably works to flatten different qualities into the register of market values.

In the following, I will analyze commercial culture in terms of the deep imbrication of equality and the dominance of markets in order to vindicate Marx's belief that egalitarianism cannot furnish an effective weapon against capitalism. I will undertake this analysis from both historical and theoretical perspectives. I will then briefly explore two recent failed efforts to reconcile the preeminence of equality with a commitment to human cultivation. We will then be in a position to understand how market egalitarianism has endowed the question of expert aesthetic judgment with an unprecedented political salience, and we will understand, as well, the social implications of judgment's qualification of equality.

*

The idea that all cultural tastes and preferences are equal is so counterintuitive, and so anomalous historically, that it raises the question, How did we ever come to believe it? A key moment in the intellectual history of capitalism provides one answer. The late nineteenth-century transition from classical to neoclassical economics, which presaged neoclassical domination of both economic education and economic policy, discloses how the project of giving markets unrestricted control over society required elevating equality to the preeminent social value. It also illustrates the convergence of economic questions with questions of cultural and aesthetic values. This watershed in economic history coincides with a broader dispute within liberalism itself. Establishing the dominance of markets as the means of coordinating values in a liberal order involved a radicalization of the liberal commitment to equality. The neoclassicals triumphed over their classical liberal foes by placing all consumer preferences on an equal plane, snuffing the effort to distinguish between better and worse preferences.

In the final decades of the nineteenth century, a group of economists carried out a dramatic revision of the discipline that has been compared to the Copernican Revolution in astronomy. Classical economics understood values in terms of "natural," objective properties, such as the amount of labor necessary, under prevailing social and technological conditions, to create a given commodity. The neoclassical revolution, operating through the key concept of marginal utility, understands value in terms of the subjective preferences of consumers. In this model, the ultimate source of value lies in the utility, or satisfaction or pleasure, an individual receives by acquiring an additional unit of a given commodity. The idea of marginal utility appeared to solve, among many other problems, the celebrated water and diamonds paradox, which asked why water—while infinitely more necessary to human health, life, and happiness than diamonds—was nevertheless of (nearly) infinitely lower price.

The key feature of the complex transition to neoclassicism I wish to highlight lies in its relation to utilitarianism, particularly to J. S. Mill's revision of Bentham's utilitarian calculus. Mill, by qualitatively distinguishing between higher and lower forms of pleasure, addressed the most devastating attack on Bentham: that his equalization of all the varieties of pleasure in a simple quantitative measure represents a gross distortion of human psychology. "Mill, in his distinction of higher and lower pleasures, tries to correct for the naivete of Bentham's simple hedonistic calculus."[23] In distinguishing between better and worse pleasures, Mill developed an "enlarged utilitarian philosophy that goes beyond Benthamism to accommodate a more complex psychology (involving higher moral and aesthetic kinds of motivations that may trump narrow self-interest)."[24]

Mill's embrace of qualitative distinctions between forms of pleasure has an important corollary that will prove to be one of his sharpest contrasts with the neoclassicals who succeeded him. Mill believed there should be a limit to economic growth, that technological development should eventually lead to a "stationary state."[25] The implication is that growth in human cultivation, once a certain economic level is reached, can be achieved without economic growth and the consequent environmental degradation. "Mill's philosophical novelty lies in part in his view that a stationary state is compatible with, even essential to, the advance of civilization." In such a state, "most persons . . . attach more importance to certain 'higher pursuits' than to further labour, investment, and the exploitation of natural resources."[26] Mill believed that the capacity to distinguish between higher and lower pleasures is required to detach the pursuit of human cultivation from the endlessness of profit-driven economic growth.

Alfred Marshall, who with William Stanley Jevons represents the main English exponent of neoclassicism, was at first sympathetic to Mill's views. But he later altered his position in a way that reveals the tendencies of the broader neoclassical movement. Marshall is especially interesting because of his deep background and interest in psychology—which distinguishes him from other neoclassical luminaries like Jevons and Leon Walras. Marshall's break with Mill came when he rejected Mill's distinction between higher and lower tastes. He believed that "Mill's qualitative distinction between higher and lower pleasures, introduced to counter accusations of putting every action on the same footing, meant giving up every possibility of their measurement and scientific treatment."[27]

The idea that distinguishing between pleasures on the basis of quality would destroy the ambition to make economics a science both links and separates Marshall from the other neoclassicals. Philip Mirowski, in his influential study of the origins of neoclassicism, notes the "irony" of the fact that the marginal revolution that displaced value from the physical world to the subjective was patterned after "the premier model of the external physical world in the nineteenth century," energy physics.[28] As Jevons wrote, "The notion of value is to our science what that of energy is to mechanics."[29] For most neoclassicals, the equalization of utility was motivated not by psychological considerations at all but by the desire to discover in the human world a force amenable to measurement in the way energy was for the new physics.

Marshall, however, had a psychological motive, as well as a scientistic one, for wishing to jettison Mill's way of distinguishing between lower pleasures—those associated with the appetites, self-interest, or the desire for accumulation—from higher pleasures—those associated with the fine arts, nature, literature, philosophy, or altruistic action. Marshall believed in the difference between higher and lower motives and satisfactions. But he found in the other great scientific movement of the time—evolution—a model for psychological progress which obviated the need for conscious, public distinctions in ethics or aesthetics.

For Marshall, "evolution supplanted utilitarianism." "In evolutionary ethics, higher levels—like moral standards—are not the product of separate authorities but grow from within."[30] Society doesn't require the disciplines of literary, ethical, or philosophical expertise to aid in distinguishing better from worse ways of spending our time and effort. Our existing preferences, interacting with one another through the market, will naturally evolve into better forms. Interference with these existing preferences—interference with the operation of the market—can only distort the evolutionary process. Later free market advocates like F. A. Hayek would expand Marshall's hints into the idea that the market is a self-organizing system, a kind of organism that should be left to evolve on its own without the meddling of ethical, social, or aesthetic values originating from processes outside the scope of the market's action.[31]

Mill's particular way of distinguishing between higher and lower utilities is open to critique; I will defer to the next chapter my own understanding of the methods by which the "separate authorities" of disciplines can make valid value judgments.[32] For now, I wish to emphasize how in the late nineteenth-century debate over utility the idea that all consumer preferences are equal is defended as a way of protecting the market's role as the sole means of coordinating human values. Today, we tend to reject the idea that one person's aesthetic preference is better than another's on egalitarian grounds. But in the neoclassical debate, the victors defend equality itself as a value necessary to the unimpeded flourishing of markets. We must consider all preferences equivalent, Marshall argues, not because we actually believe them to be so, but because treating them as equal will enable the market process to sort the adaptive from the maladaptive, the evolutionary from the decadent. All the market wants to know from you is what you want and how much you are willing to pay for it. For the factory owner, the shopkeeper, the advertiser, and the neoclassical policy maker, individual preference is the only relevant source of value.

By the early decades of the twentieth century, the equality of all preferences had become the foundational assumption of microeconomics.[33] But just as Mill objected to both Benthamite and neoclassical conceptions of utility on psychological grounds, so modern microeconomics has been subjected to critique by behavioral psychologists. The "behavioral revolution" sparked by Kahneman and Tversky in the 1970s focused attention on "possible discrepancies between experienced utility and decision utility."[34] In many contexts, this research showed, individuals are poor judges of what will give them pleasure. Our preferences often do not correspond to experienced pleasure or well-being in a manner necessary to justify the neoclassical picture of market agents as rational utility maximizers. Using a method by which subjects were asked to briefly rate their well-being throughout the day, psychologists found that people consistently chose to pursue commodities and activities that gave them less pleasure than others. This contemporary psychological critique challenges the neoclassical belief in the rationality of market decisions; the pursuit of my preferences will frequently fail to bring me the happiness I expect. Yet the psychological critique—and the nature of its proposed interventions in the market—is limited in scale. Psychologists typically rely on measures of intensity and duration that tend to equalize experiences of very different quality. In some cases, of course, a measure like the intensity of pain is quite useful: for example, when trying to design medical procedures that will minimize patients' memory of pain. But adopting as the sole public standard a measure like self-reported well-being creates the illusion of rendering very different experiences comparable. It is possible to imagine a self-assessment of pleasure by a person who's enjoying *The Apprentice* matching that of a person enjoying *Middlemarch*. But this conceals the fact that the different pleasures are linked to different values. To say that the difference between the two experiences can't be measured doesn't mean that it doesn't exist. It just means that the relation cannot be discerned by the kinds of measures available in the current state of psychology or neuroscience.

The differences between the experiences of different objects are real, but they require judgment to discern. Absent such qualitative judgments, the psychological critique of neoclassical economics tends to express itself in a "liberal paternalist" approach to policy, in which, for example, instead of having to choose to opt in to your company's 401(k), you opt in by default.[35] Just as Marshall felt that distinguishing between higher and lower pleasures would make it impossible to perform large-scale calculations, so in the recent psychological critique of neoclassicism a sense of how the market limits human flourishing is itself limited by current methods of measuring flourishing. The deeper principle on which neoclassical market fundamentalism is based—that a given pleasure is no better and no worse than any other—remains as powerful, and as devoid of justification, as ever.

What has this brief sketch of two prominent liberal challenges to neoclassical hegemony shown us? As Marx might have foreseen, liberal efforts to limit the scope of capitalist markets—to envision a future in which the progress of civilization and the progress of markets might be decoupled—repeatedly run aground on capitalist equality. The principle of viewing all desires as equal and equivalent restricts the capacity to distinguish between goods that involve the untrammeled, environment-consuming proliferation of tawdry commodities and the degrading forms of work required to produce them—and goods such as leisure enriched by art and thought that don't. To be sure, the past century has confirmed Marshall's—and Marx's—belief that the development of markets will enormously expand productive capacity, lift masses from abject poverty, and free hundreds of millions from what Marx called "the idiocy of rural life."[36] But time has also disclosed good reasons for rejecting Marshall's faith in the evolutionary refinement of the human and natural environments.

For both their own good and that of others, the preferences of individual consumers benefit from shaping by the kinds of "separate authorities" the neoclassicals reject. But the doctrine of the market—all desires are equal, all value is only private opinion—defeats the effort to create a better world by teaching people to want better things. The principle of equality has an important role to play in the unfinished liberal process of countering discrimination against various historically oppressed groups. But the struggle against the specific ills generated by the domination of markets requires the courage to defy the market's dominant passion, dogmatic equality.

*

I have been suggesting that the extension of equality to individuals' preferences militates against human cultivation by making the public distinction between better and worse objects of human desire impossible. But if this distinction isn't measurable given the current tools of psychology and is denied by mainstream economics, then how can we bring it into discourse in a manner capable of convincing the skeptic? I turn now to philosophical considerations in order to get a more vivid picture of the kind of goods blocked by the egalitarianism of commercial culture.

Agnes Callard has recently provided a lucid account of education as a process that involves suspending individuals' current preferences. She understands education in terms of a person's effort to acquire new values: "When one teaches art history or physics or French at the college level, one is trying to give students access to a different domain of aesthetic, scientific, or literary value. We aren't selling them something they already want; instead, we are trying to help them learn to want something, or to strengthen and deepen a pre-existing but weak desire."[37] "The process of substantive value-change," she writes elsewhere, "has a distinctive rational form that is not the rationality of deliberation, calculation, preference, or decision."[38] Callard argues that current philosophical and psychological decision theory is powerless to describe this process. The theory—which includes both neoclassical rational choice theory as well as behavioral psychology of the kind practiced by Kahneman—understands education in one of two ways. Either the individual *does* have a preexisting preference for the subject in question—Renaissance literature, for example—or the preference isn't the subject's at all but the result of indoctrination or social pressure.

Yet Callard persuasively argues that what is at stake in liberal arts education is the individual's desire to acquire a kind of value that person currently doesn't possess. Referring to someone taking music classes in an effort to appreciate opera, she writes, "Though she looks forward to a time when she will no longer find operas boring, the aspiring opera-lover does not currently find her boredom external or alien" (11). Her current preferences, in other words, are not satisfied by opera. But neither is it correct to say that her effort to understand opera is therefore the alien imposition of someone else's values. The individual feels that her current preferences are limited; she believes that by undertaking the process of education, she will acquire new kinds of perceptions, animated by values currently inaccessible to her. "On an aspirational account of self-creation, the creator does not determine, choose, or shape the created self; rather she looks up to, imitates, and seeks to become the created self. *The source of normativity lies at the end of the process rather than at the beginning*" (13; my emphasis).

One suspends one's current values in the expectation of acquiring better values. The motivation for education lies in the kind of person one wants to become, not in the kind of person one is. Callard distinguishes modes of aspiration originating in a preexisting value—the desire to lose weight, for example—from modes of aspiration that aim at the acquisition of new values—such as the effort to appreciate great music or literature. She argues that the aspirants' motivations are often impure, which one would expect given the difficulty of motivating oneself to come to appreciate forms of experience one currently feels indifferent or even negatively toward. Callard distinguishes between "proleptic reasons" for taking a class about classical music, for example, and non-proleptic reasons. Competitiveness, pretense, the desire for good grades, or a fuzzy view of the value of great music or literature can all be proleptic, if these desires help motivate and foster a learning process aimed at acquiring the new value. They can be non-proleptic if one's sole motivation, is, say, to impress one's parents with good grades. In proleptic cases, "competitiveness is a way of holding open a door for the person I'm trying to become. I'm competing in order to become excellent rather than to show that I already am . . . this form of competitiveness is *proleptic competitiveness*" (83).

Callard thus suggests a limit to the rationality of market preference more profound than that identified by Kahneman. It is perfectly rational for me, if I have never received the benefit of aesthetic education, to come to believe that my current values and preferences are not as good as they could be. It is also perfectly rational for me to then expect that by pursuing aesthetic education, I will learn to appreciate art, music, or literature in a way that is richer, more powerful. I understand that the process of coming to acquire these values will in some respects make me a different person than I am today. I will see and hear things I currently am unable to see and hear; I will acquire a taste for qualities I am currently unable to distinguish.

Of course it is possible that at some point in this education, I will come to understand enough of the object of study to determine to my satisfaction that I will never like it, or that it's not worth the effort for me to try to acquire a taste for it. It is also possible that I will be motivated to continue to pursue this process from curiosity, or from a desire to free myself from what I perceive as the limits of my upbringing, or from a desire to emulate someone I admire. While for some people these motivations will constitute the entirety of their desire to learn about art or literature, for many these desires will serve instead to motivate the difficult process of learning new values. The skeptic—the one who must deny that people ever have a reason to pursue a value they currently don't hold—is in the difficult position of demonstrating the irrationality of those feeling that their current values are deficient. He must show that competitiveness or status seeking is the *sole* motivation for the pursuit of values one doesn't currently possess. How could the skeptic make such an argument? What principle can he point to as proof of the necessarily inauthentic, deluded nature of any effort to transform one's values? He can only point to the principle of equality. All preferences are equal; one taste or value is no better and no worse than any other. The skeptic now stands revealed as a dogmatist. He denies a priori, as a matter of first principle, the distinction between higher and lower pleasures. He is prepared to redescribe all aspirants as suffering from a pernicious ideological delusion. He will ignore their testimony; he will not trouble to investigate the methods and processes of the disciplines that pretend to refine and improve judgment.[39]

The dogmatic egalitarianism of the market thus offers the strongest barrier to aspiration of the kind analyzed by Callard. It does not, it is true, erect any legal barrier to aspiration. It is still legal to major in English or art history—although the efforts of republican state legislatures place this in doubt in many public institutions. If one is wealthy enough, one can still send one's child to a private high school in which education in the arts is still cultivated. But throughout our society, in university administrations' policies, politicians' rhetoric, state education standards, intellectuals' dogmatic skepticism, the constant pressures of advertising, multiplied and concealed through new digital technologies—through all these forces circulates a simple message. Whatever you want is good. Look around, see what you want, then work for it. If you don't like it, don't click on it.

It is futile to define commercial culture in terms of the specific qualities of the goods or services it produces.[40] You can find anything on the market. Herman Melville and *Twilight* are both available on Amazon. The difference between good and bad art, between higher and lower pleasures, cannot be determined in advance of particular acts of judgment. To discern the secret of commercial culture, we must look not to the objective features of the goods it generates but to the structure of desire it enforces. The dogmatic equality of the market works to neutralize any value not derived from the subjective preferences of consumers. But progress in human cultivation takes the form of a value that calls to us, that calls us out of our current likes and dislikes, that calls us to undertake a discipline to transform, refine, and enrich our capacities and desires.[41]

This form of progress is blocked by the equalization of preferences and values. The nature of commercial culture cannot be seen from within. From outside, from the perspective of a form of judgment that transcends preference, the chilling effects of the eradication of public, trans-subjective standards of value become visible. From the perspective of the aspirant's frustrated desire to escape one's self and one's desires, we see what commercial culture is: the Eden, using Marx's term, of equality.

*

But perhaps these philosophical and historical reflections operate at too abstract a level. Does the commercial culture we currently inhabit actually militate against the transformation of consumers' values? Is it really so cut off from all standards of value external to the dynamics of the marketplace? One thinks, for example, of the network of sources of aesthetic judgment that mediate consumers' access to culture. Arts reviewers employed by newspapers and magazines, book clubs, the subcultural expertise developed around science fiction, horror, or rap, the editors of publishing houses: surely these represent sources of judgment organic to the market, embedded in its cycles of production and dissemination.[42] Do these sources shape aesthetic taste in a way that obviates the need for a sphere of aesthetic education external to the marketplace?

It is certainly true that all these sources—and many others—seek to provide public standards of judgment and to mediate the decisions of consumers. Yet everywhere in our culture today, we find them under assault. By the very fact of claiming to offer valuations different from the empirical "votes" for products registered by the market, these institutions incur the animus of dogmatic equality. As the editors of *n + 1* noted in 2013:

> We've reached the point at which the CEO of Amazon, a giant corporation, in his attempt to integrate bookselling and book production, has perfectly adapted the language of a critique of the cultural sphere that views any claim to "expertise" as a mere mask of prejudice, class, and cultural privilege. Writing in praise of his self-publishing initiative, Jeff Bezos notes that "even well-meaning gatekeepers slow innovation. . . . Authors that might have been rejected by establishment publishing channels now get

their chance in the marketplace." . . . Publishers have responded by reducing the number of their own "well-meaning gatekeepers," actual editors actually editing books, since quality or standards are deemed less important than a work's potential appeal to various communities of readers.[43]

We see the same process in book reviewing. Christian Lorentzen, in his 2019 *Harper's* essay "Like This or Die," describes how the reviewing professions have become adjuncts of publishers' and producers' marketing divisions:

> No doubt a consumerist mode of engagement with the arts has always been with us. Its current manifestation mimics the grammar of social media: the likable, the shareable, the trending, the quantifiable, the bite-size. It is no surprise that this set of gestures has become dominant. What jars is the self-satisfaction expressed by people who should know better. Editors and critics belong to a profession with a duty of skepticism. Instead, we find a class of journalists drunk on the gush. In television, it takes the form of triumphalism: a junk medium has matured into respectability and its critics with it. In music, there is poptimism, a faith that whatever the marketplace sends to the top must be good. Film and art writing were corrupted so long ago by slavish fixations on the box office and the auction price that it's now hard to imagine them otherwise.[44]

Market egalitarianism long predates the internet, but digital pressures have accelerated the dissolution of sources of judgment that do more than reflect current consumer preferences. As Lorentzen in particular shows, this process increasingly cuts across the sociological divide between pop and high culture. The difference now refers to a marketing distinction rather than to different modes of valuing. In many ways, the high/low culture distinction was always fraught precisely because it was a sociological distinction rather than a value judgment. The increasing colonization of literary fiction and classical music by the frankly market-driven dynamics long characteristic of popular music or Hollywood film underlines the fact that the essence of commercial culture can no longer—if it ever could—be sought in the opposition of criteria: simple/complex, narrative closure/

narrative aperture, formally conservative/formally novel.[45] The key distinction today is between modes of judgment that give individuals access to forms of value different from those they already possess, and modes that seek only to give consumers the kinds of things they already want.

And we see that the sources of transformational judgment once embedded within the cultural marketplace are becoming less secure by the year. The increasing paralysis of aesthetic judgment in the academy—documented in the previous chapter—affects these extra-academic sources of judgment even as it reflects the market equality of the broader culture. The traditional circuit of exchanges between English departments, creative writing departments, literary agents, editors, and book reviewers has often been marked by tensions, but the presence of people with English BAs and even MAs and PhDs at all levels of the publishing industry remains common. The dogmatic egalitarianism current in academia therefore doesn't simply lend itself to the rhetoric of CEOs like Jeff Bezos; it shapes the self-conception of the editors *n + 1* discusses and of the reviewers that Lorentzen analyzes. On the one hand, the crisis of judgment in the literary academy reflects the attitudes of the commercial sphere; on the other hand, the academic rationalization of the rejection of judgment provides key agents of that sphere with a new conception of their task as a kind of embodied algorithm, showing people things they might like on the basis of their current preferences. What all this suggests is that while commercial culture has in the past proved compatible with critical judgment, the immanent dynamics of the market tend gradually to marginalize any source of judgment that makes a claim on the tastes of others. The factors which mediated cultural consumption are gradually eroding; cultural life is increasingly being reduced to a relation between a buyer and a seller.

Therefore, the important question is, Does the buyer-seller transaction itself possess properties that can transform individual taste? Tyler Cowen, in his influential *In Praise of Commercial Culture*, thinks it does. While celebrations of popular culture have become more common in the academy in recent years, Cowen—as an economist—is clear about the philosophical entailments of a commitment to capitalist mass art in a way that makes engagement with his work fruitful in this context. Cowen is interesting and even courageous among defenders of commercial culture because he doesn't claim to be agnostic about the existence of aesthetic values determined without reference to consumers' actual tastes. He differentiates between two approaches to value—one based on popular taste and the other based in expert judgment—and claims that commercial culture can satisfy on both counts.

Regarding the first form of value, he quotes Orson Welles to draw a familiar connection between market choice and democratic process: "The audience votes by buying tickets . . . I can think of nothing that an audience won't understand. The only problem is to interest them. Once they are interested, they understand anything in the world."[46] Cowen doesn't remark on the fact that Welles, whose masterpiece *Citizen Kane* was a box-office flop, is an unusual spokesman for this position. It is likely that a great proportion of the millions who have seen *Kane* in subsequent decades—whether in film classes, at art house revivals, or privately—have done so largely on the basis of its high critical and academic reputation. Indeed, one can see in the rescue of *Kane* from popular oblivion an example of how aesthetic judgment, operating on pop cultural materials, provides them with popular audiences they initially lacked. The rescue of H. P. Lovecraft's writing represents a similar case. Such rescues, of course, depend on the kind of robust extra-academic sources of judgment that Lorentzen depicts as under assault as well as academic sources.

Whatever the ironies, Cowen understands Welles to be arguing "for the supremacy of consumer opinion in judging aesthetic value."[47] This seems to be something that the market can indeed do well, although one might raise several objections even here. As Kahneman and Tversky's research has shown, consumer choice doesn't always accurately record, let alone satisfy, consumer preferences. To this objection we might add that it is a question, to say the least, whether the purchase of a given movie ticket or novel indicates a positive judgment on the consumer's part. It may well reflect no more than the consumer's susceptibility to a misleading piece of advertising or even boredom. Nothing is more common than to hear someone say of some show or book, "It's just crap, but it helps pass the time."

So we should perhaps qualify our acceptance of the market's capacity to respond effectively to consumer judgment. Clearly there are many popular works that many people love and find deeply meaningful. But such works coexist with many others that, while popular, may not in fact be highly valued by the consumers who, in the language Cowen borrows from Welles, "voted" for them. I don't think there's enough evidence to be able to say that *in itself* a purchase decision reflects a positive aesthetic judgment.

Cowen's argument that the market reflects consumer judgment is common enough among free market advocates and often implicit in academic celebrations of popular culture. But in his suggestion that the market also advances a second form of judgment, Cowen makes a more unexpected claim about the market's relation to culture. He acknowledges that there are better and worse forms of aesthetic value; he believes that there is a valid, expert perspective from which the difference in quality between two works is independent of audience preferences. Cowen argues that "market mechanisms do more than simply give consumers what they want . . . the market incentive to conclude a profitable sale simultaneously provides an incentive to engage producers and consumers in a process of want refinement."[48] In adopting this line of argument, Cowen resembles Alfred Marshall, who accepted Mill's distinction between higher and lower pleasures but felt that the evolutionary process of market exchange would itself gradually lead people toward the high and away from the low.

It's worth considering this claim closely. Certainly, there is a sense in which one can, in certain contexts, discern something like an educational process in the relation of producers to consumers. A personal anecdote might serve to illustrate how this could work. In my own lifetime, middle-class consumer attitudes toward coffee have changed for the better. The coffee I drink today is certainly preferable to the coffee I drank as a teenager in the 1990s. I remember how, when Starbucks began its inexorable spread, the residents of my middle- and working-class Illinois suburb thought the multinational chain's coffee tasted "too strong" or "bitter." But Starbucks claimed this was better coffee than we were used to, even if we didn't presently like it. It would be possible to argue that this was simply a case of a seller trying to convince buyers of a falsehood. But after our tastes adapted, my family and I came to believe that Starbucks was right—we could see that the coffee we used to like was in fact terrible. I couldn't always afford Starbucks, but when I could, I appreciated it.

In this case, the seller's motivation to make a higher profit, to charge more for a cup of coffee than the buyer was used to, entailed an advertising campaign that sought to convince people that certain kinds of coffee were dramatically superior to the kinds currently on offer. You might not like the taste at first, they were told, but you will grow to like it. And then you'll see that Starbucks blends are superior to Folgers. And people did. Bracketing the various problems external to the core question that concerns us here—how Starbucks drove out independent stores, its extraordinary profits extracted through arguably quasi-monopolistic methods, and so on—I think the changes in middle-class coffee consumption serve as a good example of a process in which consumer taste is refined by the market.

Is a similar process detectable in the cultural sphere? Cowen's own examples involve artists like Jasper Johns, whom he represents as giving up higher earnings early in his career in order to slowly educate the market to prefer his radical new work. This kind of example is complicated in several ways due to unusual features of the art market. The sums involved place it beyond all but a few buyers. The tiny group of consumers of sophisticated modern art tend to possess college-level aesthetic educations, and they often employ PhDs as advisers on their purchases. So the fact that this particular market might be more responsive to a change of values like that proposed by Johns isn't surprising. But this has less to do with the transactional buyer-seller relationship and more to do with the unusually intense impact of critical discourse on the art market, especially in the mid-twentieth century, when individual critics like Clement Greenberg enjoyed an influence rarely if ever witnessed since. We can perhaps see a roughly similar dynamic on a different scale in the current market for literary fiction, largely composed of college-educated readers and, despite the trends documented by Lorentzen, still with access to a dwindling number of venues of expert critical judgment.[49]

In both these instances, the purported capacity of the market to educate consumers depends on the educational activities of experts. And these sources do not derive their aesthetic judgments from market dynamics. Cowen admits this, writing that "critics . . . contribute powerfully to the vitality of market art."[50] In markets like those for abstract art or classic literature or poetry, the supply and demand of high-quality works reflect aesthetic judgments made by experts of various kinds, from critics to editors. Writing in 1998, Cowen can perhaps be forgiven for thinking that professional, expert criticism is so embedded in the market that one can consider the judgments of critics an intrinsic part of the transaction between buyer and seller. But in 2019, it is much more difficult to make this assumption with the same confidence, in part because of the destruction of the journalism industry and in part because of the process, analyzed by Lorentzen, by which the remaining critics' understanding of their function has become more algorithmic than discerning.

The development of capitalism has created a situation in which we must understand Cowen's claim that "the market incentive to conclude a profitable sale" itself can bring about a refinement of tastes more literally than he perhaps intended it twenty years ago. I believe that making the market relation between producer and consumer the primary, often the sole, space for the formation of aesthetic value greatly reduces people's capacity to acquire values they don't already have. Cowen provides no examples that would demonstrate the contrary, and it hasn't been easy for me to think of any.

The kind of transformation at which aesthetic education aims seems to me unlike my coffee example in a number of respects. First, the likely profit wouldn't seem enough to encourage investment in many aesthetic forms, superior examples of which wouldn't necessarily sell for more, or sell more, than inferior ones. Second, the transformation in taste involved in switching from Folgers to Starbucks seems qualitatively different from that involved in imbuing someone who currently prefers young adult fiction with the capacity to appreciate Marilynne Robinson. The latter represents the outcome of an educational process more extensive, more uncertain, and more time intensive than the kinds of marketing strategies justified by reasonable projections about their impact on the bottom line. Aesthetic education involves a transformation of values sometimes so intensive, as Callard argues, as to entail a transformation of the person.

But perhaps gradual refinement over relatively long periods of time does, as Marshall believed, eventually produce higher values. The superiority of contemporary television is often invoked to demonstrate the market's capacity to evolve dramatically better forms of art. When comparing a popular and acclaimed 1990s TV cop drama like *NYPD Blue* to a contemporary popular and acclaimed TV cop drama like *Bosch*, we can see that the latter is refined in a variety of ways, from production values to acting to narrative. But all these improvements answer the preferences of people who already like police television dramas; they represent improved versions of the same kind of thing. This kind of example would thus seem to more closely resemble the coffee example than to provide an instance in which the market was able to instill new aesthetic values in its audience.

Perhaps some readers object to my use of examples such as *The Apprentice* or *Fifty Shades of Grey* or even *Bosch* to characterize market culture. Yet my point is not to deny that some popular works are better than others. Rather, it is to show that any such discrimination relies on a judgment that does more than simply refer to empirical consumer choices; moreover, such judgment necessarily violates the dogmatic equality of commercial culture. Part of the reason I have dwelled on Cowen's argument so extensively is because he believes what one *must* believe to argue that commercial culture can distinguish between significantly better and worse works without reference to external sources of judgment.

Again, I am not arguing that popular, profitable art cannot possess extraordinary vitality and power. The contemporary popular form I have studied most closely—rap music—expresses its orientation toward the market in figures that represent some of its most aesthetically powerful achievements.[51] But arbiters of taste within this community have developed robust forms of judgment that always make it possible to distinguish between market success and quality as well as between degrees of quality in artists of roughly similar market success. Rap's capacity to educate its consumers is predicated on these sources of judgment. In addition, its success in educating consumers is always partial and often in tension with actual consumer preferences, as seen in examples of wildly successful rap artists despised by rap critics, from Vanilla Ice and MC Hammer in the early 1990s through Macklemore and Soulja Boy in the 2010s.

Thus, while the market relation may in some instances contribute to the "refinement" of existing desires, Cowen provides little evidence that it possesses the capacity to give consumers values they don't already possess, and I have not been able to discover such evidence for myself. But why is this necessarily a bad thing? What's wrong with giving people steadily refined versions of the things they already like?

Here I think we need to recall that aspect of Adorno and Horkheimer's seminal critique of the culture industry that retains its power today. Certainly parts of their critique, developed at a time of far fewer content producers and providers, are no longer relevant.

Despite recent industry consolidations and mergers, we confront a more diverse mass entertainment environment than that of the mid-twentieth century, one more responsive to consumer choice. Yet Adorno and Horkheimer's contention that consumer preference is shaped by deprivation far more than commercial culture cheerleaders like to admit has lost none of its force. The consumption of large portions of most people's days by the dullness and emptiness of modern work constrains both the amount and the quality of time people can devote to the experience of cultural works.[52] Indeed, as David Graeber has recently argued, today's ubiquitous office work may be even more soul destroying than the factory work Adorno and Horkheimer analyzed.[53]

Work disfigures the times in life before individuals fully enter the workforce. Ever-larger segments of even the middle class are steered away from aesthetic education by the increasing emphasis on vocational training. And the high school arts education that nourished much of the best of early postwar popular culture—one thinks of the testimony of Smokey Robinson and other future Motown greats to the impact of music education in the Detroit public schools—has been steadily demolished.[54] What consumers "naturally" want is thus negatively determined by their being deprived of both aesthetic education and the free time in which to appreciate its objects. It is positively determined by advertising, which grows daily more insidious through the manipulation of internet search and automatic product suggestion. Therefore, judging the market by its capacity to provide people with values that transcend their existing preferences isn't a case of opposing the better to the good; it's often a case of opposing meaningful cultural experience to the experience of deprivation and manipulation.[55]

Cowen is certainly correct in his observations about other ways the market has fostered culture—such as how the enormous wealth created by capitalism makes possible university and orchestra and museum endowments that shelter valuable forms of art from the marketplace. (Although one might suggest that public support of such institutions provides them with a more secure and democratic foundation.) Yet a close examination of his argument in light of the development of commercial culture over the past two decades suggests that the spread of market egalitarianism, by steadily eroding sources of judgment external to the market transaction, also erodes the access of individuals to richer forms of culture.

*

There are two ways to avoid Marx's insistence that the ills of market-dominated society can only be addressed by qualifying our commitment to the principle of equality that has dominated the politics of the Left since the French Revolution. The first is to insist that the market actually encourages human cultivation. In considering and rejecting Cowen's nuanced argument for this position, I hope to have given good reasons for the market's inadequacies in this regard. The other method is the opposite of Cowen's. One might accept that market dominance now hinders human cultivation and nevertheless believe that we can rid ourselves of this dominance without compromising our primary devotion to equality. Martin Hagglund, in his recent book *This Life*, makes a powerful argument for this latter position.

Freedom, Hagglund argues, is the capacity "to ask ourselves what we *ought* to do with our time."[56] And this freedom in turn depends on liberation from our imprisonment in degrading, meaningless, poorly paid, and/or socially and environmentally destructive forms of work. Choose socialism, Hagglund argues, because your time on earth is short and precious, and capitalism systematically wastes it. The style of his thinking about socialism, its constant intimacy with basic, existential concerns, represents a model for how a literary and philosophical perspective might illuminate some of the most pressing problems of our time.

Hagglund wants to argue that socialism is simply the freedom to decide what we want to do with our lives. But it is quite obviously not. The freedom to do whatever we want is a capitalist, not a socialist, freedom. There are strong arguments for why a socialist approach to health care, for example, would simply level some economic inequalities and provide better health for the community. But this isn't the case Hagglund makes. He argues that socialism is the order appropriate to spiritual freedom. He defines spiritual freedom in terms of a life led according to personally meaningful commitments. All his book's many examples of such commitments—from the care of a child to the writing of a book—present people making their lives matter through creative, interpersonal engagement.

But what if what I want most is to have a more expensive car than you? What if I'd prefer to spend my time not working my boring job at the post office but collecting rare examples of high-powered automatic rifles? What if I want to spend my days gambling? Or drinking and watching reruns of *The Apprentice*? Fulfilling any of these desires would—in different ways—motivate an economic system that would be more accurately called capitalist than socialist.

So Hagglund is in the position of having to say to people: A commitment to having a better car than your neighbor isn't a good commitment. Watching *The Apprentice* reruns all day isn't a good use of your time. It's a waste of your time. Many of the ways people currently spend their free time are bad. You should instead devote your finite lives to the kind of creative, interpersonal engagement that makes our shared world a better place.

Yet Hagglund doesn't appear to entirely recognize that his position entails such claims. He doesn't distinguish between better and worse ways of spending one's free time, at least not as explicitly as the structure of his argument calls for. He largely avoids it. And the means he uses to avoid it are the same venerable means used by Marxists from Engels to Fredric Jameson: the labor theory of value. Early on, Hagglund claims that he doesn't believe in the labor theory of value, but this is only because he imagines that this theory entails a transhistorical argument that value must always be measured in terms of labor. But when people describe the old Marxist labor theory of value, they are describing the position Hagglund in fact holds.

His argument goes like this. Time is valuable under capitalism; it is the source of the value of the various commodities we fill our empty lives with. Since our time is the ultimate source of value, then a system that restores our time to ourselves by abolishing wage labor simply returns the source of what we value—our time—to us. Hagglund's prose gets uncharacteristically cramped in presenting this position: "The measure of social wealth in terms of free time is not an ideal that I impose as an external alternative to the measure of social wealth in terms of labor time. On the contrary, the value of having time in the realm of freedom—the value of disposable time—is the real measure of wealth because it is internal to the value and measure of labor time in the realm of necessity."[57]

Note that Hagglund—like Marshall—is concerned to deny that he imagines any "external" ideal or value. The argument about labor time serves an important function in this respect. It ensures that neither he nor anyone else needs to distinguish between better and worse ways of spending our free time. Our free time itself is intrinsically valuable as a fact about economic life. Therefore, he is able to make the case for socialism without violating what Marx called capitalism's "dogmatic" form of equality. This is an equality that says you can do anything you want to do, that all desires are equally legitimate, that society plays no role in judging what form of life you should adopt, so long as you don't harm anyone else in certain carefully delimited ways.

There are two problems with Hagglund's commitment to the labor theory of value. The first is a technical problem. Value in capitalism is not a matter of socially necessary labor time, and therefore the value of free time isn't "internal" to capitalist valuation. Hagglund is not alone among humanists interested in economics in imagining that the weakness of neoclassical economic models means that the nineteenth-century theory of value displaced by those models is therefore correct. Because the labor theory of value has been considered dead for so long in the social sciences, relatively few recent economists—at least since Erik Olin Wright's work in the 1980s—have taken the trouble to explain its flaws to humanists. I recommend chapter 17 of Steve Keen's *Debunking Economics* as a lucid explanation of the flaws of the value theory Hagglund adopts from the perspective of a contemporary progressive economist.[58] David Harvey, writing from a humanist-oriented Marxist perspective, argues, in ways that echo some points made by Keen, that Marx's mature economic analysis dispenses with the labor theory of value.[59]

In a fundamentally humanist book such as Hagglund's, these technical economic issues are not important in themselves. Economics is important because it serves a philosophical function in *This Life*. The labor theory of value, by making the value of free time look self-evident, enables Hagglund to avoid showing us why we should value free time more than the kind of work and rewards capitalism offers us, which in turn involves arguing for the value of certain ways of spending free time over others.

Hagglund quotes Marx's vision of socialism as making possible the "free development of individualities . . . scientific, artistic, etc."[60] A particular conception of the good life underlies and supports this idea. One of the many virtues of Hagglund's book is its wealth of examples of such projects. These examples may make it seem obvious that all people will naturally throw themselves into the oceans of free time socialism offers, eager to advance their various positive projects for self- and world improvement. But I'm not so sure.

I have no doubt that I personally exemplify someone unusually prone to bad desires. At various times in my life, I have (1) been addicted to heroin; (2) gone broke buying worthless consumer goods; (3) engaged in heroic, albeit unsuccessful, efforts to one-up my close friends; and, lest you imagine that this kind of thing is an artifact of my distant past, (4) spent over three hundred hours of the year 2018 playing the computer game *Slay the Spire* (according to my Steam account, which irritatingly tracks these hours).

I would be the first to agree that the kinds of worthy projects that Hagglund describes are better than the kinds of things I've spent too much of my life doing. But insofar as I've succeeded in moving some of my time from worthless pursuits to better pursuits, this has been through processes—some of them court mandated—that can be loosely described as educational. Without various forms of education, not only would my free time not be more valuable to me than one of the several meaningless jobs I've held in my life, it would certainly be less valuable.

Hagglund takes socialism to offer a certain kind of life, a different and better kind of life than capitalism offers. But in calling this kind of life "spiritual freedom," he doesn't devote enough attention to the hard problem here. That problem is how to make the case that some forms of life, and some kinds of desires, are superior to others. If one doesn't want to restrict socialism's benefit to the people (unlike me) naturally attracted to higher pleasures, one must then consider how to embed these values in educational institutions of various kinds.

Hagglund writes that the "transformation of our practices should be determined by our democratic participation rather than be dictated to us by the dynamic of capital."[61] He thus suggests that decisions about the kinds of projects our society will support will be circumscribed by democratic decision-making at the collective level. But this presents another hard problem. The distinctiveness of liberal capitalism is that it is neutral about the worthiness of individual desires. Those desires are generally coordinated through markets, not through collective institutions. I can drive a big gas-guzzling, carbon-emitting SUV if I want, as long as I have the money to pay for it and can afford the taxes a reasonably progressive liberal order will place on gas.

A move to democratic socialism of the kind Hagglund envisions, on the other hand, will involve introducing people to a challenging concept: your individual desires will be bound by the results of collective decisions in a much more intense manner than is the case under capitalism. You're going, for example, to have a lot more free time now, and the choices of things to buy on Amazon are going to be a lot smaller. The endlessness of human desire, which constitutes the theory of capitalism and drives its increasingly empty dynamism, will be limited, shaped and constrained in a socialist order. You can't waste your time if you want, at least not in some of the principal ways we waste time now. In many ways, Hagglund's vision resembles J. S. Mill's in that it imagines human collective progress detached from endless economic growth. But Mill, as we've seen, predicated this prospect on a distinction between higher and lower desires. And as we have seen, dogmatic equality blocks this distinction. Hagglund's vision of the transition to socialism tacitly depends on a distinction between better and worse forms of desire and ways of life—but he doesn't seem to realize the kinds of arguments this distinction entails.

It is possible, of course, to argue for a kind of socialism in which people can buy whatever they want, in which Amazon's virtual shelves are stocked just as high as now, perhaps through enhanced redistribution schemes that leave markets intact but ensure that market power is more democratically distributed. But Hagglund envisions a more radical form of socialism, one that will genuinely liberate our time. At the heart of his book is the idea that free time is more valuable than working unsatisfying jobs in order to accumulate mountains of consumer goods and services. This is socialist freedom. Advocating for this socialist freedom, however, means transforming some—perhaps most—of the desires that currently drive capitalism. And dogmatic equality, by placing all individuals' values on a single plane, neutralizes any effort to oppose what people *should* want to what they *do* want.

Hagglund's case for free socialist time thus requires a willingness to move beyond the capitalist equality that views all desires equally. And this in turn requires making the kinds of arguments that Hagglund mistakenly believes the labor theory of value renders unnecessary.

Any theory of socialism must also be a theory of the kinds of collective institutions and practices of judgment that will make freedom a blessing rather than a curse, as it all too often is under commercial culture. The commitment to equality is as disabling to Hagglund's project of socialist flourishing as it is to Cowen's project of capitalist flourishing.

Certainly, the benefits of judgment will reach their full democratic potential only when conditions of work have been transformed so as to free us of the degrading labor that consumes much of most people's lives. But the belief that the development of forms of value beyond consumer preference can wait for this transformation is a delusion. As the flaws of Hagglund's argument reveal, the distinction between better and worse ways of spending our time is a precondition for a robust vision of a transformed work world and a necessity to motivate broad commitment to this vision. Today, the debate over expert artistic judgment poses the question of a standard of value beyond the market with unique force. Not only is that practice the form of political intervention to which the education of humanities professors is best suited, but the unprecedented oppressive force of dogmatic equality endows this political struggle with unprecedented interest.

*

The ever-proliferating venues of the culture industry justify themselves with an impeccably egalitarian argument. People like this stuff. They choose it. The corporations couldn't afford to produce it if people didn't like it. Who is to say that one person's choice is any less valid than anyone else's? No one is forced to watch *The Apprentice*.

The prized works of aesthetic education are distinguished from the dogmatic equality of the market in that their value is not accessible to just anyone. These works claim a value independent of the subjective preference of consumers. As we have seen, to appreciate Henry James's superiority requires education; that education requires submission to expert judgment. Equality is here the *outcome* of the process of education—its promise, not its starting point. If you undertake this process, the professor tells us, you will become endowed with the same enriched modes of perception and insight that I enjoy. The kind of equality aesthetic education promises is thus quite different from dogmatic equality's insistence that we not discriminate between educated and uneducated taste.

Insofar as dogmatic equality succeeds in undermining the moral validity of the claims of expert judgment, the accessibility of superior forms of life dwindles. This is equality's paradox: it denies people the opportunity of surpassing the modes of subjective preference shaped by the contemporary capitalist environment. The discipline of aesthetic education, with its norms, traditions, and modes of practice, represents, like every discipline, a relatively autonomous method of producing judgments. Dogmatic equality condemns this autonomy. The capitalist "passion for equality" conceals a hollowness at its core. It is a formal, desiccated equality, pushing itself into every sphere of existence, eradicating all hierarchies inassimilable to market exchange.

Marx's perception of the imbrication of equality and capitalism has been abundantly verified in our history and our present. We are in a position to appreciate his reasons for describing equality as a dogma and rejecting it in the name of better, freer forms of human life. Aesthetic education is a discipline of discovering such forms. It consists of the sifting and selecting of different objects of engagement, the development of enhanced forms of attention and perception. The paralysis of aesthetic education by equality is an index of the need to reframe that principle.

We should qualify our commitment to equality, distinguishing opposition to material oppression, on the one hand, from dogmatic resistance to any valuation not resulting from the formally democratic index of market choice. We must distinguish the effort to provide equal access to richer forms of life from the effort to deny the existence of any value that can't be registered by the market. Such a qualification means that aesthetic education won't remain paralyzed by its double bind, won't crumple the instant it's faced with the scandal of judgment's suspension of equality. In marking this difference, we acknowledge that the total commitment to equality that still characterizes the Left's politics renders that politics powerless to contest the neoliberal dominance of markets.

A liberal Left perspective might seek to save the principle of equality by distinguishing between formal and substantive equality. If you tell me my preference for *Fifty Shades of Grey* or SUVs is neither better nor worse than a preference for Emily Brontë or public transportation, you are robbing me of the opportunity to enrich my life by transforming my values. You're giving me a desiccated formal equality. On the other hand, substantive equality extends aesthetic education to everyone, regardless of class or race.

Yet I prefer Marx's term. Dogmatic equality expresses the religious intensity and uncontrollable force of equality, its capacity to consume all differences and distinctions along with any politics inassimilable to the dominance of markets. The formal/substantive distinction is useful, but because of the subversive force of dogmatic equality, we must declare forthrightly: Equality is not our highest value. Our highest value is a better life for everyone.

When we pass from market preference to aesthetic judgment, we abandon the principle of equality that places all preferences, all aesthetic experiences, and all cultural works on the same plane. This doesn't mean that we should stem our efforts to eliminate the prejudices and exclusions derived from a history of oppression from the scenes of expert judgment. This effort is part of the work of aesthetic education. And the new world that education creates for our publics is the best argument for limiting equality's scope. We choose judgment over equality when we face our students and our publics and say: we will show you a better way to live.

Judgment and Expertise I:
Attention and Incorporation

How do experts judge works of art? Why should people trust them? In the course of addressing varieties of evaluative skepticism, I have given some initial reasons for why the core principles of David Hume's aesthetics underlie some of the best features of current professional practice in the study of the arts, and I have suggested how to overcome some of the obstacles this practice faces. But to get a clearer view of the nature of aesthetic education, we need to explore these principles in greater depth and in the process give them a significance and application Hume couldn't imagine. His eighteenth-century model requires adaptation to the very different circumstances confronted by aesthetic education in the twenty-first century. These differences can be grouped under three general headings.

First, the suspension of equality by the practice of judgment has given this practice a social and political significance that it couldn't possess in Hume's time. While the philosophical foundations of both classical economics and liberalism were then visible—Hume and his fellow Scot Adam Smith represent perhaps the foremost contemporaries in this regard—no one could have foreseen the effects of the coevolution of the market economy and liberal democracy that have concerned us in the preceding two chapters. These effects, as I have argued, first become notable to especially acute observers in the mid- and late nineteenth century, and they continue to unfold in surprising ways—as in the acceleration of market egalitarianism by digital technologies that we explored in the previous chapter. While we've already addressed the most obvious and important ways judgment works to counter the reduction of all value to market value, we will continue to observe the tensions between judgment and equality in our investigation of aesthetic expertise in the present chapter.

The second heading under which we might organize the manifold historical differences between aesthetic education in Hume's time and ours concerns the incorporation of criticism by educational institutions. The qualities and background of Hume's "best critics" may now be understood in terms of the academic training of aesthetic experts. Ideally, professors of literature, art historians, or musicologists exist as part of an ecology of judgment, which also includes editors, producers, curators, professional reviewers working for newspapers, magazines, and websites, and the amateur criticism that gathers around and sustains various genres and mediums.

But as we have seen, market egalitarianism, combined with the devastation of the journalism profession, has steadily eroded the factors—other than marketing devices—that mediate between existing consumer preference and content providers. Academic institutions—however beleaguered—currently represent the sturdiest shelter for aesthetic education as well as a crucial potential resource in the preservation and revitalization of extra-academic forms. We must adapt and extend Hume's principles to describe how literature, art, and music departments serve as a source and standard of values outside the market. While my focus is on the discipline of literary studies, key features of the model of aesthetic expertise I will elaborate may, I believe, be fruitfully modified to describe other disciplines of artistic judgment.

The third category of relevant differences between Hume's time and ours concerns the dramatic transformation of the objects of study—the various arts—over the past two hundred and fifty years. While this difference is arguably the most significant of all, Hume's model may stand in least need of adjustment here. The artistic world we encounter today is immeasurably richer and more diverse than that of Hume's time. Many important national traditions had hardly begun in the eighteenth century—including American literature, Russian literature, and the Latin American literatures. The traditions of Asia and Africa were known to Hume's Britain only in the most distorted forms. Romanticism and modernism lay in the future, as did the mature forms of the realist novel, the slave narrative, free verse, the postcolonial novel, and science fiction. The literary world of the eighteenth century was overwhelmingly dominated by white men. And while the interchange between popular songs and folktales and literature has an ancient pedigree, there was little indication of the variety of popular literary forms—from the romance novel to the detective story—that would emerge with the advent of mass literacy and widespread secondary education.

And yet Hume's model, formed at a time of comparatively homogenous tastes, is nevertheless conceptually adequate to this artistic diversity in a way that most later models are not. The New Critics, to take one prominent example, adopted criteria of organic unity or formal complexity appropriate mainly to their primary canon of modernist and seventeenth-century poetry. Adorno's criteria, to take another influential example, valued the capacity of quintessentially modernist, difficult forms to gain critical distance from society. His theory possesses few resources for valuing other traditions—jazz, most notoriously. Hume's model, however, doesn't specify criteria in advance of the critical encounter with a given work. As we shall see, this lends it unique flexibility. A Humean orientation to criteria formation encourages a deeper, more complex account of both the subjective and the objective dimensions of expert aesthetic attention.

The present chapter will primarily address the second of these three historical differences by supplementing Hume's aesthetics with a theory of expertise. I present Michael Polanyi's theory of tacit knowledge as the best model for the specific shape of expert judgment in literature. With a detailed model in hand, I then address some common objections to the claims of expertise as such. In the next chapter, I delve more deeply into the specific qualities of expert aesthetic judgment and the complex question of criteria.

While a key source of my model of aesthetic expertise is the current practice of literary education, that practice has not yet been adequately theorized—in part because of the egalitarian taboo causing literature professors to pretend that their enterprise doesn't involve judgment. The elaboration of this model will often serve as a defense of current practices. It will also identify practices that can be made more rational and less vulnerable to distortion by prejudice or authority.

*

The chemist Michael Polanyi developed his influential theory of expertise as tacit knowing in a series of works, with his 1966 book

The Tacit Dimension serving as perhaps the most lucid exposition of his mature views. His theory, which influenced philosophers of science from Kuhn to Feyerabend to Dreyfus, begins with "the fact that we can know more than we can tell."[1] Polanyi acknowledges the contribution of explicit, formalizable knowledge to expertise, but he emphasizes the kinds of background knowledges and experiences that are brought to bear in the performance of skills.

When scholars account for expertise, the nature of tacit knowledge has led them to dismiss it in favor of rule-based reasoning or rule-based procedures. Its "functional structure" consists in attending "from" something, a "proximal" entity close to us and of which we aren't explicitly aware, "to" a distal entity of which we *are* explicitly aware (10). The tacit, proximal, and internal basis of our knowledge appears for us only in the appearance of the object. "We are aware of that *from* which we are attending *to* another thing, in the *appearance* of that thing. We may call this the phenomenal structure of tacit knowing" (11). This structure can make it easy to miss the crucial role of background knowledges and to overemphasize the rules and knowledges of which we are focally aware.

If I have a mathematical background in algebra, an equation will look differently to me than it will to someone without this background. I may immediately see a solution; I might grasp the equation in terms of some use to which it might be put. I am not aware of applying my understanding of mathematical theory to the object; I simply notice certain features of it. In such scenes of expertise, the "interiorization" of knowledge serves as the "tacit framework" for "acts and judgments" (17). "This is why mathematical theory can be learned only by practicing its application. . . . [We] are aware of the theory, while thus using it, in terms of the spectacle that it serves to explain" (17). We can't learn a theory by contemplating the theory alone. To acquire expertise, the student must interiorize it, such that she can view mathematical expressions through the lens of the theory. This is why it is a mistake to imagine—as contemporary educational discourse often does—that one can divorce "skills" from "content," as if literary studies defined a set of skills transmittable regardless of the qualities of its objects. The capacity to transmit a skill depends on engagement with particular kinds of content.

Sometimes Polanyi discusses the proximal component of tacit knowledge—the entity from which I perceive the object—in terms of knowledge like that of a mathematical theory or of English poetry (two of his examples). But sometimes he discusses the proximal entity in terms of a thing. Like his contemporary Merleau-Ponty, Polanyi takes the example of a blind person's cane to show how expertise incorporates things. A blind person becomes an expert in the use of the cane through a process by which he comes to sense the world directly through the tapping of the stick. "In this sense we can say that when we make a thing function as the proximal term of tacit knowing, we incorporate it in our body—or extend our body to include it—so that we come to dwell in it" (16). Polanyi names the process by which experts incorporate tools, devices, or theories "indwelling."

Polanyi draws from an example close to our concerns when he writes of expertise in terms of "aesthetic appreciation as an entering into a work of art" (16–17). His brief comments suggest that he understands this process in terms of a phenomenological criticism in which the critic recovers the author's experience from the shape of the work.[2] But we can generalize his insight in ways that don't depend on this narrow view of appreciation. The expertise of the qualified reader or viewer of the artwork partly consists in the skillful opening of the self to the work and allowing the work to organize one's experience of the world. One might then look *from* the novel or painting or film *out* at the world.

In part 2 of this book, I will give concrete examples of entering and then looking out from literary works in order to discover new things about death, value, and race respectively. Here I want to highlight several features of Polanyi's model that bear especially on aesthetic expertise. First, he is by no means the first to understand aesthetic perception in terms of the use of a tool. Martin Heidegger's thoroughly anti-Kantian "Origin of the Work of Art" contains a broadly similar conception, most visible in his use of architecture as the primary example for showing how art organizes the experience of the viewer.[3] Many people have been struck, upon entering a cathedral, by an experience of space that seems vaster than the objectively limitless space experienced outside the structure. The cathedral's organization of the experience of space might stand as an example of the dynamic Heidegger has in mind when he shows how artworks make "worlds" out of "earth." In their different ways, Marcel Proust and Viktor Shklovsky, to take further examples, view the work of art as a technology enabling us to see the world outside the encrustations of habit, a technology we use by inhabiting it, seeing the world from its perspective.[4]

If his conception of the structure of the artwork is familiar, Polanyi's originality lies in making this structure exemplary of the structure of expertise in general. He argues that art critics who explored "tacit knowing, as applied to the understanding of man and of works of art . . . were mistaken in asserting that this sharply distinguished the humanities from the natural sciences. Indwelling, as derived from the structure of tacit knowing, is a far more precisely defined act than is empathy, and it underlies all observations" (*The Tacit Dimension*, 16–17). On the one hand, Polanyi carefully shows how scientific forms of expertise rely on tacit knowing far more than has been previously acknowledged. On the other hand, he shows how the appreciation of artworks is a matter of expertise, something often denied or understated.[5]

Polanyi's model also suggests something crucial about the dynamics of expert practice. The subjectivity of the expert, in the performance of expert skill, takes its structure from key features of an object. When I view the equation from a background knowledge of algebra, or when I sense the world through the tapping of a stick, or when I look at death from the perspective of Emily Dickinson's "I heard a Fly buzz—when I died—," my perception of the world is shaped by an object. Thus, the subjectivity of expert knowing has a curious structure. On the one hand, the subject determines the object—the equation seen by the mathematician is not the equation seen by the novice. But on the other hand, this subject is itself shaped by the object in a variety of distinct but related senses.

First, the nature of the object will determine which of my various background knowledges will be activated. As an English professor, I won't see a Renaissance sonnet in the same way as twenty-first-century free verse. The work calls forth a different set of tacit knowledges and skills in each case. Second, those knowledges themselves are objects incorporated by my subjectivity, objects that deprivatize my experience in some respects, and ensure a broad range of commonalities in the possibilities that mathematicians, for instance, discover in identical equations. To take a literary example, people familiar with the nineteenth-century realist novel will instantly be able to spot a dramatic departure from the norms of that genre as an occasion of possible thought and interest in a way that novice readers will not.

Third, the capacity to enter the work or the tool and make further observations and discoveries from its perspective represents a way in which the expert subject becomes involved with its object. Indeed, for Polanyi expertise at its heart consists in just this capacity to transform and extend the self through objects. Expert judgment does not take the form of an individual subject's reaction to an object. It represents a space in which the boundaries between subject and object are reorganized so as to enable perceptions, discoveries, and actions otherwise impossible. This shows us yet again how judgment is not to be confused with the simple attribution of value to an object that presents the same face to expert and novice. The sense of a value—of beauty or strangeness or comfort or complexity or surprise—is itself often a tacit component of the perception of a feature. And this perception takes place on the basis of transformed, extended expert attention.

Polanyi doesn't deny the importance of explicit, formal knowledge and procedures to expertise. But he argues that the knowledge of how and when to apply formal knowledge itself rests on tacit knowledge. "In order that we may formalize the relations that constitute a comprehensive entity, for example, the relations that constitute a frog, this entity, i.e. the frog, must first be identified informally by tacit knowing; and indeed the meaning of a mathematical theory of the frog lies in its continued bearing on this still tacitly known frog" (*The Tacit Dimension*, 20). The constitutive role of tacit knowledge means that the idea of a fully "objective" science is a fantasy; expertise cannot do without the "personal" capacity of the subject to incorporate proximal entities so as to perceive distal entities in special ways (20). Polanyi thus gives a philosophical foundation to the conflict we explored in the first chapter with Jerry Muller's description of metrics-obsessed managers' efforts to supersede "subjective" professional judgment. The fact that subjectivity remains an ineradicable element of any form of expertise is balanced by the sense in which expert subjectivity is itself constituted by the incorporation of various kinds of objects in consistent ways. Expert judgment is thus not equivalent to private opinion.

Polanyi's understanding of expertise has important consequences for how he understands teaching. The explicit and the tacit must be carefully balanced. Using the example of a pianist who attempts to concentrate on his fingers, he writes that "an unbridled lucidity can destroy our understanding of complex matters" (18). This mistake—a mistake that metrics fixation shares—derives from "the popular conception of science [that] teaches that science is a collection of observable facts, which anybody can verify for himself . . . this is not true in the case of expert knowledge" (63). Referring to the capacity of the expert to incorporate knowledges and objects, Polanyi writes, "In order to share this indwelling, the pupil must presume that a teaching which appears meaningless to start with has in fact a meaning which can be discovered by hitting on the same kind of indwelling as the teacher is practicing. Such an effort is based on accepting the teacher's authority" (61).

In part, Polanyi's conception of teaching is simply a gloss on what it means to follow an example. When attempting to learn tennis, for instance, a rule book and a list of strategies won't get me very far. When I want to learn how to play tennis, or to learn how to play tennis better, I identify an expert. Then I watch her. I take her movements, gestures, and explanatory words as indicating an invisible structure—the background knowledge and experience that tacitly organize her moves and enable her to see possibilities in the court that I cannot. Perhaps at first, I mechanically imitate her moves. But I am constantly looking for that which her moves make manifest and which is not identical to them. Her knowledge appears in her moves, but it is something different from what appears. My capacity to learn any expert skill depends on the faith that what appears meaningless or obscure to me initially is in fact the manifestation of a knowledge that I can acquire.

A student who asks, "What is so great about this poem?" or "Tell me the reasons for that move" is asking for a kind of knowledge that cannot be fully disclosed, or in some cases even partially disclosed, in advance of a sometimes lengthy educational process. This is not to say that the expert won't have an answer. But as Evan Selinger and Robert Crease put it in their study of Dreyfus's similar conception of expertise, "Rational reconstruction of expert decision making . . . inaccurately represents a process that in principle is unrepresentable."[6] The authors examine the case of a ballistics expert who gives his opinion in court that a certain weapon fired a certain round, a determination he makes largely on the basis of tacit knowledge. When on cross-examination the expert is asked to explain to the jury how he arrived at this conclusion, he is being asked to "produce derivative, and ultimately false, representations of his or her expertise."[7]

The structures necessary for the transmission of expertise leave ample space for the abuse of authority. The effort to squeeze out these spaces by reducing expert knowledges and skills to formalizable rules produces the kinds of unintended consequences that Muller describes and that are to be expected by a process destructive of expert judgment. If a novice tries to understand the climate, for example, on the sole basis of the explicit language of peer-reviewed studies, he is apt to arrive at perverse conclusions.

Yet it is equally dangerous to simply trust that experts will do what's best. Arguments like Polanyi's and Dreyfus's may appear to leave "no grounds for understanding how an expert might be legitimately challenged."[8] Thus, the kinds of internal and external checks I will shortly explore are critical in protecting the integrity of a discipline or field of expertise, the field's students, and other affected groups. While it may be impossible to make the grounds of expert judgments fully available to novices over the course of a semester or even the span of a college major, it should certainly be possible to do so to one's peers. One malign effect of the widespread view that professional publications in literary studies should not concern aesthetic judgment is to effectively give the individual professor unchecked classroom authority with respect to judgment. In addition to the kinds of checks provided by robust peer review, students themselves must be able to put the professor's judgments to Hume's test. If the professor fails to transmit to students at least some degree of the capacity to test the insight or quality of the work for themselves, then it is legitimate to question that professor's own knowledge and skill.

Before turning to a consideration of some common objections to the claims of expertise, I want to highlight one final feature of Polanyi's general model. This feature is related to the questions we have been considering, as it raises the problem of how expertise is able to transcend the accumulated knowledge and experience of a field. If the expert recognizes the object on the basis of tacit knowledge, then how can experts come to see the object in new ways? How can they come to appreciate new kinds of objects? How will the limits of current expert knowledge become apparent? How can the tradition concentrated in tacit knowledge be challenged? Most basically: How does change come to fields of expertise?

Polanyi writes that any tradition or field of expertise must "teach its current ideas as stages leading to unknown truths which, when discovered, might dissent from the very teachings which engendered them. Such a tradition assures the independence of its followers by transmitting the conviction that thought has intrinsic powers" (*The Tacit Dimension*, 82). For Polanyi, the skills and knowledges that constitute tacit knowledge are not simply means for experts to see the kinds of things they've always seen. Rather, expert practice is a mode of thought that is itself open to constant revision; viable expertise should be uniquely sensitive to registering features of its object that require a new approach.

This view cuts against the sense, derived from Thomas Kuhn, that the transition between "paradigms" of expert practice is marked by discontinuity. The celebrated historian of science Fredric Lawrence Holmes develops a view closer to Polanyi's. As Jed Buchenwald renders the conclusion of Holmes's detailed case studies of scientific discovery, "A community's apparently surprising support for what might appear in hindsight to be novel and even unorthodox work frequently derives neither from the community's inability to perceive a possible challenge nor from its desire to support novelty. It may rather have much to do with the methodological canons that the new work embodies."[9]

There is something about the methods, the skills, and the tacit knowledge of solid expert practice that puts it in contact with the world. Respect for these methods provides a means for overcoming the barriers that prejudice, tradition, and complacency always present to new ideas, new forms, new traditions. As studies like Holmes's show, genuine novelty—the discovery of outlandish, weird, impossible states, concepts, and effects, the shattering of prejudice, the opening of canons—typically derives not from a leap past existing expert practice but from adherence to it. As we will see, expert discipline functions as a kind of negative capability, a means of countering projection, enabling us to see anew. When radical results are produced, they usually derive from a conservative approach to method. In literary studies, the patient application of that network of tacit practices and knowledges known by the famously vague term *close reading*, sometimes coupled with responsible interdisciplinary work, has been the primary means of creating valuable and original insights.

Polanyi discusses the problem of novelty in the classic terms of Meno's paradox. If my capacity to discover something new is dependent on my existing knowledge, then how am I to recognize the new thing? "To search for the solution to a problem is an absurdity; for either you know what you are looking for, and then there is no problem, or you do not know what you are looking for, and then you cannot expect to find anything" (*The Tacit Dimension*, 22). Yet Polanyi argues that the kinds of perception cultivated by expertise don't simply enable one to see things in terms of the familiar categories of expert knowledge. It is rather that the tacit underpinnings of any robust discipline's practice will be of a nature to clarify rather than to distort, to enable closer contact with the object than is possible for untutored perception. He dissolves Meno's paradox by writing that "we can have a tacit foreknowledge of as yet undiscovered things" (23).

We can clarify Polanyi's somewhat mysterious formula with respect to the peculiar form of expertise that concerns us. If the natural human tendency is to reduce the unknown to the known as quickly as possible, one aspect of literary expertise is the capacity to stay with forms or ideas one is currently unable to recognize. Nothing is more common for the novice student of literature than to find in the work ideas or even sentences that are not there and that represent the projection of what the reader already knows onto the work. Contemporary psychology has shown how people are naturally vulnerable to "affective realism," which, in Lisa Feldman Barrett's words, means that "you experience what you believe."[10] Your experience—of people, of books, of landscapes—is determined by what concepts you have.

The cluster of tacit knowledges and methods indicated by "close reading" represents an expert practice that can help defeat one's projections.[11] The first step for creating a new conceptual model adequate to a new work is to actually perceive the unfamiliar features of this work. Close reading, in bringing unfamiliar features vividly to consciousness, can make acute the tension between one's current knowledge and the as-yet-unknown knowledge required to make sense of these features. In such instances, expertise doesn't simply involve seeing the work through the lens of familiar concepts. It also entails the training of vision to get a grasp on the work beyond the constraints of these concepts.

A related way in which aesthetic expertise points beyond the expert's limits is in the expert capacity to ascertain the richness of a work in terms of the presence of perspectives, insights, or qualities that have not yet become manifest. An expert reader can often sense a richness in a work without being able to yet say exactly where this richness lies. One might approach a familiar, canonical work with a sense that all that has yet been written about it nevertheless fails to exhaust its capacity to turn new facets to careful attention or to generate new insights in new contexts.

In these cases, we see how tacit knowledge preformats the work for us—it prepares the work for our attention in a certain way. Yet far from enclosing the work within a narrow set of preconceptions, this tacit foreknowledge often serves to illuminate the limits of our knowledge. The extent of expert knowledge is often felt as an intensification of mystery and doubt. There's something here, we sometimes say to our students, but I don't know just what it is. If the work has a tool-like structure, it is the structure of a tool whose use we don't always yet understand, a tool that shapes the hand that grasps it. Expert judgment sets itself apart from commercial culture in terms of offering a mode of value other than market value. But it also sets itself apart by the inner mechanisms of expertise, the capacity to reach beyond one's preferences and preconceptions.

*

Before proceeding in the next chapter to further delineate the components of literary expertise, it might be worth pausing to consider some sources of the widespread resistance to expertise as such. Any claim for the authority of expert knowledge—regardless of the particular model of expertise adopted—today meets with suspicion, even occasionally among academics whose position is predicated on expertise.[12] This resistance is neither new nor confined to academia. The question of expertise has long been considered to be among the central problems confronting modern democracies. On the one hand, as Stephen Turner writes, there is broad agreement that "cognitive authority and the acceptance of expertise, in modern conditions, is a condition of genuine public discourse."[13] Not only can lives be improved and transformed by the expertise collected in fields ranging from medicine to music, but many of the questions on which our common life depends—from the climate to food safety—require clarification by expert methods and knowledges.

On the other hand, as Selinger and Crease put it, "The authority so conferred on experts seems to collide with the democratic and anti-elitist urge to accord equality to all opinions."[14] The question of expertise thus invokes the conflict between judgment and equality we've been exploring. The nature of aesthetic expertise brings it into conflict with the rival valuations of the marketplace—and with market egalitarianism—in a way not fully shared by many other forms of expertise. But some reflections on the tension between equality and expert judgment at the most general level will provide a guide to the peculiar challenges faced by aesthetic expertise.

Experts possess knowledge that can enrich and preserve life, thereby bringing enormous benefits to the community. Yet expertise can also function as a mask for special interests, a means of rationalizing prejudice, and a way of concealing the groundlessness of expert claims. Given that the nature of expertise resists making its special methods and knowledges transparent to outsiders, how is the public to determine which experts—and which fields of expertise—deserve the claims they make on the public to have their findings treated as "neutral fact"?[15] The grievous failure of mainstream economists to anticipate the 2008 recession—and their advocacy of policies that can be seen retrospectively to have exacerbated the recession's human misery—represents perhaps one of the most dramatic recent failures of expertise. The flourishing of climate denialism and the widespread, unfounded suspicion of vaccines represent two contemporaneous manifestations of the opposite danger—the reflexive suspicion of expertise.[16]

No form of expertise is immune to skepticism or impervious to prejudice and distortion. However, fields can take measures to enhance their claim to be heard and respected by the public. To establish a basis for public trust, the expertise of a given field requires both internal and external checks. The internal checks range from methods of correcting the errors of individual experts, to measures countering discrimination and harassment, to procedures for testing and challenging dominant expert ideas or practices. The external checks can range from legal regulations governing educational standards and admission procedures, to measures identifying and discouraging conflicts of interest, to the various informal factors that qualify or enhance a field's prestige, such as the success of a field's predictions or the capacity of its practitioners to obtain the results they claim.

We need look no further than the recent history of the discipline of literary studies to find an example of how expert dogmatism, on the one hand, and public contempt, on the other, flow from the absence of internal checks on expert claims. Over the past three decades, the discipline has been periodically roiled by public scandals, highlighting the tendency of literature professors to make economic, biological, psychological, statistical, or historical claims rejected by economists, biologists, psychologists, statisticians, and historians. Some literature departments sheltered a space I have called a "bizarro world," in which certain kinds of discipline-specific knowledge flourish, protected from the methods of verification characteristic of those disciplines.[17]

Certainly, experts in one field might have insights that correct the errors of another field—the impact of Kahneman's psychological research in exposing the flaws of neoclassical economics represents one example we've considered. The problem is that literature professors frequently have no idea of the nature of the objections their arguments about psychology or economics will encounter, because they insulate themselves from meaningful exchange with those disciplines. Meanwhile, graduate students and non-tenured faculty are regularly forced to accept work ranging from Fredric Jameson's historical fantasies to Andrew Piper's statistical fantasies as dogma, with no clearly defined method for challenging the accuracy of those claims on their own terms.[18] It's important to emphasize that this problem isn't exclusive to the bygone era of "theory," of which Jameson was a prominent representative, but is equally manifest in the empirical, antitheoretical orientation of computational literary studies, which Piper represents.

Paradoxically, this bizarro world was erected on the basis of an animus toward expertise. By affecting to disdain the expertise of other disciplines, literature professors ensured that their own expert discourse was freed from the checks that could prevent its decay into authoritarianism. But periodic public exposure opened the field to the external check of widespread contempt, ensuring that putatively "interdisciplinary" literary work found little support beyond a shrinking enforced audience of graduate students and non-tenured faculty in literature and closely adjacent fields.

The work of scholars like Jameson or Piper represents extreme examples of expertise as dogma, and this model never achieved the domination of the profession that the field's critics have sometimes alleged. While it is important to institute responsible modes of interdisciplinary work, authoritarianism in literary studies doesn't always involve the protection of mistaken views about the objects of other academic disciplines. Within the subset of scholars interested in aesthetic education, we find a different example of the way hostility to expertise—often justified through egalitarian ideals—erodes the internal checks that make experts accountable.

Mark Edmundson, in his 2004 book, *Why Read?*, is eloquent on the capacity of literary education to transform lives. He dismisses a misguided individualism that would limit this capacity, quoting an observation by Proust that richly illuminates how literature often works:

> The mediocre usually imagine that to let ourselves be guided by the books we admire robs our faculty of judgment of part of its independence. "What can it matter to you what Ruskin feels: feel for yourself." Such a view rests on a psychological error which will be discounted by all those who have accepted a spiritual discipline and feel thereby that their power of understanding and of feeling is infinitely enhanced, and their critical sense never paralyzed. . . . There is no better way of coming to be aware of what one feels oneself than by trying to recreate in oneself what a master has felt. In this profound effort it is our own thought itself that we bring out into the light, together with his.[19]

This answers those who argue that allowing oneself to be guided by another in aesthetic experience violates the integrity of that experience.[20] Yet when it comes to the hard question of by what authority these "masters" are to be identified and presented to students, Edmundson takes a suddenly egalitarian tone: "I would largely leave the question of what to teach up to individual teachers, who could offer those books that they think can change their students' lives for the better. Let them choose the works that they themselves have been transformed by and that they think, now, can have the greatest effect on students. . . . Teachers must not be guided by . . . what they sense might become the subject of a bracing essay for *PMLA*."[21]

The libertarianism of this passage functions in defense of professorial authority without limit. Abstracting judgment from the collective exchanges and professional forms of the discipline deprives the teacher of any check on his opinion. The professor must ask himself: What about this work, which I feel so strongly about, has value for others? What features does my response depend on, and how can

I make these features visible to students and peers? Edmundson writes that "an essay on Shakespeare and love ought not to unfold the 'ideology' of Shakespearean love, but let us know what, if anything, the author has to teach us about Eros."[22] But how is the professor to know whether these supposed insights into love are valuable without recourse to the knowledge of both literary history and criticism, as well as such disciplines that bear on this question as philosophy, psychology, or history? If the professor's view is not exposed to illumination or correction by solid disciplinary practices, the classroom risks devolving into a space of tyranny, with an interpretation of a novel or poem serving as the dogmatic expression of the professor's pet views.

Edmundson's emphatic distinction between a vivifying aesthetic education and the dry, tedious exercises of peer review and scholarly research actually erases the distinction between expert judgment and private opinion. As I will argue in the next chapter, we should reverse Edmundson's position. If you can't even imagine an academic essay being written on the feature of a work that causes you to judge it positively, then you have no disciplinary ground for your judgment; your judgment has no claim on your students and merits no authority.

David Bromwich, in his very different study of these questions, *Politics by Other Means*, combines a distaste for expertise with some telling criticisms of expert practices in literary studies. He persuasively condemns the hypocrisy that characterized prominent exponents of a cultural studies approach to literature in the 1980s and is still occasionally visible today. This approach was egalitarian with respect to aesthetic value but devoted its energies to criticizing the malign ideologies shaping mass culture. He ventriloquizes a representative critic of this school as saying, "My generous endorsement of all your present habits is thus matched by my unselfish willingness to tell you which of those habits are depraved."[23]

Bromwich argues that Hume is a superior model for an approach to artistic value. Yet his interpretation of Hume makes the latter an exponent of an essentially amateur practice lacking the disciplinary methods that might justify it in the face of skepticism. In a discussion of Hume's "Of the Standard of Taste," he writes, "Who then sets the standard? A general culture such as the enlightenment imagined to be possible and desirable—a culture, that is, defined by its cosmopolitanism, its practice of toleration, and its respect for the achievement of different talents in different walks of life. These talents we may think of broadly as 'callings'" (213). Bromwich weakens any connection between Hume's conception of standards and something like expert practice by defining the former as "certain habits that seem by long use and assimilation to have joined our nature itself" (213). He thus suggests that aesthetic standards are indissociable from a given culture, that to be a qualified judge is to follow a "calling" rather than to practice a profession, and that there is no way to justify critical judgment to people who come to works from outside the relevant culture.

Bromwich accepts that judgment derives from a process of education, yet he makes this education seem closer to nature than culture. "Though artificial, because manmade . . . [aesthetic standards are] also necessarily natural, being suited to the ways of human nature as they are modified by a given society" (213). His ostensibly Humean program is vulnerable to the critique Bourdieu aimed at Kantian accounts, in that it conceals the contribution of formal education to taste and gives those who are raised outside a particular cultural formation no means of ascertaining the validity of these standards. The undercurrent of suspicion of expertise in Bromwich's account is therefore accompanied by an image of "lay" reading and judgment that effectively restricts the latter to those with an education that has managed to conceal itself as nature, habit, character.

Yet Bromwich's representation of Hume omits those features that render the latter a uniquely effective guide to the problem of endowing populations that have not been raised in this liberal, cosmopolitan, and literary culture—such as many people from lower-class backgrounds, immigrants, and minorities—with access to what Mill called the "higher pleasures." Hume emphasizes the role of "practice," of an education based on the "comparison" of a wide variety of works.[24] And he argues that the educated critic should be able to show features of a work to a novice audience in such a way as to obtain the assent of that audience. These aspects of Hume's model supply us with a way of understanding expert practice as transcending the total determination of judgment by a single informally transmitted cultural tradition.

Aspects of the field of early 1990s literary studies Bromwich confronts make understandable his temptation to dismiss the expertise of literary studies as the preserve of self-righteous, conformist hypocrites possessed by an ideological contempt for aesthetic values. Yet the dismissal of expertise contains its own risks for hypocrisy and involves a lamentably effective restriction of aesthetic values to upper-middle-class cosmopolitan aesthetes. Bromwich's preference for those with a "calling" over mere "professionals" ultimately distorts what is most progressive in Hume's account, and it tacitly endorses a mechanical, superficial view of professional expertise. The pathologies of expertise in literary studies call for a better understanding of expertise, not its wholesale rejection.

The final example of literary studies' resistance to expertise that we will examine—and perhaps the most influential—stems from the Kantian tradition. Vivasvan Soni beautifully articulates the relevant aspect of that philosophy: "For Kant . . . understanding aesthetic judgment can help us make sense of how we are able to judge (and communicate our judgments to others) in the absence of rules, norms, or laws."[25] Kant largely takes this idea that aesthetic judgment isn't based on rules from Hume, but as Soni shows, he develops it in a more exclusionary manner. For Soni, Kant's account of judgment makes it look as if any expert practice—based on norms and defined methods—violates essential aspects of judgment. He thus discovers examples of the "suspension" of judgment everywhere, from the hard sciences to the New Criticism. Discussing the New Critics, he finds both "a suspension of judgment . . . [and] an absolute norm specified in advance as a criterion for judgment."[26]

Insofar as some New Critical practice was committed to a single rigidly defined criterion—or else a very restricted series, Soni is right to say that they failed to understand that aesthetic values cannot be determined by principles applied to cases. But he carries the implications of Kant's position to a logical conclusion, going so far as to imply that judgment cannot be an object of education.[27] "As both Kant and Aristotle knew, judgment cannot be taught, though it can be learned through example and experience."[28] Yet this view depends on a model of education and expert practice as depending more on the formal application of rules than on "example and experience." Soni's aversion to expertise manifests in a recurrent, if qualified, suspicion of science. "It is not my task here to determine to what extent the sciences are complicit in concealing the space of judgment. It is sufficient that this is effectively the role they have come to play in contemporary society, largely at the expense of humanistic inquiry."[29] Later, he wonders whether "the methodological premises of science require a certain suspension of judgment."[30]

Soni suspects that expertise—paradigmatically exemplified by the sciences—is incompatible with judgment; he thinks there cannot be an expert practice of judgment. The hostility we've observed in Bromwich and Edmundson has now been refined and sharpened into a verifiable claim. Judgment involves the discrimination of value through a process not reducible to the consistent application of rules. Therefore, judgment contains intrinsically subjective and intuitive elements that disqualify it as the subject of expert practice.

We will now test this proposition. In this chapter, I have presented a broad model of expertise that is tacit and example-driven, and it supports an intersubjectivity based on a transformed relation to objects. We will now proceed to examine key dynamics of the expert judgment of literature. Many of the positive elements that writers like Edmundson, Bromwich, and Soni find in judgment will thus be conserved, while the drawbacks of their promotion of amateur judgment—as vulnerable to authoritarianism, underdevelopment, hypocrisy, or concealed prejudice—will be minimized.

Judgment and Expertise II: Concepts and Criteria

We might begin by listing thirteen of the elements of expertise broadly shared by literature professors:

1 Deep knowledge of at least one literary period or national tradition, along with a broad knowledge of other literatures
2 Knowledge of the dynamics of a number of different genres
3 A deep knowledge of at least one historical period, along with a broad historical knowledge of other periods
4 The capacity to interpret a work against the background of these knowledges
5 The capacity to detect meaningful patterns of image and language
6 A broad and thin knowledge of developments in a range of other disciplines
7 The capacity to perceive the world through the forms, patterns, or concepts of a literary work
8 The capacity to put your criteria in question when engaging a work
9 The capacity to use techniques of close reading to identify elements either unrecognizable or incompletely captured by current means of recognition
10 The ability to articulate your interpretations and judgments and to defend them in a professional context
11 The ability to show students what you are seeing in a work
12 Deep and reasonably current knowledge of the critical tradition

on at least one literary period, along with a broad knowledge of
significant critical approaches, problems, methods, and debates

13 The ability to perceive and demonstrate aesthetic qualities
like delicacy, brutality, mystery, sublimity, abruptness, heavy-
handedness, obscurity, or surprise

This list—by no means intended to be complete—may nevertheless be sufficiently robust to allow us to make certain observations.
The first question a reader is likely to have is, Where on this list is the
expertise appropriate to judgment? As I have been arguing throughout this book, expert judgment doesn't take the form of a naked
claim about the value of an object. Judgment is a process of disclosing particular features and qualities. The value of what is disclosed is
sometimes implicit—as in qualities like "a beautiful line," "a surprising
word choice"—and sometimes established with respect to a particular context—as when making a claim for a historical, philosophical,
or political insight expressed or embodied by a character, metaphor,
or description. Borrowing a term from physics, we can regard judgment as an emergent property, arising from the interaction of two or
more of the elements listed above. Yet in other cases, as we will see,
judgment constitutes the tacit ground on which the other skills and
knowledges operate. Judgment is thus alternately the ground of interpretation or an emergent property of interpretive skills. Putting it this
way risks obscurity, but the point is a simple one. Expert judgment,
as opposed to private judgment, cannot be isolated from interpretive
skills and disciplinary knowledges.

While the content of many of the elements of literary expertise
listed above can be formalized and made explicit, each also functions
as a proximal object in Michael Polanyi's sense. By internalizing, for
instance, the history of twentieth-century America, certain features
of a text show up for the expert as possessing a salience in terms of
that history. The reader becomes aware of this knowledge through the
identification of the feature. Thus, knowledge creates a background
against which certain aspects of a work appear in distinctive ways.
They would not appear this way for people ignorant of the history. But
neither would they appear this way to people who know the history
but have not learned how to internalize it as a means of transforming
and extending their perception of a literary work. So I list historical
or literary knowledge separately from the capacity to view the work

through that knowledge. Only the former can be transmitted in terms of explicit contents; the latter is learned in the same way it is applied—tacitly, through example.

As is inevitably the case when discussing the tacit elements constitutive of expert practice, my formulations in the following discussion are likely to occasionally appear abstract and vague. I appeal to the reader to judge my claims first with respect to your own experience as a student, teacher, and reader. Second, I refer the reader to part 2 of this book, which contains three extended examples of judgment. In the present chapter, I will sometimes leaven the abstraction of my descriptions with reference to some aspect of the practical criticism of the final three chapters. Some readers may wish for a more concrete understanding of judgment without having to read accounts of poems and novels. But if the model of expertise I have been presenting is correct, there is no other way. In the final analysis, a chapter like the present can simply indicate some general tendencies of the kind of skillful engagement that is made fully present only in relation to a specific work.

The two Gwendolyn Brooks poems I study in my seventh chapter, for instance, become salient on the basis of an understanding of certain features of the history of mid-twentieth-century American urban life (elements 3 and 4). Yet a countering skill is also at work. The capacity to suspend projecting that historical understanding onto the poems depends on the capacity to identify features of these poems that seem discrepant in that context (elements 5 and 9). My judgment that these poems contain valuable historical insights ultimately emerges from an explicit consideration of the implications of this discrepancy, of how differently the midcentury urban world looks from their perspective (element 7). But my identification of which extradisciplinary knowledges to investigate further—political science, psychology, urban planning (element 6)—depends on features that are themselves disclosed through tacit literary knowledges. Finally, the interest of Gwendolyn Brooks herself is not something I discovered; her work forms an enduring part of the canon of twentieth-century American poetry (elements 1 and 12).

My argument for a new kind of value in Brooks's work, therefore, takes place against a horizon in which the general interest of her work has already been established. Although it is certainly possible to undertake an investigation tending to diminish or qualify the value of a canonical author, this also would take place against the same horizon, albeit with a different orientation. All this is simply to say that my agency as a critic is embedded within, and shaped by, the tacit knowledges and skills I share with other experts, who are able to affirm or dissent rationally from my various claims in a way that a thoroughly subjective model of aesthetic judgment would make impossible (element 10).

One way to express the imbrication of expert judgment, perception, knowledge, and interpretation is to say, as John Frow does, that judgment takes place on the basis of interpretation.[1] My sense of the value of Brooks's historical insights depends on a particular interpretation of her work, an interpretation itself predicated on the various tacit knowledges I bring to the poetry (which are hardly unique to me—no aspect of the tacit knowledges or skills I bring to bear on the poems cannot be found in the practice of my teachers or colleagues). What is disclosed through expert judgment is not a raw value, attaching to a distinct object, but rather a feature of a work, the value of which is either a quality that feature possesses—like a delicate transition—or one it accrues by virtue of being placed in some context—as is the case with the insightful quality of Brooks's lines.

But another way to express this imbrication is to say that interpretation takes place on the basis of judgment. As an empirical fact, my tacit recognition of the interest and power of Brooks's lines came *before* my interpretation of the meaning of those lines. This illustrates Polanyi's response to Meno's paradox. If the value of a given feature depends on its disclosure of something we don't already know, then how can we recognize that feature at all? Experts, Polanyi writes, "can have a tacit foreknowledge of as yet undiscovered things."[2] My sense that there was something about these lines of poetry, out of all the thousands of lines of Brooks's poetry I've read, that made them worth especially careful and close interpretation precedes that interpretation. It is no more possible in this case to detach interpretation from judgment than the reverse. We will see that the precedence of judgment with respect to interpretation isn't confined to this kind of example but takes a range of forms.

I think enough has already been said, both above and in the preceding chapters, about several of the elements that constitute literary expertise to enable the reader to observe their operation in more detail in the second half of this book. In the remainder of this chapter,

I wish to provide fuller descriptions of three elements that may be less familiar or more controversial. The first is the nature of aesthetic concepts. The second is the role of scholarship—the complex of skills involved in producing and evaluating peer-reviewed books and articles—in relation to judgment as an educational practice. And the third is the capacity to allow a work to put one's criteria for judgment into question.

*

The capacity to recognize and use aesthetic concepts is a key component of aesthetic expertise. Frank Sibley's classic discussion of this topic represents one of the monuments of twentieth-century aesthetics, and among the least known outside philosophy departments. Sibley defines the term as follows: "When a word or expression is such that taste or perceptiveness is required in order to apply it, I shall call it an *aesthetic* term or expression, and I shall, correspondingly, speak of *aesthetic* concepts."[3] Beautiful, graceful, zany, delicate, crude: these are real qualities of things in the world, but they require judgment or "taste" in order to discern. "When I speak of taste in this paper, I shall not be dealing with questions which centre upon expressions like 'a matter of taste' (meaning, roughly, a matter of personal preference or liking). It is with an ability to notice or see or tell that things have certain qualities that I am concerned."[4]

When he says that one requires judgment to discern that a thing possesses the quality of delicacy, Sibley means something quite specific. "There are no non-aesthetic features which serve in any circumstances as logically *sufficient conditions* for applying aesthetic terms."[5] You can never supply someone with a list of conditions for something having the quality of "delicacy."[6] "No description in non-aesthetic terms permits us to claim that these or any other aesthetic terms must undeniably apply to it."[7] In Sibley's discussion we hear an echo of Hume's argument—one later taken up by Kant—that no rules furnish adequate reasons for judgment. You cannot produce a set of conditions that will enable someone to identify a "fine stroke." Yet unlike Kant, for Sibley the capacity to identify these qualities doesn't depend on an innate "sensus communis." It can be taught by those who have it to those who don't.

Sibley's description of aesthetic education is worth considering in some detail. The critic, he writes, "cannot be represented either wholly or even mainly as providing new interpretations. His task quite as often is simply to help us to appreciate qualities which other critics have regularly found in the works he discusses."[8] If we rely exclusively on the publications of aesthetic experts for our understanding of aesthetic expertise, the truth of Sibley's observation can be easy to miss, because the skill he has in mind typically shows up in expert publications, if it shows up at all, in implicit ways. Such publications typically have the function of presenting new interpretations and judgments to the criticism and evaluation of peers.

Of course if a critic wants to show how a work typically interpreted in terms of one set of aesthetic qualities actually possesses a quite different set of qualities, aesthetic concepts become explicit. Nabokov, to take one well-known instance, shows that Gogol's fiction doesn't possess the qualities of the realist novel, as had been alleged, but quite different qualities. His argument depends on communicating to his audience the Russian aesthetic concept "poshlust," which he loosely translates as "vulgarity" and which he defines not through rules but through a series of examples drawn from Gogol's prose.[9] Other examples of new interpretations that involve revised aesthetic concepts include Harding's description of Austen's novels in terms of "regulated hatred," or the discovery in slave narratives of aesthetic qualities in what had been supposed to be purely documentary works.[10] My fifth and sixth chapters in part 2 of this book adopt a roughly similar procedure.

But when teaching, one frequently wishes to show students qualities in works that would come as no surprise to other experts. Sibley describes methods of teaching students to recognize these elements, which most teachers will immediately recognize. "By merely drawing attention to those easily discernible features which make the painting luminous or warm or dynamic, we often succeed in bringing someone to see these aesthetic qualities. . . . In mentioning features which may be discerned by anyone with normal ears, eyes, and intelligence, we are singling out what may serve as a kind of key to grasping or seeing something else (and the key may not be the same for each person)."[11] The teacher may say: Look at how ridiculous this statement by Anne's father in *Persuasion* is! Do you hear the quiet fury of this sentence of Harriet Jacobs's? Isn't Plath's comparison of the sun to a bleeding woman in "Poppies in October" bizarre, horrible, beautiful? In each case, the teacher points to a feature the students can see—a series of words, a sentence, a line. Then she describes that object by using an aesthetic concept. But what if the student were to ask, "What features make Sir Walter Elliot's language here ridiculous? I ask because I want to create a list that will enable me to identify future instances of the ridiculous in the comic novel"? The teacher would have no reply. She might offer various kinds of explanation relevant to the example before them, but this would not give the student what he was asking for.

Yet by simply showing the student something that possesses a certain quality, and describing it in terms of that quality, that student would gradually come to have an eye, or an ear, for the ridiculous which he didn't previously possess. "Besides our verbal performances, the rest of our behavior is important . . . tones of voice, expression, nods, looks, and gestures."[12] In this way, the fundamentally tacit knowledge of aesthetic qualities can be communicated.

Perception of these qualities underlies judgment. The judgment of the comic brilliance of passages of *Persuasion*, for example, follows directly from recognition of a quality like the sublime ridiculousness of Sir Walter Elliot's character. The very capacity to interpret a work like *Persuasion* depends on the ability to identify qualities like the ridiculousness of Sir Walter's language, qualities that cannot be proved through the enumeration of sufficient conditions in the passage. It is not uncommon, in my experience teaching this novel, for students to fail to detect the silliness of Sir Walter's lines. But it wouldn't be quite right to describe such a response as a different interpretation from mine (for example, an interpretation of Elliot's lines as just the way fathers back then tended to speak). The novice simply fails to hear the ridiculous quality of Austen's passage in the same way that a color-blind person might fail to perceive the structure of a Matisse. Interpretation is possible, as Polanyi shows in the example of the frog, only on the basis of a prior identification of the object through tacit processes. The interpretations of novice and expert are based on fuzzier and clearer perceptions of the object. It would of course be possible to interpret the passage differently from the way most expert readers of Austen do, but this would first involve recognizing the quality of the lines that leads others to hear them as silly and teasing from them a new quality—of hatred, for example.

It is not difficult, in my experience, to bring students to hear the ridiculous quality in such passages. Perhaps it is more accurate, in speaking of *Persuasion*'s comedy, to say that students lack not the aesthetic concept of the ridiculous as such but the curious variant of that quality discernible in Sir Walter's speech. Perhaps a more effective name for that quality might be "Pompous/preposterous/hyperbolic/ ridiculous/simultaneously-expressive-of-an-exquisite-sensitivity-to-one's-own-perceptions-while-manifesting-total-obliviousness-to-the-feelings-of-others." The challenge of trying to define such a quality underlines Sibley's basic point about how the knowledge of aesthetic concepts is conveyed—language is more gestural here than definitive. We probably lack names for most of the best literary qualities; the expressive ingenuity of the professor is tasked when trying to awaken students to a sense of them, as when I point to the opening metaphor of "Poppies in October" and say, incoherently but not ineffectively: bizarre, horrible, beautiful!

The Kantian subject, upon perceiving a beautiful object, can only point at it and expect agreement on the basis of the other's innate capacity to represent the object in a similar way to himself. Instead, Sibley's novice learns to appreciate and to identify the quality through the example of the teacher. The aesthetic expert models the kind of person capable of appreciating qualities and values that the student may not initially sense and that cannot be demonstrated to the student outside gradual, tacit, and indirect educational processes.

Some aspects of literary expertise—the knowledge of a critical tradition, the knowledge of the norms of a genre—function tacitly but can if needed be made explicit. But the basis for identifying aesthetic concepts cannot be made explicit even in principle. This doesn't mean such concepts are private or that they aren't qualities of objects. Aesthetic concepts describe real qualities of objects, which require a certain quality of subjectivity to become visible. People with a taste for the ridiculous in literature will recognize this quality in Sir Walter's discourse. It is possible to bring those who cannot initially appreciate this quality to do so through aesthetic education. Aesthetic concepts thus function as examples of the entities Polanyi identifies, the "proximate" entities through which the expert views "distal" objects to reveal qualities often unavailable from a novice perspective. Because aesthetic concepts are public, not private, it is always possible to challenge a given expert's identification, in the way that

Harding, for example, revises what we see by showing us the qualities of hatred and aggression lurking within Austen's depiction of Sir
Walter's absurd speech.

Another element of aesthetic expertise with an irreducibly tacit
component is the capacity to take the work itself as the proximate
term for looking at the world. When, in my chapter on Dickinson
and Keats, I say that "the poem *invites us* to imagine death by *directing us* to reflect on our own experiences of absorbed listening," this
invitation and this direction are not something a novice reader will
hear or see. Yet the capacity to take features of a work as capable of
incorporation by the reader, as a way of transforming subjectivity in
order to obtain insights not easily achievable otherwise, is an important means of disclosing the riches of cultural objects.

This capacity runs across a spectrum, from the relatively simple
ability to use Sir Walter's speech to interpret certain kinds of speech
in one's own world, to the more complex cases I explore in this book's
second part. It is hardly necessary to add that not all works will repay
incorporation by the reader in terms of what they disclose. The vast
majority of works produced in all periods disintegrate under the pressure of judgment as the curious, searching intelligence of a reader
seeks to make of the work a second body and mind.

*

The status of the professional scholarship and criticism produced by
academic literary experts has been a perennial source of conflict and
confusion. From the perspective of the kind of aesthetic education
I have been describing and defending, professional publication—in
peer-reviewed journals and books—serves a crucial function. It
defines a space in which critics' judgments are exposed to critique,
comment, and revision, on the one hand, and in which other experts
may broaden or transform their own judgments, on the other. This
is a primary space in which individual experts' judgments encounter
checks. Participation in this space ensures the distinction between
professional judgment and private opinion. The classroom is always a
potential space of authoritarian domination; the gap between novice
and expert means that it is easy to abuse the credulity of the student.
Rendering the grounds for our judgments completely transparent to
nonexperts is, as we have seen, impossible. This makes it all the more

crucial that professors be able, in both theory and practice, to defend their judgments before their peers.

I will repeat the formula I previously introduced: if I can't imagine an academic article describing the features and qualities that give rise to my judgment, then my judgment is not an expert one, and it has no claim on my students. The idea—often heard when I was a graduate student—that professional publication involves analysis rather than appreciation is exploded by reflection on the processes of expert judgment we've been exploring. Expert judgment is not the naked attribution of value; it is not the expression of a private sense of ineffable qualities. Expert judgment is bound up with the elements of expertise enumerated above; it involves the disclosure of features, insights, or qualities that can be shown to other experts in sufficient detail so as to enable them to agree or disagree and to give reasons for their verdicts. It is true that these reasons frequently depend on the tacit knowledges constitutive of expert discourse and that it is often difficult to transmit them clearly to outsiders to the field. But these tacit knowledges are not private, and if they are subjective, they represent structures of subjectivity shared by other experts in the field.

The three examples of practical criticism found in the following chapters had their origin in the classroom, where my inchoate sense of the interest and value of literary features was forced into greater definition through engagement with students. The students put my judgments to Hume's test, with varied but generally affirmative results. I then turned these judgments into a form appropriate for peer review and submitted them to the evaluation of my peers through audience questions and reader's reports. These peer evaluations led me to revise and tighten my analyses and judgments, which improved how I teach these works. I think this feedback loop represents a means by which expert aesthetic judgment becomes a collective process, with several internal checks for ensuring the viability of expert judgments.[13]

There are good histories of the profession—Gerald Graff's *Professing Literature* is one acknowledged classic, Joseph North's *Literary Criticism* is a more recent and even more germane one—that document the struggle between philologists who believed that evaluation was "only subjective opinion" and critics who believed that criticism represented an extension of aesthetic education.[14] To delineate more clearly the shape of my conception of the role of professional writing by literature teachers, I want to contrast it with a more recent model not fully grappled with by either Graff or North.

Rita Felski has been among the most forceful critics of the tendency of literature professors over the past few decades to adopt a dismissive, skeptical view of their objects of study. Her recent books explore a range of literary qualities neglected by the prevalent attitudes of academic criticism.[15] She speaks of "professional pessimism" as a component of the kind of expertise associated with "critique," a perverse formation which provides career incentives for individuals to get ahead by undermining the social basis of the profession.[16]

But Felski's remedy for this problem is to adopt a "perspective less dismissive of lay experiences of reading."[17] In this vision, professional articles and books on literature would express and explore some of the same kinds of experiences—of wonder, of beauty—that "lay" readers express. While Felski doesn't imagine that professional writing will simply imitate "lay" writing, it as if, for her, professional and lay experiences of literature lay along parallel tracks. But surely the point of literature professors is to *teach* students to read and to read better, not to appreciate elements of student response that we can then adapt in our own writing. When one reflects that many lay readers, the overwhelming majority of readers of literary fiction and nonfiction, have themselves attended college and received high-level aesthetic educations, then one grasps a more robust causal relation between professional and nonprofessional reading practices.

Similarly, Tim Aubry, in a book charged with powerful aesthetic insights, argues that the aesthetic dimension of literary studies has migrated from its object of study to the form of academic criticism itself, involving appreciations of qualities like "the complexity and rhetorical verve of [Jameson's] analysis."[18] Here academic literary criticism sets itself up as a kind of competitor to literature, perhaps on the principle that it offends dogmatic equality less to present one's own writing for aesthetic judgment than to judge the writing of another. This strategy is of course not new, and in 1980 Geoffrey Hartman was already diagnosing the periodic efforts of criticism to escape its secondary status by becoming a kind of creative writing.[19] What is different now is how the crisis of judgment has prevented scholars from understanding the important social, cultural, and political role played by academic criticism *as* criticism.

Academic literary criticism will only rarely reach an audience large enough to make it a vehicle of aesthetic education in itself. The excellence of academic criticism *as writing* will always be circumscribed by and subordinated to its role within the larger ecology of aesthetic education. This is not of course to diminish the interest of creative forms of criticism by professors; the hybrid forms of memoir, criticism, and cultural history of Maggie Nelson's *The Argonauts* and Aaron Kunin's *Love Three* constitute extraordinary recent instances.[20] But to praise this work doesn't mean that all writing about the arts by professors should take this form.

Academic criticism plays a crucial role as the space of the collective refinement, enlargement, and transformation of the expert judgments guiding students' education. When we speak of the consensus of experts as the ultimate standard of knowledge and value in a field, we refer to the practices of peer review, the norms governing what counts as evidence, the venues of professional exchange. These are some of the means by which individual discovery takes a form amenable to collective recognition and response.

Consensus in literary studies refers less to a singular decision than to a spectrum. On one end lies broad or even tacit acceptance of some truth or judgment. At the other extreme lies the half-formulated preference of an individual professor. Between these extremes lies a field vital with tensions, dynamic with disagreements, and connected by a shared sense of what is required to make a judgment and interpretation public and present to the expert community. A judgment that achieves this public status, that places itself before the eyes of other experts for argument and evaluation, participates in the collective process of expert judgment.

This understanding of consensus enables a diversity of expert judgments. It is not necessary for every professor of American literature to agree with my sense of the meaning and significance of one of Emily Dickinson's poems. But it is necessary, for the validity of my judgment as expert judgment, that they understand how and why I see the poem as I do. If by *consensus* we understand a final and binding decision about the value of a given work or even about the kind of value it possesses, then we misunderstand the meaning of this term in this context. Consensus is the movement toward a common sense; it is the never-completed forging of something like the "sensus communis" Kant imagined as an innate property of every human mind.

The particular works we read, and the skills and concepts through which we read them, slowly change with the arguments of the professional discourse sheltered by the venues of the discipline. These are the spaces in which the collective knowledges and skills that constitute aesthetic expertise develop, coevolving with the discovery of new aesthetic traditions and the creation of new aesthetic works. One of the aims of a defense of judgment is thus to secure a renewed sense of the value of academic writing, not in competition or by analogy with creative writing, but in its institutional role as a source and test of extra-commercial values, an agent of the perceptual transformation of populations.

*

The final element of expertise I wish to explore before proceeding to examples involves criteria. Judgments are made on the basis of criteria. Criteria are the forms of value; when aesthetic experts claim to give people access to new kinds of value, we are often speaking of showing them new criteria. The work satisfies a desire we didn't know we could have; it exemplifies a principle we didn't know existed; it manifests a new quality.

The Humean thesis that the standard of value is the consensus of qualified critics derives from the impossibility of creating rules for applying even a familiar criterion—such as sublimity—to any individual instance. A painting of a mountain in a thunderstorm might be sublime, or it might be ridiculous. I want to extend Hume's thesis to suggest that the same principle applies to the question of *which* criteria are appropriate for a given work.

Here, too, there is no rule. The right criterion for a novel with a wedding at the end might be comic brilliance. Or it might be sublime terror. Or political insight. Or all three. It might be best judged in terms of a quality we don't yet have a name for. The novel might represent the pedestrian expression of common ideologies of the time tied together with threadbare conventions, a source of no knowledge one couldn't get more directly and clearly from a history or political science or gender studies text. A novel's jokes and metaphors might be dead past all hope of resuscitation. The novel might be a good example of a kind of thing we don't know how to value anymore, a reminder of how alien people in the past are. It might be the only example of its kind, with a quality unlike anything else. We might be wrong about it.

Academic criticism has consistently encountered difficulties due to its restriction of judgment to a narrow set of criteria. The New Criticism is exemplary in this regard. After decades of abuse, the New Criticism has seen something of a revival over the past decade or so. As Aubry writes, "The New Critics helped to support . . . the democratization on an unpreceded scale of nonproductive forms of aesthetic sensitivity that had been mostly reserved up until that point for members of the leisure class."[21] He argues that despite the polemics, the theory generation conserved the aesthetic values of the New Critics. Critics of the 1970s, 1980s, and 1990s "reject[ed] any firm distinction between literature and other texts . . . but continue[d] to seek out the experience of ambiguity, irony, and paradox."[22] These criteria, Aubry argues, shape critics' approach to historical, philosophical, or cultural matters, and they provide the values for the presentation of academic criticism itself as a species of creative writing. Aubry thus demonstrates that New Critical criteria survive the collapse of the New Critical project of aesthetic education.

Ambiguity, irony, complexity, formal integrity: these criteria exclude a vast range of aesthetic works, the value and power of which require different measures. Yet this restriction paradoxically accompanies the opposite problem, the bending of these criteria to show that any work is valuable. As Graff observes of the New Critical era, "The prospective evaluator was logically restricted to questions of formal coherence. And since what counted as the formal criterion was presumably whatever the poem itself was organically trying to be, even formal criticism was disarmed, in principle if not in practice."[23] Graff cites R. S. Crane's contemporaneous complaint that "a method needs to have some way . . . of producing counterexamples as well as examples."[24]

The New Criticism, as the last robust, intentional educational program of literary judgment, thus poses the challenge of criteria starkly. On the one hand, formalist criteria can easily be made to justify any work the professor or the profession happens to teach. On the other hand, insofar as formalist criteria can be made sufficiently rigorous, judgment risks sacrificing huge swathes of great literature.

This is a real problem, and not one that can be solved in advance or in principle. It can, however, be approached through the flexible, Humean model of expertise we've been exploring. Aesthetic experts should be familiar with a range of criteria; but they should also be capable of allowing the work to put their criteria in question. In this case, as in so many others, the critic's greatest strength can often be weakness, a kind of negative capability that enables alertness to unfamiliar modes of value, along with readiness to surrender current criteria. In the expert's capacity to derive her criteria from the work, we see again a profound truth of aesthetic expertise. The expert engagement with a work of art does not represent the encounter of a subject with an object. Expertise consists precisely in the capacity to encounter the work as constitutive of subjectivity. The expert approaches the work as the bearer of subjective qualities and capacities. She sees through the work's forms; she thinks with its concepts.

At the same time, this capacity has a critical side; this perceiving through the work is also a testing. We don't blindly accept the value of any work presented, nor do we accept its criteria for itself without putting it to the test. The same test we discovered for the evaluation of individual works should apply to the formulation of criteria. Does this form of value open the work in such a way as to reveal insights, aesthetic concepts, or forms that enrich our perception, knowledge, experience?

This flexible approach to criteria renders a Humean model uniquely capable of responding to the signal difference of literature today compared with Hume's time: its diversity. No fixed set of criteria will enable experts to come to terms with the varieties of genres, periods, and traditions. Furthermore, according to the paradoxical principle of literary history enunciated by Borges—"every writer creates his precursors"—we often find that criteria suggested by later periods illuminate the value of earlier, neglected works.[25] And the rediscovery of an earlier period's values might inspire new insights, new ways of approaching present-day works.

The capacity to adopt new criteria is especially pressing when considering that certain kinds of criteria have sometimes served to suppress the recognition of minority literatures. In a classic essay, Cheryl Wall describes Zora Neale Hurston's call for rejecting "conventional standards" that had obscured the appreciation of Black writing. Contributing to this neglect was the fact that "from its beginnings in the United States, black writing has been defined as having *only* an ideological importance."[26] "Departing from the work of mainly white scholars and critics of an earlier generation, much of the work in African American literary study has been devoted to defining aesthetic principles and to demonstrating the dual quests for freedom and for beauty in black writing."[27]

This activity of "defining aesthetic principles" describes the work of aesthetic expertise in discovering different values through the encounter with different kinds of work. But to recognize that appreciation of Black art frequently requires the formulation of new criteria certainly does not preclude the discovery of valuable features in these works through the application of modernist criteria, as the examples of bebop or Ralph Ellison in their different ways make clear. To take another example, Merve Emre has suggested we might learn alternate criteria from the "paraliterary" institutions that flourished alongside the New Critical academy in the mid-twentieth century. "What if, under certain circumstances, literature could teach us how to imitate fictional characters? . . . Which authors and texts would lend themselves to imitation? . . . What if reading could . . . teach us how to feel or amplify certain feelings?"[28]

Viable criteria will suggest a test, a way of ensuring that criteria don't decay into the dogmatic justification of whatever affective, aesthetic, intellectual, or political convictions the professor wishes to transmit. We thus need to ask of the criteria above, Show us an example of a work that teaches us how to feel. How does this work? Why would we want to amplify certain feelings? Show us a work that attempts to amplify certain feelings and fails. The role of the counter-example has perhaps been too little pursued in aesthetic education. But the practice of coming up with counterfactual sentences that would ruin the effect of a given passage, for example, can be one way of preventing criteria from sliding into vague affirmation.[29]

As Graff argues, the history of aesthetic education shows the risk that the professor's techniques can devolve into engines for justifying any work she chooses to put before the class. To adopt a delimited set of restrictive criteria might ameliorate this danger but only at the cost of sacrificing much of the interest of past literature, as well as the profession's openness to cultural change. Part of the solution is to understand the capacity of the venues of professional exchange to function as processes for the discovery and testing of new forms of value. The skepticism with which any profession greets proclamations of new forms of value can, if carried too far, serve to repress. But in moderation this tendency has the benign effect of forcing practitioners to demonstrate and to defend their claim for the value and interest of a kind of work obscured by existing criteria.

I want to conclude this chapter by exploring the resistance literary studies has offered to one particular criterion. The prospect of judging works by the quality of the ideas they contain cuts against the perennial formalism of the field, the tendency—derived from Kantian aesthetics—to turn every question about the artistic value of literature into a question about form.[30] While formalism may appear to provide literary studies with a specific expertise, in practice it prevents literary scholars from constructing viable interdisciplinary methods adequate to literary content's inevitable traversal of disciplinary boundaries. Since this problem involves basic assumptions about the nature of literary studies as a discipline, it represents a particularly revealing demonstration of the dangers of restrictive criteria.

*

Caroline Levine's recent book *Forms* is an influential example of the resurgence of formalism. The novelty of her approach lies in her attempt to show that literary form, in addition to representing the discipline's object of study, also represents our best way of projecting the interest of our work beyond the bounds of the discipline. Her argument is simple. All spheres of human life are organized by form. Since literary critics have a special competence with form, therefore "it is time to export . . . to take our traditional skills to new objects— the social structures and institutions that are among the most crucial sites of political efficacy."[31] Evaluating works according to exclusively formalist criteria will give our judgments the widest influence.

Chief among the virtues of Levine's book is its demonstration of how dynamic formalism looks next to the dominant desiccated historicism. But her program for proving and projecting the interest of literary studies, by attempting to fit different kinds of criteria under the heading of form, both renders form vaporous and obscures the work necessary to test the virtues she claims for it. First, the forms on which her argument hinges are not forms at all but ideas described as forms. Second, these ideas are secondhand, derived from other fields. These issues are not due to carelessness; she presents the formalist case powerfully. As I will show, her book's problems are bound to attend any effort to make literary form the primary basis of literary interest.

The problems are starkly evident in the extended reading of Elizabeth Barrett Browning's "The Young Queen" that occupies the heart of *Forms* (74–81). Levine's argument unfolds in two stages. First, she describes the ideational content of the poem, then she redescribes that content in terms of form. Barrett Browning stages the conflict between two different kinds of institutional time: the time of mourning following the king's death and the political rhythms of the monarchy. Levine states that the way the poet handles this conflict "anticipates the work of the New Institutionalists" (74).

The New Institutionalism is a twentieth-century school of thought in the social sciences that rejects totalizing ideological or economic analyses in order to focus on how relations between and within institutions shape society. Where Marxist sociologists or neoclassical economists see the social order as determined by large-scale underlying causes, New Institutionalists describe conflicts between competing and overlapping institutions. From their perspective, the world looks less monolithic, more striated and fractured. More possibilities for emancipation or constraint open up than are visible from traditional perspectives. Barrett Browning's interest in the chafing of different norms, derived from different traditions, around the death of the king seems to Levine to prefigure this view.

It's worth attending closely to Levine's claim that the nineteenth-century poet anticipates twentieth-century social science. The term *anticipation* appears designed to free the critic from the kind of work that a term like *influence* requires. Whereas a claim of influence necessitates carefully uncovering causal links between the literature and the various social scientists whose thinking was shaped by it, the claim of anticipation is merely that a certain literary idea *resembles* a later scientific idea. The claim is vulnerable to the charge that the literary idea bears only a superficial resemblance to the scientific concept and lacks the background assumptions that give the concept meaning in its scientific context.[32]

Claims of anticipation suffer from a kind of bad faith. Accept for the moment that Barrett Browning's poem does in fact express an insight about institutions deeply consonant with that of the New Institutionalists. We might wish to celebrate the poet for being in advance of social science. But the literary critic—Levine—comes to this knowledge *after* the New Institutionalists. It is only by familiarity with their ideas that she can recognize the similarity in Barrett Browning's poem. The claim of literature's priority with respect to the science masks the belatedness of literary criticism.

This isn't necessarily fatal. In a study of influence, the critic must still do the historical work of locating and describing the relevant causal chains. But what has the critic of "anticipation" done? She's simply noticed a resemblance in the literature to something she has read elsewhere. This kind of noticing is as valuable in literary studies as it is in other fields—when it plays a role supporting a judgment that also makes use of other skills and knowledges. Having noticed the resemblance, Levine might, for example, have brought the poem into critical engagement with the science, showing how Barrett Browning achieves insights that correct or transform or extend some aspect of the science.

But the claim of anticipation doesn't involve this kind of work. If there is a difference between the poet's insight and that of the social scientists, Levine doesn't explore it. She simply presents Barrett Browning's lines as exemplifying a kind of thinking robustly detailed by social scientists. Because Levine is trying to show that the literary scholar possesses knowledge about society that can be "exported" to other fields, this is a problem (*Forms*, 23). The critic's social knowledge is imported. Repackaging it as an export would seem to require some fairly inventive marketing.

Unless, that is, the second, formalist stage of Levine's argument can make good on the unfulfilled promise of the first. She proceeds to tackle the meter of "The Young Queen," arguing that it is in form that the original contribution of literature toward social understanding can be found. The argument she draws from this analysis presents a familiar problem.

Levine tells us that by attending to the poem's metrical form, we learn to reject schemes that project a "powerfully homogenizing, unifying order on the social" (80). In place of such totalizing views, the poet presents a "new hypothesis: what if the organizing forms of the world do not—cannot—unify experience?" (80) What if the social order is instead shaped by the friction of different structures and institutions? This is of course the same message that Levine has just taken from the New Institutionalists, a message she has already found "anticipated" by the poem's content.

Levine has taken the ideational content of the poem, which she understands in terms of concepts borrowed from social science, and projected it onto the poem's form. Her reading thus consists of an old literary critical move—the application of ideas drawn from another discipline to interpret a poem. For readers who already value Barrett Browning's poetry, such a move may prove useful in elucidating its meaning. But such people aren't Levine's audience. Her criterion for judging the poem is simple: what does its form teach us about society? She explicitly addresses her book to those in our field who want to use literary critical knowledge to intervene in other spheres. Her book can offer nothing to such an audience. It contains no social or political perspective that can't be gotten directly from the works of the New Institutionalists. According to her own criteria, rigorously applied, the poems she presents as valuable are valueless.

Levine's translation of the idea into form produces the illusion of discovery. This is a risk of the formalist method. Instead of interpreting ideas, the formalist critic recognizes forms. "Once we recognize the organizing principles of different literary forms . . . they are themselves no longer matters of interpretive activity or debate" (13). Here Levine draws from Frances Ferguson, who, as an example of literary form, chooses the sonnet in *Romeo and Juliet*. Ferguson's point is that the status of a given arrangement of words as a sonnet doesn't require interpretation: it either is or it isn't. Levine tries to treat ideas as if they could be approached in the same way as metrical patterns. Underlying this approach is a process the Marxists used to call reification—the transformation of a flexible, inventive human activity into an object. As soon as an idea is spotted in a literary work, the critic's basilisk eye casts it in the stone of form. Why this antipathy toward literary ideas?

I think the root of this fear lies in the move, foundational for the modern discipline of literary studies, by which the New Critics described the expertise of literature professors. Critics deserve to occupy a special place in the modern research institution, so the argument went, by virtue of our special knowledge of and capacity to judge literary form. Historically, literary formalism's primary institutional function has been to mark off the boundaries of the discipline.

The new formalist project thus confronts a basic paradox. Critics want to use tools designed to enforce the boundaries of literary studies as a means of making those boundaries permeable. Books like Levine's are dominated by the silent imperative inherited from disciplinary history: treat every idea as an effect of form. This treatment requires the critic to translate semantic material that might express concerns shared with other disciplines into a form meaningful within literary studies alone. The imperative makes it impossible to achieve the goal of demonstrating the value of literary studies in terms of its capacity for extraliterary knowledge. It explains why critics' accounts of literature's social knowledge must in the end turn to another discipline for its ideas about society.

The formalism practiced by literary critics has no extraliterary significance. This isn't a bug, it's a feature. When formalism fails to yield exportable ideas, it's just doing what it was designed to do. But literature's concerns have never been confined to the boundaries of any academic discipline. Therefore, an important element of literary expertise is the capacity to evaluate works when the relevant criteria require interaction with other disciplines. A broad and thin knowledge of a range of other disciplines, as well as an understanding of how to get deeper knowledge when the evaluation of a work requires it, is just as important to literary expertise as the capacity to notice patterns of images. We should jettison the residue of Kantian and New Critical prejudice by admitting that the judgment of artworks isn't confined to formal features but embraces a range of criteria. If we are interested, as Levine and many others are, in engagement with the wider world of knowledge and action without being shamed or ignored, we should explore the resource that has always interested people beyond literary studies: literary ideas.

The possibilities can be demonstrated by James Gleik's recent book *Time Travel*. Gleik shows how H. G. Wells was the first to ever conjoin the words *time* and *travel*, and then he shows how Wells's underlying conception of time in terms of space shaped developments in theoretical physics.[33] Reviewed glowingly everywhere from *Nature* to the *New York Review of Books*, the book's reception is everything that Levine might wish.

At a dinner after a recent talk on a topic in the natural sciences, I found myself surrounded by colleagues from philosophy, history, economics, physics, and chemistry, all of whom were familiar with Gleik's book. A few had been surprised to learn of this instance of the power and influence of a literary idea, but most were not. And why should they be? Literature is full of the most astonishing ideas on every imaginable topic.

Literally opening my volume of Emily Dickinson's *Poems* at random, I find 419, "A Toad, can die of Light." The poem expresses the idea that death is a "right," the rightful possession of each individual living thing. A toad has a right to his death, just as I have to mine. "Life," on the other hand, is a kind of common substance, one that fails to individuate. Dickinson expresses this idea by imagining blood-red wine broken out of its separate casks. "Which Ruby's mine?"[34]

Here, among others, we have the idea—one Dickinson also develops in better-known poems—that we have a right to die, but life can't be thought of in terms of rights. Granted, to say this is to commit the heresy of paraphrase, to fail to understand the complex ways the forms of Dickinson's lines interact with the meaning. But so what? When faced with a group of undergraduates, or colleagues from a different field, wanting to know why they should care about this poem, we might start with the ideas. And we can use other ideas—Arendt's, Agamben's, Aristotle's—to create a context in which to establish the literary idea's resemblances and differences, its strengths and weaknesses, with respect to the philosophy. The evaluation of some literary values may not have any specific "aesthetic" component, and they may not look different from the processes of evaluation in other fields—may, in the case of some literary ideas, be identical to those processes. Unlike such aesthetic ideas as the sublime, the ridiculous, or the beautiful, there is nothing particularly "aesthetic" about the concepts I have in mind here. But the discovery of literary ideas is embedded in the tacit structure of literary expertise, and it often requires judgment to discern. Aesthetic expertise will thus often take a hybrid form when compared to a model of expertise seeking to circumscribe expert access to artworks by a prior understanding of the limits of the aesthetic.

The ideas in "A Toad, can die of Light" are not encoded, they are expressed. Perhaps an ingenious formalist might be able to show how the ideas are somehow canceled or ironized by the line breaks or dashes. I doubt this enterprise could succeed in the case of this poem. But we should be clear that the motive of such a reading could only be to destroy the possibility of bringing Dickinson's work into contact with the concerns of anyone who isn't professionally committed to reducing literary values to formal criteria.

I sometimes think of literature in the way scientists working on new medications think of the rain forest: the chances are that the next great idea—of philosophy, economics, history, neuroscience, or political science—lies buried somewhere in the literature section of the library. If nothing else, the critics who've found so many of the signature ideas of other fields "anticipated" by literature have given us compelling evidence that this might be the case. Why should critics always be condemned to belatedness with respect to literary knowledge?

To overcome this belatedness, we need to recognize that the power of the ideas and insights found in literature represents a distinctive criterion for judging literary works. This enables us to clearly see the work involved in evaluating these ideas. The capacity to interpret and evaluate the formal dimensions of works is important. But formalist skills are largely irrelevant to the interdisciplinary work required to evaluate a literary idea in terms of the fields it touches. When publishing a literary idea in a neuroscience journal, for instance, I suppress reflections on the formal structures of its literary context, simply because such structures don't matter here.[35] Naturally, this isn't to say that there aren't many interesting interactions between form and idea. My fifth chapter focuses on how the effort to forge certain aesthetic effects involves writers in hard philosophical and psychological thinking. The results of this thinking can be brought into fruitful relation—not "anticipation"—with the ideas of other disciplines.

Such a relation requires hard work on the critic's part. Levine's nuanced understanding of the New Institutionalism exemplifies the kind of extradisciplinary research the judgment of literary ideas will pursue. But this is only half the work. We need to develop the capacity to lay down our formalist tools at times to cultivate a different kind of reading. Adorno derided the ideas expressed by literary works as mere "opinions."[36] His sense that what the work expresses is less valuable than what it encodes has been tacitly endorsed by formalist criticism, which identifies professional expertise with techniques of decoding.[37]

But there are other interpretive techniques. To identify and understand the ideas a poem like "A Toad, can die of Light" expresses is no easy task; it requires the capacity to suspend our projections, to develop new ways of responding to new criteria, along with an alertness, a hunger for new thoughts. The discovery, evaluation, and explication of these ideas promise to both project the work of our field to new audiences and serve as a needed check on educational practices. Pretending that literary study is identical to the study of form represents another pitfall of literary expertise in blinding us to the work needed to evaluate the ideas on which literary education inevitably depends.

The problem of restricting judgment to formalist criteria rehearses once again the Kantian error of beginning with a restricted range of experience or particular human capacity we call aesthetic, then interpreting artworks insofar as they can be brought under those headings. But if we start instead from engagement with the object of study, we adapt our criteria to the values we discover in the object.[38]

The following extended examples of expert judgment illustrate the elements of expertise described in this and the preceding chapters. I've chosen my emphases in part to counter the bias that literary judgment is limited to form. In the fifth and seventh chapters, the criterion is the power of specific literary ideas. In the sixth chapter, the work of judgment discloses a criterion suggested by the literary work itself.

PART 2

The Practice of Judgment

✳ 5 ✳

How Poems Know
What It's Like to Die

What does literature know, and how does it know it? A prominent philosopher of science has recently argued that literature aims to produce not knowledge but certain aesthetic or emotional effects.[1] Literary critics, therefore, should abandon their efforts to create knowledge and return to cultivating literary appreciation. But even if we restrict our attention to literature's aesthetic qualities, can we abandon philosophical and scientific problems of knowledge? In some cases, the judgment of a work's aesthetic qualities is inextricable from the evaluation of its ideas. In judging that poems by Emily Dickinson and John Keats create compelling depictions of what it is like to die, I will show how they have taught us something new about life and death.

The poets' strategy is to present an experience of listening as an analogue to the experience of dying. We are familiar with the sensation of "losing ourselves" in sound. In describing this familiar experience, the writers locate surprising aspects of it. These aspects align absorbed listening with some of our intuitions about what death is like. The authors of "I heard a Fly buzz—when I died—" and "Ode to a Nightingale" find a depiction of listening to be analogous to the experience of death because they have discovered something extraordinary about this ordinary experience. I think we can learn something about how literature generates new knowledge by attending to this discovery.

> I heard a Fly buzz—when I died—
> The Stillness in the Room

Was like the Stillness in the Air—
Between the Heaves of Storm—

The Eyes around—had wrung them dry—
And Breaths were gathering firm
For that last Onset—when the King
Be witnessed—in the Room—

I willed my Keepsakes—Signed away
What portion of me be
Assignable—and then it was
There interposed a Fly—

With Blue—uncertain—stumbling Buzz—
Between the light—and me—
And then the Windows failed—and then
I could not see to see—[2]

The poem's first line indicates that its subject is the experience of crossing from life to death. Dickinson describes the experience of dying by way of a certain experience of listening. The speaker experiences the sound of the fly as an interruption. She has been thinking of other things—in particular, about her imminent death. A group of people are in the room with her, and they are thinking about death in a familiar way. From their perspective, death marks a dramatic break with ordinary life. It is awaited as one awaits the dramatic entrance of a "King," a transcendent being whose entrance creates a sharp discontinuity. Immediately before she hears the fly, the speaker has been thinking about her death in another familiar way: death as the dissolution of the person's objective, public existence. She has been making her will, distributing the material dimension of her legal and social identity to her heirs.

At this point her thoughts are interrupted, not by a "King" but by the sound of a fly buzzing in the quiet room. She becomes absorbed in the experience of listening; she hears the fine-grained contours of the sound: "uncertain—stumbling Buzz." At the apex of her absorption, the experience of listening eclipses the experience of sight; the buzz comes "between the light—and me." Sound replaces vision. And the poem ends.

Freud famously affirmed that our own death is "unimaginable, and whenever we make the attempt to imagine it we can perceive that we really remain as spectators."[3] Dickinson here proves Freud wrong. She imagines death, and she imagines it without having to imagine herself remaining as a spectator. She imagines the experience of crossing from life to death entirely from within, as an experience of absorption in sound. We have all had this captivating experience. We sometimes describe it by saying we have "lost ourselves" in the sound. Dickinson simply asks that we take seriously that aspect of the experience of absorbed listening that causes us to speak of "losing ourselves." Dying is just like losing oneself in sound, the poem suggests, with the difference that in the case of death, one doesn't return to oneself.

What criteria can we use to judge the adequacy of this resemblance? We do, after all, know some things about death. We have a rough sense of the kind of state it is, mostly because we have a rough sense of the kind of state it isn't. Our intuition tells us that death is unlike life in various ways. We feel that death will probably bring an end to our concern with our careers, for example. We think it will probably bring an end to our friendships, at least in their familiar form. And it probably seems reasonable to most of us to assume that death will bring an end to our various experiences.

Now the true scale of Dickinson's problem is starkly clear. Any chance of producing a compelling account of the experience of death depends on finding an analogue in living experience. But the criteria we might use to establish the similarity of the experience of life to the experience of death reflect our intuition that death is profoundly unlike life. Therefore, to bring off her aesthetic effect, *Dickinson must convince us that a certain living experience is profoundly unlike life as we understand it.*[4]

Our intuition about death is that it is a state in which we don't have experiences. The aesthetic structure of Dickinson's poem—using the experience of absorbed listening to show what the experience of death is like—depends on the idea that absorbed listening is a state in which we don't have experiences. This listening, in other words, presents a case where first-person experience gives access to an experience in which the self is not present.

Dickinson's implicit position challenges both the philosophical view that experience provides direct evidence for the existence of a self—to think is to be, as Descartes has it—as well as the literary historical view that equates descriptions of first-person experience with individualist ideology.[5] If our exploration reveals Dickinson's idea to be philosophically coherent, we might take the poem as both an exception to the common view of literary history and evidence for the separability of representations of experience from representations of individuality or identity. While I will not dwell on the literary historical implications of my argument, I understand it to develop a project pursued by Sharon Cameron in her later work, which investigates impersonality in nineteenth-century American literature. Demonstrating the separability of experience and identity may also have implications for the way we understand the role of memoir, for example, in modern literary culture.[6]

Some philosophers have written about experience in ways that support some aspects of Dickinson's implicit claim about absorbed listening. Hume, for example, observes that "I never catch myself at any time without a perception, and never can observe anything but the perception."[7] Derek Parfit has carried out perhaps the most influential recent development of Hume's thinking in this respect. Parfit cites Lichtenberg's argument that immediate experience gives me no sense of a subject, and he goes on to argue that therefore it is possible to give an "impersonal description" of experience.[8] Since nothing in my immediate experience gives evidence of a self, for Parfit we discover this sense in psychological continuity, in the felt connection of present experiences to past experiences, the sense of present experience as being consistent with past experience. Parfit redescribes death as the disappearance of psychological continuity and the persistence of other kinds of continuity.

By suppressing the kind of psychological continuity that would be displayed had the poem continued past its final line, Dickinson suppresses what Parfit takes to be the ground of our sense of ourselves. If the speaker had tried to shoo the fly away, or had begun to observe the mourners gathered around her deathbed, or had returned to thoughts of making her will, the represented experience would immediately cease to resemble what we intuit about death, because it would now include the survival of a self. Or, to follow Parfit more precisely, it would now include the condition—psychological continuity—that produces what we ordinarily refer to as a self. As it is, the poem's final lines represent an experience, but the experience is in an important sense not the speaker's experience.

Several aspects of the poem will immediately seem to qualify this assertion. First, the very existence of the poem suggests the speaker's survival. Furthermore, this survival is underlined by the poem's retrospective narration: "I heard a Fly buzz—when I died." This implies, and pretty strongly, that the "I" has survived the experience.

But I prefer to read the choice of retrospective narration as Dickinson's acknowledgment of the fundamentally illusory status of the poem's claim to represent death. It is ultimately impossible for her to deny it. Imagine that she attempted to conceal it by writing the poem in the present tense: "Hearing a fly buzz—blue, uncertain, stumbling buzz." The very fact of the poem would give it the lie. Dickinson's aesthetic effort here is not to convince us that the poem really contains the testimony of someone who has died. Rather, she wants to create a convincing experiential analogue to death. Openly acknowledging the poem's necessary fiction tends, in my view, to shift our interest to the capacity of the experience to stand as compelling analogue. Furthermore, while the narrative tense generates an implied *formal* continuity with the experience that ends the poem, Dickinson suppresses *psychological* continuity. There is no record of experiences *after* the experience of absorbed listening.

Similarly, I read the final two lines, which explicitly refer to a subject, not as a representation of the experience of absorbed listening, nor as the representation of further experiences, but as the poet's indication of the status of that experience. The sound, the speaker tells us, comes "between the light—and me." I hear a distinction between this line's characterization of the experience of absorbed listening and the description of the content of that experience in lines 11 through 13. On this reading, the final two lines occupy the same narrative space as the initial line. The poet tells us something about the status of this experience of listening: that it is an experience of death, that it involves sound eclipsing vision, that it involves sound eclipsing "me."

To be sure, this language acknowledges the fictional status of the poem's claim to represent an actual experience of death. We know that if it were an actual experience of death, there would be no one to tell us about it, no one to say: this description of listening is a description of death. But the explicit subjects—"me, I"—of the final stanza don't in my view compromise the poet's representation of the subject-lessness of absorbed listening. The speaker loses herself in a sound, and then she doesn't return to herself. In this respect, what is important is that the final lines don't record *further* experiences.

But this raises another objection. Even if the final experience is not represented as followed by subsequent experiences, the moment of listening is connected to the speaker's earlier experiences. Hearing the fly succeeds her ruminations about her will. Isn't there psychological continuity here? Recall, however, that Dickinson represents the fly's buzz as interrupting this continuity. There is no indication that, while she is absorbed in listening to the fly, the speaker is conscious of her earlier thoughts. The fly is represented as consuming her attention. We can imagine that if the poem had continued, she would again become aware of psychological continuity of previous experiences with the experience of the buzzing. But of course the fact that the poem ends amid this absorbed listening is part of what makes it a convincing analogue to death.

And yet the very fact that this experience is identifiable as the experience of a particular person might seem to make it profoundly unconvincing as a representation of death. As readers, from the outside, we identify this listening as the experience of a particular person. As we've seen, Dickinson's speaker, in the first and final lines, also occupies an external position with respect to this experience in declaring: this is the experience of *my* death. Dickinson's inclusion of other people within the poem's frame might seem to further undermine the subjectlessness of the experience. She is listening to the fly, they might think, watching her. We might reasonably demand of a compelling representation of death that no experience at all be happening inside the head of the dead woman. We might demand that all experience be represented as disappearing, yet in this poem only vision disappears. Wouldn't a representation of a slide into unconsciousness, therefore, be a better image for death than absorbed listening?

But from within that listening, within the rapt attention to the fly's buzz, there is no sense of self, no sense of the location of experience, no sense of experience as the experience of a particular person. As Parfit argues, nothing in the content of immediate experience gives evidence of the existence of a subject. A perspective outside the moment of experience is required to identify the experience with a subject, either the temporal perspective of psychological continuity with other experiences or the external perspective of an observer.

The poem fulfills our rigorous demand by offering us a perspective from which there is no detectable link between the experience and the woman who crosses from life to death. This is the perspective of absorbed listening itself.

I think Dickinson's strategy is ultimately a more plausible way of describing the experience of death than a representation of experience disappearing. The latter might seem to be the best method; the ubiquity of comparisons of dying to falling asleep shows that many have found this method satisfying. Consider the following famous examples from Shakespeare:

> After life's fitful fever, he sleeps well.[9]

> To die:—to sleep:
> No more; and, by a sleep to say we end
> The heart-ache and the thousand natural shocks
> That flesh is heir to, 'tis a consummation
> Devoutly to be wished.[10]

Sleep resembles death insofar as we understand (dreamless) sleep to be a state of unconsciousness, a state where we don't have experiences. But as Freud points out, it suffers from a fundamental flaw. To imagine our experience of death as the disappearance of experience, he notes, is to surreptitiously reintroduce ourselves into the scene as an observer, as the one who makes the judgment: now I am asleep. This of course presumes the survival of the self and furthermore conceals this survival from ourselves.

We can never experience the cessation of experience. We can only imagine looking at ourselves and saying: there is no experience in that body. In imagining death as sleep, in fact, we imagine *both* our continued experience *and* our continued subjecthood. But in absorbed listening, Dickinson suggests, we experience the extinction of the subject. And this is the closest we can come to an experiential analogue to death.

The poem invites us to imagine death by directing us to reflect on our own experiences of absorbed listening. Of course after and before such an experience, we have access to a perspective that identifies the experience with a subject. But the poem holds open a space in which experience is separate from a subject; we can judge the plausibility of the poem's representation of this experience as selfless simply by reflecting on our own experiences of absorbed listening. If the image of sleep or unconsciousness gives us neither the experience of no experience nor the experience of the loss of self, the image of absorbed listening does deliver the latter. Furthermore, when we compare the smuggling of the subject back into the picture in the case of sleep to the purely formal survival that Dickinson acknowledges by placing her narration in the past tense, I think we will prefer the latter.

We might still resist Dickinson's presentation of the experience of death in terms of an experience without terminus. But several considerations may soften this resistance. We don't, after all, imagine that all experiences will stop when we die; we just imagine that *we* will stop having experiences. The speaker recounts a state in which experience is happening, but that experience's relation to her has been severed. And this aligns with some of our basic intuitions about what death is like. If we agree with Parfit and Hume about experience, we can see how the presentation of an experience which suppresses psychological continuity—which begins with the interruption of previous sensations and thoughts, and ends without the representation of further sensations or thoughts that would serve to anchor a sense of self—can seem analogous enough with death to ensure the poem's aesthetic success. Aesthetic success doesn't require us to believe that death will really be like this. We simply need to feel that aspects of the experience of absorbed listening are sufficiently, if surprisingly, similar to some aspects of our intuition about death.

The surprise is an epistemological benefit, because it signals that the poem has discovered something. A little reflection will show that Dickinson is not merely representing experience in accordance with what philosophers after Hume tell us about the selflessness of immediate experience. Their accounts provide no basis for understanding why Dickinson chooses to analogize death by the experience of absorbed listening, as opposed to, say, absorbed looking or distracted listening. Hume's and Parfit's claims are about perception as such, not certain kinds of perception. But this poem would not be as powerful as it is were the experience one of sight, for example, or of distraction.

In fact, Parfit doesn't think that we experience our identity as a matter of psychological continuity across moments of selfless experience. He thinks, to cite the title of chapter 10 of *Reasons and Persons*, "we are not what we believe." Analysis and argument are required to show us that what we think of as our personal identity is in fact merely psychological continuity. Dickinson, on the other hand, suggests that if we attend to a certain kind of experience, the experience of absorbed listening, we will find that in this experience we have directly experienced the absence of self. In this experience we have undergone the separation of experience from subject. This feature serves to distinguish absorbed listening from most other forms of experience, which accounts for its peculiar appropriateness for Dickinson's poetic structure.[11]

In a perceptive essay, Katie Peterson has traced Dickinson's representation of hearing through a number of poems—though not the one that concerns us here. Her account is nevertheless useful in establishing a pattern in the poet's work in which "individual personhood is threatened by an intense experience in the auditory realm."[12] We can begin to specify the source of the auditory eclipse of selfhood by drawing from the phenomenological tradition.

Philosophers from Husserl to Merleau-Ponty to Shaun Gallagher have described the intentional structure of experience, the extent to which I am aware of the object of perception without being aware that it is I who is the subject of this awareness.[13] This tradition has also shown how in the course of everyday life this kind of perception is frequently, even incessantly, disrupted. In everyday life, I do indeed become aware of myself, and of my difference from the object of my perception. And this happens in ways different from the background sense of psychological continuity Parfit picks out. Think of Martin Heidegger's famous example of the worker who's absorbed in his job when his tool suddenly breaks. Before the malfunction, his experience is of utter absorption in the activity. He is not conscious of himself. The accident serves to precipitate a sense of self, and a sense of division between subject and object, from his experience.[14]

Some sense modalities appear better suited to the experience of absorption than others. Michael Fried's work on the antitheatrical tradition in French painting, for example, draws from the phenomenological tradition to argue that the motivation for minimizing the theatrical orientation of the painting to the audience is to minimize the audience's sense of the subject/object distinction.[15] When I become aware that someone is performing for me, I tend to become self-conscious. My experience of the spectacle takes on a different quality; I become aware of the location of my attention and the relative distance of that location from the object of my attention. It is as if I am unable to concentrate entirely on the object since my sense of myself as subject occupies part of my attention.

Now vision, perhaps because of the very robustness of mental resources devoted to it in the human brain, tends to provide me with a very distinct sense of my location with respect to the objects of vision. This accounts for the scale of the challenge that confronts painters who want to elicit absorption. Sight continually informs me that the painting is over there, and I am here. This constant visual sense of the difference between subject and object doesn't negate Parfit's reflections on the fundamental subjectlessness of experience. To establish the existence of a permanent self, of a substantial subject of experience, would require awareness of what Parfit calls a "further fact" besides the immediate data of experience.[16] Vision doesn't give me access to this further fact. But vision does tend to highlight the source of my experience in my body. The persistence of my body is one ground of my sense that I am a self. It is harder to experience the kind of interruption Dickinson represents when I am aware of my body.

Furthermore, since I connect the persistence of my body with my psychological continuity, this introduces a fuller sense of self into the immediate experience of sight. My awareness of my body is like a spatial emblem of the psychological continuity of my experiences across time that constitutes my sense of self. Visual experience reminds me of psychological continuity; in other words, it reminds me of my self. Vision constantly threatens to precipitate me from absorption in the moment of perception, the moment where, as Parfit argues, there is no self.

Vision is distracting with respect to the aspect of experience Dickinson means to activate. It's hard for me to "lose myself" while my eyes are open. I don't say it's impossible; we have, after all, the testimony of Chardin's enraptured audiences if not our own memory of arresting visual experiences. But it is difficult to lose oneself with open eyes, and this difficulty invalidates vision for Dickinson's effort to represent an experience that lacks a sense of self.

Compare the experience of being at a concert and listening to the music with your eyes open with attending that concert but listening with eyes closed. These are fundamentally different experiences.

Musicologists refer to sound heard without a visual sense of its source as acousmatic sound. Here the sense of distance between oneself and the source of the music is much less distinct. Brian Kane, in *Sound Unseen*, observes that in experiencing acousmatic sound, "the location of [the sound's] source as definitively located inside or outside the listener's own body . . . becomes uncertain."[17] One's muted awareness of the physical distance between oneself and the music, one's muted awareness of the distinctive place of one's body relative to phenomena, enables one to descend completely into the experience of the music as it unfolds. In this experience, there is no scaffolding for the subject of experience. There is just the experience of the music.[18]

You lose yourself in the music. You become absorbed in the music; your self is not part of the content of the experience. Now imagine that the song comes to an end, or that your friend gently touches your shoulder, or that your nose begins to itch. You open your eyes. You have returned to yourself.

Now imagine the experience without this last part. Where were you? Who were you? It might be tempting to say that your self was somehow suspended or covered up during this experience. But Parfit, Hume, and the others provide good reasons for thinking that this was not the case and that there was simply no self there. If you had to pick an experience of life that resembled death, wouldn't this be a good one?

Many poets, at any rate, have found it so. Here are passages from two famous poems that, each in a different way, use absorbed listening as a bridge to death:

> Now more than ever seems it rich to die,
> To cease upon the midnight with no pain,
> While thou art pouring forth thy soul abroad
> In such an ecstasy![19]

> She whispered a song along the keyboard
> to Mal Waldron and everyone and I stopped breathing.[20]

Dickinson's poem is hardly the only one to approach death by way of sound. But "I heard a Fly buzz—when I died—" presents what's at stake aesthetically and philosophically most clearly, even starkly.

Dickinson's representation of death in terms of the experience of listening picks out some interesting features of this kind of experience. Part of the philosophical interest of what Dickinson highlights about listening may depend less on articulating new ideas about experience, more on drawing together different existing accounts of experience in a new way.[21] The poem would then function as a kind of lens that brings a set of reflections about experience stretching from Hume to Parfit into relation with a different set of reflections about experience stretching from Husserl to Gallagher.

I think there is another, and perhaps stronger, way in which Dickinson challenges our ordinary thinking about experience. We can approach this by way of a possible objection to my discussion of Dickinson's poem. Dickinson describes the experience of hearing a fly buzz, but I have reflected on the poem by way of examples of listening to music. I use a musical example simply because it is the experience of absorbed listening that will be most familiar to most people. Certainly, it is possible to become absorbed in some nonmusical sounds, such as that of a fly buzzing; I think such absorption is similar, with respect to the relevant effects, to my musical example.

Branka Arsić's fascinating discussion of Thoreau's accounts of listening identifies several descriptions of natural sound as music that are roughly contemporaneous with Dickinson's poem. Thoreau claims that "clear and unprejudiced ears hear the sweetest and most soul-stirring melody in tinkling cowbells and the like (dogs baying at the moon). . . . Those cheap and simple sounds . . . men despise because their ears are dull and debauched."[22]

In other passages, as Arsić shows, Thoreau goes beyond saying that such natural sounds are a kind of music to saying that they are preferable to ordinary music because of their resistance to ideation. Thoreau sometimes fears that the various associations and concepts music may trigger in the listener will tend to prevent the felt dissolution of the barrier between subject and object. While it may be possible to see a similar motive behind Dickinson's depiction of the buzzing fly, I think the relevant feature of this depiction is simply the experience of absorbed listening itself. I'm not sure that the particularity of the object defines this experience.[23]

Arsić's account of some of Thoreau's writing about sound emphasizes the difficulty and rarity of a kind of listening that erases the difference between subject and object. She cites John Cage's reading of

Thoreau; Cage claims that "the whole history of the ego along with all of its habits must be undone" to experience subjectless listening.[24] But part of what poems that approach death through experiences of listening show us is that nothing like this extensive process of self-unmaking is necessary.

The loss of self in hearing is a pretty common experience. In the words of a different Thoreau quotation, Dickinson reveals the "cheap and universal" quality of this listening.[25] I understand Dickinson to be drawing out the extraordinary quality of ordinary and common experiences. In this way, she challenges the view that to directly experience the absence of self is difficult and requires various mental, sonic, or spiritual contortions. The poetic structure by which Dickinson delivers this insight is complex and sophisticated; the route that enables us to see a familiar experience in a new way is twisting. But the experience in question is simple and fairly common.

If Dickinson's poem illuminates an interesting aspect of a familiar experience, the way poetry knows what it's like to die also generates a different kind of knowledge, one perhaps more genuinely novel if also far stranger. To begin to explore this other thing that poetry knows about death, return to the memory of closing your eyes at a concert. What motivates you to do this? Perhaps it is simply to hear the music better. But perhaps there is another desire, a desire to become more fully absorbed in the music.

Now imagine that your eyes are closed and that you are listening, but you still are not as absorbed as you would like to be. At that moment, from a place entirely within this experience, what concrete form might your desire for more absorption take? Imagine that the music is just loud enough; that you aren't distracted by people shoving or talking or by cell phones going off; that your ankle isn't throbbing; that your nose isn't running. What could make the experience of the music more intense?

To pursue this question, we need now to turn to Dickinson's great predecessor in the effort to represent death by listening. In a dynamic that will appear paradoxical only to those who expect literary history to be linear, Dickinson gives a fuller picture of why absorbed listening works as a satisfying experiential analogue to death, while a prior poet, John Keats, shows how this discovery leads to a new way of desiring death.

Here is a longer excerpt from "Ode to a Nightingale":

Away! away! for I will fly to thee,
 Not charioted by Bacchus and his pards,
But on the viewless wings of Poesy,
 Though the dull brain perplexes and retards:
Already with thee! tender is the night,
 And haply the Queen-Moon is on her throne,
  Cluster'd around by all her starry Fays;
   But here there is no light,
 Save what from heaven is with the breezes blown
  Through verdurous glooms and winding mossy ways.

I cannot see what flowers are at my feet,
 Nor what soft incense hangs upon the boughs,
But, in embalmed darkness, guess each sweet
 Wherewith the seasonable month endows
The grass, the thicket, and the fruit-tree wild;
 White hawthorn, and the pastoral eglantine;
  Fast fading violets cover'd up in leaves;
   And mid-May's eldest child,
 The coming musk-rose, full of dewy wine,
  The murmurous haunt of flies on summer eves.

Darkling I listen; and, for many a time
 I have been half in love with easeful Death,
Call'd him soft names in many a mused rhyme,
 To take into the air my quiet breath;
  Now more than ever seems it rich to die,
 To cease upon the midnight with no pain,
  While thou art pouring forth thy soul abroad
   In such an ecstasy!
 Still wouldst thou sing, and I have ears in vain—
  To thy high requiem become a sod.[26]

If Dickinson's poem presents absorbed listening as an experiential analogue to death, here the experience of listening stimulates a desire for death. By presenting the consequences of the deathlike qualities of intense listening for desire, this feature of Keats's ode illuminates the problem we've been examining from a new angle.

  The excerpt begins with an experience in which the speaker feels his consciousness utterly absorbed by the song of the bird. Earlier in the poem, he's experimented with various strategies for effecting a union of the self with the nightingale. Finally, in the third line of the excerpt, he achieves this union through poetry: "Already with thee! tender is the night."

What does Keats mean by attributing agency for absorption to "Poesy?" One possibility is that the union of self and nightingale is an imaginable, but not experientially realizable, state. The disappearance of the subject/object distinction in listening is something that can happen in a poem but not in life. In a recent essay on Keats and Dickinson, Virginia Jackson argues along these lines. Repeating the central move of David Porter's and Sharon Cameron's readings of "I heard a Fly buzz," Jackson writes that "the beauty of Keats' lines will only give him access to . . . the beauty of poetic language." The represented experience is an artifact of poetic language, not a description of a possible experience. Keats's "identifications . . . with the nightingale's song . . . depend on identities that cannot die and be reborn."[27]

Jackson's judgment here depends on an unacknowledged philosophical commitment to the reality and stability of personal identity in actual experience. But as we've seen, there are philosophically compelling ways both to deny that personal identity is an impermeable box containing the self's experiences, and to affirm that absorbed listening is a state in which the division between subject and object is felt to dissolve. Jackson simply assumes a philosophical position which in fact requires argument; in the absence of such argument, her claim that Keats's lines could not represent a possible experience of absorbed listening is unconvincing.[28]

On the contrary, Keats's representation of listening here seems to be an instance of what he described in a famous letter as *negative capability*, a term which elides the difference between poetry and experience. In that letter, he equates poetic capacity with a perceptual capacity: the ability to let one's identity dissolve and to allow one's consciousness to become utterly absorbed by its object. In a classic discussion of Keats's "sympathetic absorption," Walter Jackson Bate connects Keats's idea to a broader strain of Romantic aesthetics, citing Hazlitt's essay "On Gusto," in which he writes of "an excitement of the imagination in which the perceptive identification with the object is almost complete."[29]

However evocative, these formulas remain somewhat obscure

on the dynamics of this identification with the object of perception. Bates's use of the term *sympathetic absorption* suggests that something like empathy is involved here, that the poet makes use of a special mental capacity instead of activating a potential state of ordinary perception. In a recent consideration of these issues, Linda von Pfahl understands Keats's negative capability in terms of an "expansionist urge to move outside the self, to unite with that which is not self."[30] This language conceives of the self as a kind of box and of the poet as using an empathy-like ability, which he possesses in an unusual degree, to burst through the box of self to an object that lies outside it.

But we have explored the sense in which, as Gallagher and Zahavi put it, "consciousness is not like a box."[31] As philosophers from Hume through Parfit observe, in perception I am conscious of the perception; there is no further experience of self. What we call our self is primarily a kind of background to our awareness, a sense of the psychological continuity of present experience with past experience. Of course this passive sense of continuity doesn't exhaust our sense of self; we actively construct ourselves in a number of ways, ranging from memory and expectation, to an awareness of the persistence of our body, to reflection on ourselves. But as Sartre puts it, the ego appearing in reflection is the object, not the subject, of reflection.[32]

According to this philosophical tradition, our perceptions do not include a positive experience of our subjecthood. The sense of subjecthood is, rather, derivative of various factors extrinsic to immediate experience, such as the sense of psychological continuity from moment to moment. Interrupting this continuity, and becoming sufficiently absorbed in immediate experience so as to suppress consciousness of the various memories and projects and expectations that erect a self, presents a certain challenge. But metaphors about escaping the self, or breaking out of the box of self, are misleading as to the nature of this challenge.

The self is simply not part of experience; the effort is not to get out of subjective experience to some special selfless experience but to descend into an experience sufficiently deeply to prevent the extrinsic constituents of the sense of self from taking hold. And while this is a special kind of experience, it is not rare. It's possible, as we've seen, to characterize an intense absorption in listening as an experience without a subject. There is no box that needs to be opened, no gulf that needs to be crossed. All that is required is a sufficiently total immersion in the present moment of perception.

In Keats's ode, the experience of absorption is characterized in ways that anticipate Dickinson's poem. "But here there is no light..." As many readers have noted, the felt erasure of subject and object expressed in these lines depends on the extinction of the sense of sight. Perhaps the simplest way to understand what's happened here is that the speaker has simply closed his eyes and now listens in rapt absorption to the nightingale's song. Helen Vendler asks us to contemplate the "nearly discarnate poet, his ordinary consciousness suspended in the act of listening."[33]

The key question involves the interpretation of the third stanza in the excerpt. Amid this experience of absorbed listening to acousmatic sound, the speaker suddenly voices a desire for death. How are we to understand this? At stake is not just our sense of what Dickinson takes from this classic Romantic linkage of death and listening but our sense of the implications of this linkage for desire.

Joanna Diehl, in her study of Dickinson's relation to the British Romantic poets, presents a superficially compelling gloss. "Drawn towards death," she writes, "Keats envisions dying as an ecstasy if he can 'cease upon the midnight with no pain,' while listening to the voice of the sublime nightingale. Yet, in the very process of describing this moment, Keats turns ecstasy to lament, for the voice he now hears would become silence as he would in death no longer be able to hear it."[34]

At one moment, according to this reading, Keats somehow imagines death as joyful, and he wants to die. But reflection on this desire leads him to reconsider death as the cessation of experience and then to bemoan his mortality. In a broadly similar reading, Alan Grob notes the ambiguity of the image of death here—pointing out the contrast between "easeful death," or death as dissolution of consciousness, and death as "ecstasy." He reads the vision of becoming a sod as an image of the extinction of consciousness.[35] Helen Vendler also interprets the representation of death in this stanza as a representation of unconsciousness. "Keats has come, by the time he envisages himself as a sod, to the end of his senses."[36] Vendler understands this image of death as the logical end of a process in which the listening itself is depicted as a kind of death, understood as sleep. "To listen to music, with all one's other senses laid asleep . . . is, for Keats, very nearly to be dead."[37]

The problem with all these interpretations is that they get the order of the stanza's imagery wrong. The critics argue as if the stanza had begun with the expression of a sudden, inexplicable desire for death as ecstasy, then proceeded through reflection to substitute an image of death as the cessation of consciousness for this one of ecstatic death. But in fact, the poem begins with the speaker's memory of thinking of death as "easeful" and then proceeds, starting with the exclamation "now more than ever seems it rich to die," to develop an image of death as ecstasy.

This ecstasy, furthermore, is hardly inexplicable. Death's ecstasy and richness are entirely derived from the representation of the experience of the nightingale's song. Death is rich *because* the nightingale's song is rich. The image of the self "become a sod" immediately follows the culmination of the vision of death as "ecstasy." There is no transition to thoughts of "easeful," sleeplike death. I think the critics are led to insert a phantom transitional period of reflection at this point in the stanza because of their implicit belief that sleeplike metaphors are the only aesthetically convincing experiential analogues to death.

But the poem presents the idea of becoming a sod as consistent with the idea of death as "ecstasy." The logic of the stanza, with its pattern of increasing intensity following the exclamation "now more than ever seems it rich to die," suggests that we read the final image of the self "become a sod" as the final degree of intensification, as the apex of ecstasy. Keats imagines that to die will constitute an enrichment. This is of course a theme in his poetry. Perhaps the most relevant example comes from the final lines of "Why did I laugh to-night?":

> Verse, Fame, and Beauty are intense indeed,
> But Death intenser—Death is Life's high meed.[38]

Notable here is Keats's disassociation of the opposition life/death from the opposition intense/dull. But in this poem, he simply asserts that death is "intenser." In "Ode to a Nightingale," the poet explores the imaginative linkage of death with intensity through acousmatic listening, an exploration revealing the logic underlying the seeming perversity of "Why did I laugh to-night?" The source of richness and intensity in the "Ode" is the nightingale's song. Keats imagines that his death will constitute an enrichment of the song's ecstatic quality. The question now is, How can it make sense for Keats to imagine that his death will increase the richness of the nightingale's song?

The answer, I think, is that Keats imagines that his death will increase the intensity of the *experience* of listening to the nightingale. That experience is rich; to become a sod would make it still richer. On its face, this answer sounds absurd, but our reflections on the dynamics of Dickinson's comparison of death to absorbed listening provide us with the tools to take it seriously. We explored philosophically and psychologically compelling reasons why absorbed listening is a good way to imagine getting rid of the self. A new way of desiring death is implicit in the poetic insight into listening's deathlike qualities. It follows from two underlying beliefs, each of them fairly intuitive: (1) intensified experience corresponds to diminished self-consciousness; (2) death involves the extinction of the self. With these beliefs, it is possible for Keats's speaker to imagine that the extinction of the self yields intensified experience.

My reading, which understands Keats to imagine that death, by turning the self into a sod, does not end the experience of listening, finds support in the final stanza's description of what does end that experience:

> Forlorn! the very word is like a bell
> To toll me back from Thee to my sole self![39]

Keats finds himself precipitated out of absorption by thoughts of himself. He emerges from absorption into a depressing self-consciousness, characterized by a sense of his distinctness from the nightingale's song. One might say that the experience of self tends to dull and diminish the intensity of experience. In this sense, not death but self-consciousness resembles sleep, the gradual cessation of experience. This sense of self begins to stir almost immediately upon the poem's triumphant declaration of union with the song, culminating in the memories of past thoughts of death that open the third stanza. But the words "*now* more than ever seems it rich to die" mark a transformation in the poet's image of death. Death no longer seems easeful to him; now it seems rich, and the awareness of the self seems like sleep.[40]

This reversal is not an artifact of poetic language but a result of poetry's insight into the structure of experience. Keats's aesthetic effort to describe absorbed listening results in the discovery of a new way to love death. Perhaps this discovery will seem less useful than the insights about experience generated by Dickinson's effort to create an aesthetically convincing representation of what it's like to die. Yet it seems clear, as many critics have argued, that she knew Keats's poem well. It seems likely that she worked out her own poetic version of absorbed hearing and death with the earlier poet's example in mind. Dickinson's illumination of surprising features of the experience of absorbed listening—her literary knowledge—may well have arisen from her examination of literary desire—Keats's surprising way of longing for death.

Keats holds open a desire that perhaps we have all felt, without giving it a name and without allowing it to linger. Imagine again that you are at a concert. Your eyes are closed, and you are listening to music that enthralls and absorbs your attention. Suddenly, you find that you are not quite as absorbed as you would like to be.

You become conscious of a kind of intermittent flutter, interrupting, fracturing your absorption. A vague, background irritation, a creeping self-consciousness, fugitive thoughts: "Here I am, listening to this music." "I wonder how long this piece lasts." "Did I remember to feed the meter?"

Your sense of self appears *over* the experience after a certain amount of time, like mold on bread. And you wish the experience of the music were a little cleaner, a little more intense. But the sense of self is now an insistent, discordant note, interrupting the music. Keats compares it to a bell, a slowly tolling bell, a new sound that works against the sound of the music, calling you away from it.

The most natural thing in the world would be to grasp the tongue of the bell, to still it, to snuff the discordant note, to eliminate the self, to turn it into a sod, so the experience of the song could intensify, and never stop.

✳ 6 ✳

Bernhard's Way

O Lord God grant me the grace to produce a few good verses, which
shall prove to myself that I am not the lowest of men, that I am not
inferior to those whom I despise.

CHARLES BAUDELAIRE,
"At One O'Clock in the Morning"[1]

What would a commitment to art that has passed *through* the post-modern critique of art look like? The recent return to aesthetics has largely proceeded by either denying or ignoring this critique. Pierre Bourdieu presents the postmodern case in perhaps its most elegantly distilled form. The tradition declares art to be about experience; actually, it is about status. The tradition declares great art to be timeless; actually, its motives, meanings, and effects are circumscribed by the conditions of its production. The tradition declares the value of art to be produced by formal relations within the work; actually, it is produced by social relations between antagonistic groups.[2]

The new aesthetic criticism reverses these reversals. The experiences and affects provoked by art are not covert claims of status; they have their basis in living bodies.[3] Artistic form is not a disguise for social relations; it offers an opportunity for analyzing those relations.[4] The aesthetic is not the means of establishing social distinctions; it is "the site of an unprecedented equality."[5] The artwork is not bound to its social context; artistic form enables the work to maintain relations across time and space.[6]

The extrication of art from the postmodern critique has been aided by the critics' critics. We have learned from critics like Bruno Latour and John Guillory how to be suspicious of the epistemological grounds of postmodern suspicions.[7] We have learned from critics like Michael Fried and Rita Felski to be suspicious of the sleight of hand with which postmodern writers and artists make the possibility of absorption or defamiliarization vanish from their works, thus showing what postmodern theorists cannot prove.[8] With the help of these critics, we are learning how to carry art over or around the postmodern morass.

But what would it mean for art go through it? How can art accept that every aesthetic judgment is a fraudulent disguise for social relations without becoming anti-art, without dedicating itself to the exhaustive (and now exhausted) exemplification of the critique?[9] How might art learn from the postmodern critique? How might it benefit from the exposure of the falseness of its effort to defeat time, to create experience, to renew sensation? How can it possibly learn from this exposure without dying of it? In this chapter, I will argue that Thomas Bernhard paradoxically draws a new aesthetic criterion from the critique of artistic value. I then pose the hard question, What would it mean to judge an artwork by this new criterion?

From the depths of the postwar period's most rigorous critique of art, amid its most relentless exposure of every actual and imaginable artwork as "pseudo-art," Thomas Bernhard looks around at the assembled cultural elite of Vienna and finds them guilty of "pretense," "social climbing," "lies," and "desperate" bids for "social recognition."[10] This Austrian writer, who began life under the Nazis, devoted his late work to exposing the experience of absorption in a work of art as a form of social domination, and the creation and consumption of artworks as concealed pleas for social distinction.[11] And yet this dismissal of every artwork that passes before him is not only compatible with a commitment to art as the highest human value, that commitment motivates the critique. His most damning attack on his contemporaries is that "they've quite simply failed to achieve *the highest*, and as I see it *only the highest* can bring real *satisfaction*" (*Woodcutters*, 54; here and subsequently, italics in the original).

Written in the 1980s, Bernhard's *Woodcutters* is not unusual in its insistence that the audience's relation to artworks is a disguised way of relating to others. It is unusual in taking this condition as a challenge to art to realize its pretensions. The urgency of this challenge is not purely or merely artistic. The postmodern critique of art relations as disguised social relations is so damning to art precisely because the social relations in question convulse with anxiety, compulsion, degradation, and pain. Imbrication in the social world compromises art because the social world described by the postmodern critique is inherently compromising.

Bernhard agrees with critics like Bourdieu in denouncing art's covert parasitism on the networks of social status. But he disagrees about what to do. Bourdieu wants to jettison the ideal of the aesthetic as disinterested attention to form. This might annihilate some forms of snobbery. But it is hard to imagine that settling accounts with Kant will do much to change the social world's basic nature as a hierarchy founded on fear and pain.[12] Bernhard, with a deep understanding of how art has been infected by the social relations described by postmodern critics, reacts more rationally. Don't get rid of art; get rid of social relations.

The satisfaction of the highest art for Bernhard thus defines a human space both replete with value and outside society. In this it does not look so different from the Kantian ideal of aesthetic judgment. But there is a crucial difference. For Bernhard, accepting the truth of the postmodern critique means accepting that every relation between an artwork and an audience becomes enmeshed in status relations. Bernhard faces the consequences squarely. The "real *satisfaction*" of art can never be achieved by the audience of a work but only and solely by its creator.

*

The speaker of Thomas Bernhard's *Woodcutters*—whom I follow the Austrian courts in identifying as Thomas Bernhard himself—has been invited to an "*artistic dinner*" following the funeral of an old friend.[13] His hosts, the Auersbergers, are friends he broke with several decades ago. Upon entering the Auersbergers' apartment, Bernhard takes a seat in the semidarkness of the anteroom, a position that affords him a view of the music room, where the other guests have assembled. As readers of the novel have noted, his position is that of a critic viewing a performance.[14] He proceeds over nearly two hundred pages, without paragraph breaks, to present his damning judgment on the Auersbergers, their friends, himself, and all actually existing art.

A typical passage, on the furnishing of the music room, will illustrate his procedure. He notes that the chamber is furnished with priceless antiques. But these objects are compromised by the Auersbergers' intention in displaying them, which is to convey to others their own superior taste. "The Auersbergers, who have always been credited with what is called taste, have never had any real taste, but only a secondhand surrogate, just as they have no life, but only a secondhand surrogate" (*Woodcutters*, 138).

Why is their taste "secondhand?" Because they want people to admire them, "when in fact people admire only their polished cabinets and sideboards, their tables and chairs, the many oil paintings on their walls, and their money" (138). Their taste is "tasteless" because it is an effort to acquire social distinction by means of the distinction possessed by art objects. The dim lighting of the apartment accentuates the objects' role as status symbols. Bernhard can recognize the famous names, the celebrated styles. But there is light enough only for him to identify the aura of prestige, not to become absorbed in the forms.

Literature, philosophy, and music are not immune to the mania for self-aggrandizement that degrades the furniture and paintings. Bernhard recalls the scene when the Auersbergers forced themselves on his attention in the street in order to invite him to their tasteless party on the eve of their mutual friend's funeral. "Before rushing off with all their parcels they told me that they have bought *everything by Ludwig Wittgenstein, so that they could immerse themselves in Wittgenstein during the coming weeks*" (*Woodcutters*, 10).

But to describe the works as compromised by the use to which the Auersbergers put them is to leave open the possibility that the beautiful works themselves are worthy objects of genuinely good taste. To remove the Auersbergers' paintings from the Auersbergers' clutches—to install them in a well-lit museum, perhaps—would be to free them for disinterested contemplation. Bernhard quickly forestalls this possibility. He expresses gratitude that the dim lighting prevents his being able to see "these art treasures" properly, "for I would undoubtedly have been sickened by the sight" (139). The very perfection of the art treasures is another, distinct source of their tastelessness. "Such perfection, which hits you in the eye and crowds in upon you from every side, is simply repellent" (139).[15]

Here the sociological critique joins with an older antitheatrical critique to proclaim that taste itself is tasteless.[16] It is practically impossible to escape the fact that the sole function of these art treasures is to proclaim the wealth and sophistication of the social-climbing couple. But even if you could bring yourself somehow to bracket the Auersbergers completely, and to place yourself before these masterpieces in rapt attention, the objects themselves would betray an intrinsic tastelessness. Masterpieces demonstrate their "ostentatious" lack of taste in the brutal way their very beauties force themselves on you in a desperate effort to compel your attention (*Woodcutters*, 139).

One of the innovations of Bernhard's novel is to house the sociological critique of taste in the context of the antitheatrical critique. Most of the novel unfolds while the dinner party is suspended, its guests waiting for hours for a "celebrated actor from the Burgtheater" to appear. Some of *Woodcutters'* funniest pages are devoted to attacking the theater, describing, for example, how not just the "sensitive Kleist" but "even the great Shakespeare falls victim to the butchers of the Burgtheater" (17). Bernhard's critique of the Burgtheater follows the same procedure as his critique of the Auersbergers' "art treasures." The Burgtheater is known to be one of Europe's best theaters. This distinction is tastelessly exploited by the Austrian nation to distinguish itself as a center of world culture. But even were one able to bracket the Burgtheater's function in the cultural status hierarchy of Europe, the very perfection of Burgtheater acting would "sicken" you by the way each word and gesture proclaims its "pretense."

Bernhard can link a Bourdieu-style sociological critique of art to an antitheatrical critique of art because both the sophisticated collector and the actor depend on the pretense that they are not doing what in fact they are doing: asking you to recognize them. People make judgments of taste in order to be recognized by others. Painters paint paintings, actors deliver lines, poets write poems in order to be recognized by others. The objects they create come into the world deformed by their attention-grabbing fineness of line, color, and phrase.

The antitheatrical critique can contain the sociological critique because it is more radical, more wide-reaching. The Auersbergers' taste is tasteless because they want you to recognize them as superior, and this claim to be superior is offensive. The ostentatious perfection of their art treasures is tasteless because they clamor to be recognized, and this clamor to be recognized is itself offensive.

The Auersbergers' demand for recognition turns the half-lit masterpieces they own into monsters. The masterpieces' own demand for recognition turns them into monsters. And social life, oriented as it is around the demand for recognition, turns people into monsters. "For

more than two decades," Bernhard writes, he had avoided the Auersbergers and thus avoided "any further contact *with these monsters* as
I could not help calling them privately" (*Woodcutters*, 44). Later, he
describes people with a noun that more accurately represents the
"unnatural" distortions caused by the desire for recognition. People
are "gargoyles" (172–73).

Art is infected with the social disease.[17] The problem with artworks is that they ask to be treated like people. The problem with
people is that they demand to be recognized. As Michael Fried has
shown, the history of art is tolerable for the antitheatrical critic only
insofar as he allows himself to be convinced by a given work's pretense. The pretense is that it is not asking the viewer to recognize it.
Art thus pretends that it is not pretense. Bernhard tries this out as a
social strategy:

> Actually I've always dissembled with the Auersbergers, I thought,
> sitting in the wing chair, and here I am again, sitting in the wing
> chair and dissembling once more: I'm not really here in their
> apartment in the Gentzgasse, I'm only pretending to be in the
> Gentzgasse, only pretending to be in their apartment, I said to
> myself. I've always pretended to them about everything—I've pre-
> tended to everybody about everything. My whole life has been a
> pretense . . . I drew a deep breath and said to myself, in such a way
> that the people in the music room were bound to hear it: *You've
> always lived a life of pretense, not a real life—a simulated existence,
> not a real existence.* (*Woodcutters*, 60)

To be present at a social gathering is to present a claim for social
recognition. Bernhard, despising the social demand that one must
turn oneself into an object to be appreciated by others, tries to duck
making this claim. So he pretends not to be at the artistic dinner.
Structurally, this is identical with how the viewer before the work of
art tries to forget his position in front of the work. The viewer with
good taste tries to *lose himself* in contemplation of the work. So Bernhard sits in the semidarkness, observing the dinner as theater. He tries
to lose himself in this observation. He gradually becomes absorbed
in the pretense that he is not there. Finally, he becomes so absorbed
in his pretense that he succeeds, he truly does forget himself. At this
point he begins speaking aloud, attracts the attention of the other

guests, and thus spectacularly demonstrates the failure of his pretense and the reality of his social presence.

Bernhard is a gargoyle. His own social being as a subject tied to a pathetically recognition-soliciting object is just as monstrous as everyone else's. This is vividly brought home in an episode where he remembers seeing Auersberger and a companion in the street:

> I recalled how I had turned around, quivering with revulsion, and set off towards the Stephanplatz after the pair had disappeared into that dilapidated building. I was so sickened by what I had just witnessed that I turned to throw up against the wall in front of the Aida coffeehouse; but then I looked into one of the mirrors of the coffeehouse and found myself staring at my own dissipated face, and my own debauched body, and I felt more sickened by myself than I had been by Auersberger and his companion. (*Woodcutters*, 14)

*

Art has a social problem. Art has caught the social disease. This is the truth of the postmodern critique. Relations to artworks are always disguised forms of relations between persons. The passage where Bernhard pretends not to be in the Auersbergers' apartment is his experiment with the solution proposed by antitheatrical aesthetics. Seen "accurately and radically," absorption is, in the end, only pretense.[18] After and before its tricks, the work stands there, asking to be looked at. In the same way, even so vehemently antisocial a man as Bernhard is, is, in the end, just another person begging pathetically for our recognition.

He struggles mightily against the social problem. He tells us that he has perfected "the art of being left alone" (*Woodcutters*, 24). "At precisely the right moment," when he is listening to someone speak to him, he looks down at the ground. But of course this behavior only succeeds in making a spectacle of himself. His "art of being left alone" suffers the same fate as the Auersbergers' "art treasures." In Bernhard's prose, we overhear art telling itself the postmodern truth: "*You've always lived a life of pretense, not a real life.*"

And yet one of the works Bernhard describes in *Woodcutters* does attain a partial solution and represents a partially effective cure for the social disease. One work is presented as not "totally" bankrupt. He tells us that Joana, the friend whose suicide provided the occasion

for the "*artistic dinner*," was once married to a "tapestry artist" named
Fritz. Joana was "not cut out for a career" herself (77). Instead, she put
all her considerable artistic energy, all her artistic effort, into shaping
and advancing Fritz's career. And Fritz's work was transformed. His
tapestries became famous, now hanging in the best "museums and . . .
executive suites" all over the world (78).

For Joana, "Fritz was her one work of art" (78). "She fashioned
Fritz into this colossal work of art" (79). The narrator is utterly unim-
pressed by the value the world finds in what he disparagingly calls
Fritz's "carpets." But he is fascinated by Joana's creation of this Fritz
work. His reflections generate this remarkable passage:

> I will go further and say that Fritz's art, the works he created, all
> the tapestries which now hang in famous museums throughout
> the world, are really Joana's, just as everything he is today derives
> from Joana, is Joana. But obviously nobody takes an idea like this
> seriously, even though of course such ideas, which are not taken
> seriously, are actually the only serious ideas and always will be. It is
> only in order to survive, it seems to me, that we have such serious
> ideas which are not taken seriously. (79)

Bernhard spares Joana's artwork from the intense sarcasm drip-
ping from all his other references to art. But he cannot describe Fritz's
career as an "artwork" entirely seriously, either. Here we see a modulation in Bernhard's description of art, from sarcasm to "unserious-
ness." In this modulation, we discern the outlines of a new vision,
the ultimate achievement of which we will see reflected not in the
content but in the form of the novel. Yet even here, in this provisional
and only partially successful art, the outlines of the "highest" form
become clear. Joana's Fritz work is different from other works in that
it is structurally impossible for Joana to gain or expect recognition
from this work. In channeling her creativity through Fritz, she has set
up the visible form of the work at a distance from her creative relation to that work. Fritz's visible authorship acts as a kind of fetish; he
is a sacrificial victim taking upon himself the degrading recognition
dynamic that is the fate of all art in the social world. What the audience sees in Fritz's work is the work of Fritz. Joana's animating intention remains concealed.

Joana's Fritz work lies outside the networks of recognition. Its very existence as a work is not recognizable but must be put forward as a kind of serious joke. Her authorship is concealed in a much deeper way than that of an artist who uses a pseudonym, or who allows another to claim authorship of a work she has created with her own hands. Joana does not create Fritz's work with her own hands. She creates by somehow causing Fritz to create, by subtly influencing him in a thousand small ways over a period of years. This kind of authorship is something no court could recognize, something that no one could take seriously.

The aesthetic value Bernhard judges Joana's Fritz work to possess—its authenticity, its lack of pretense, its purity—lies in Joana's relation to that work. She is the creator of a work immune to recognition. And yet the concealment of authorship is not the only criterion. The form of the work also plays a role. Bernhard's treatment of the aesthetic value of the tapestries themselves is very subtle. He acknowledges that they are acclaimed as beautiful. He does not admire this beauty; far from it, they possess exactly the kind of "perfection" that makes all taste—even the best taste—fundamentally tasteless. And yet this beauty is not irrelevant to the status Joana's Fritz work has for him. One can imagine that if Fritz produced tapestries which left everyone cold, Bernhard would not consider Joana's creation of this career to be a "colossal work of art."

Aesthetic values are formed in public, in the social world, and the aesthetic properties of observable artworks are fundamentally social phenomena. Here Bernhard is in entire agreement with Bourdieu, for example, and against Kant. Aesthetic values, however, are not extrinsic to the "highest" art, the art free of recognition. They matter, but only insofar as they provide evidence of the quality of the act of creation. Their value as something to be looked at, something accessible to an audience, is for Bernhard below negligible.

In fact, Joana's Fritz work is only partially successful. Eventually this work, so far from providing "real satisfaction," simply "crushed and destroyed her" (*Woodcutters*, 78). This is because the work's freedom from public relations is ultimately parasitic on a relation that is, if not public, nevertheless intractably social: her marriage to Fritz. Intimacy, and especially the "matrimonial hell," is not a valued space for Bernhard in any case (87). But in this instance, Joana's inflation of Fritz's career brought him the adoring attention of the world, which made him susceptible to the wiles of a younger woman, with whom he absconded to Mexico, leaving his wife to the consolation prize Bernhard reserves for those who have searched nobly for satisfaction but failed. She commits suicide.

But reflecting on her one artwork has led Bernhard to articulate, for practically the only time in his late work, the core of his belief in the possibility of the highest art. The "serious idea which [is] not taken seriously" is that of a work of art not oriented to recognition and the benefit of which is entirely realized by its creator.

Here we confront a problem that the thematic level of this text will be of only limited assistance in solving. The aesthetic value of Fritz's tapestries is valuable to Bernhard only insofar as the works speak to the quality of Joana's act of creation. But what is this quality? It cannot be the Kantian quality, the disinterested feeling of pleasure in contemplation of the beautiful. Rather, we will see that this quality is fundamentally transformative. The satisfaction of the highest art is the feeling the creator has of becoming something other than a monster. The form of the work is the visible channel of this transformation.

*

Once the artistic dinner has finally come to an end, Bernhard takes his leave. He tells his hostess what a pleasant time he has had while cursing himself inwardly for his nauseating pretense. Once he exits the building, he begins to run. He runs through the streets, possessed by a strange excitement, a sudden feeling of "love." Here is how the novel ends: "And as I went on running I thought: I'll write something *at once*, no matter what—I'll write about this *artistic dinner* in the Gentzgasse *at once, now. Now*, I thought—*at once*, I told myself over and over again as I ran through the Inner City—*at once*, I told myself, *now*—*at once, at once*, before it's too late" (*Woodcutters*, 181).

Like Proust's *In Search of Lost Time*, *Woodcutters* ends with the narrator about to write the narrative we've just read. The joy and urgency he now associates with writing, so anomalous in the context of the 181 pages of excoriation of art and artists that precede them, present a puzzle. Facing the prospect of composing the novel we've just read, the narrator seems enthralled by a premonition of the "real satisfaction" of the "highest" art. This satisfaction is, after all, almost the only positive affect that Bernhard has named in the course of delivering his stream of invective against the Auersbergers, their guests, and himself. It seems, then, an appropriate name to give to the prospect that excites him as he heads home to begin the process of composition. So the deep question that confronts the reader at the end of *Woodcutters* is, Has Bernhard been justified in his premonition? Has the transformation that Joana approached actually been realized by Bernhard in writing the work we've just finished?

We have only the evidence of the novel. We know beforehand that we will not find the "real satisfaction" as a possible affective response by the reader to the work. So our own experience is quite irrelevant as an index of Bernhard's success at attaining "the highest." The satisfaction of the highest, if it exists, is foreclosed to us as readers from the outset.

We must instead seek traces of Bernhard's satisfaction. We must go back over the book, looking for signs of the author's successful disappearance from the social world, looking for evidence of the social Bernhard—the gargoyle Bernhard—giving up the ghost. Approached in this way, the form of the novel might betray traces of what Bernhard has declared, at the level of content, the only "real satisfaction" possible in art and life.

In form, the novel is uninterrupted first-person narration. No quotation marks divide the unbroken speech of the narrator. He reports the speech of others without notation of any kind and without departing from his characteristic tone and style. We have no access to others save through the narrator's language.

A problem intrinsic to narratives of this form is the difficulty of discerning the difference between the narrator's sense of things and the way things might appear to others. Critics have traditionally dealt with this problem under the heading of the unreliable narrator. But in the closest ancestor of Bernhard's novel—the fiction of Samuel Beckett—this problem becomes magnified to a degree that "unreliability" undergoes a change in kind. Here the problem of the novel's enclosure within its narrator's subjectivity takes on metaphysical features. The first-person narration developed by Beckett and brought to its highest pitch in his trilogy brings into the world a kind of subjectivity that cannot be identified with—that cannot identify itself as—any object. Further, as we shall see, the closer this subject comes to any object, including any object (face, body, voice) likely to house another subject, the border where the self stops and the other starts vanishes.

Formally, *Woodcutters* represents a precise and limited transformation of the mode of first-person narration defined by Beckett's fiction.

This transformation offers us the best evidence of the novel's success in terms of Bernhard's particular and demanding criteria. But why should our interpretation of *Woodcutters* privilege Beckett? At one level, of course, Bernhard's indebtedness to Beckett's work is obvious and has been noticed by most readers. The negativity, the pared-down language, the dark humor, the characters' obsession with mysterious projects, mark Bernhard as among Beckett's successors in both prose and drama. But *Woodcutters* goes beyond these family resemblances in establishing a specific relation to one of Beckett's texts in particular. This relation is worked out through one of the novel's most peculiar formal features: the uncanny symmetry between the narrator and the actor from the Burgtheater. This symmetry replicates how Beckett's *Molloy* is balanced between the first-person narration of Molloy and Moran.

Earlier, I described how Bernhard's hostility to the actor helps situate the novel's critique of art in the antitheatrical tradition. Now I want to examine how his view of the actor undergoes a transformation. Bernhard's expression of his thoughts regarding the bankruptcy of art, of Austria, of society, and of the Auersbergers dominates the first half of *Woodcutters*. The actor's expression of his thoughts regarding the bankruptcy of art, of Austria, of society, and of the Auersbergers dominates the second half. The content of those thoughts is identical. The actor, repulsed by the Auersbergers and their guests, tells them, "You talk incessantly about art without having the faintest notion of what art is" (*Woodcutters*, 167). He addresses a guest particularly odious to Bernhard in terms she "deserved" and which the narrator reflects that he himself could have used. "Words like *vicious, rude, insolent, hypocritical, infamous, megalomaniac, stupid*, rained down on the company" to the narrator's delight but also to his bafflement, given that these are *his* thoughts and feelings the actor is so uncharacteristically expressing (167).

The actor expresses both Bernhard's abundant social disgust and his positive commitments. "We don't attain the highest just by wanting it," he says (117). "Absurd ideas are the only true ideas," he declares, mirroring Bernhard's private insistence that only "unserious" ideas are worth taking seriously (161). Finally, the actor links disgust with society with belief in art: "How I hate gatherings like this. . . . How I long to be left in peace" (169). Like Bernhard, he understands that escape from the social cannot be simply a matter of misanthropy and solipsism but entails a radical transformation of the self. "If only I'd become a completely different person from the one I have become, a person who is left in peace" (170).

It is important to note that Bernhard does not exactly hear the actor delivering these lines. He *overhears* them as the actor speaks, as it were, to himself.[19] The actor really gets going only when he realizes that he has completely lost his audience, that he is no longer "inhibited" by the other guests (*Woodcutters*, 118). Bernhard describes his audience thus: "Every now and then they nodded, either looking straight at the actor or gazing down at the tablecloth, or else staring in bewilderment at the person sitting opposite; they had no chance whatever of participating in the actor's performance, with which he was regaling them so uninhibitedly, knowing that none of them could inhibit him" (118). This is more than a performance animated by the fiction of an unawareness of audience. The actor's speech is made possible by the audience's incomprehension.

This "performance" scrupulously avoids both ordinary social intercourse and audience-oriented drama. Thus, the actor's speech has the same structure as the narrator's own in the passage when he forgets himself, causing his private monologue to break into audibility. Earlier, I used this passage as an example of Bernhard's failure to completely disappear from the social situation. The actor, who wishes he had "become a completely different person," also suffers from this failure. Uncomprehending staring is, after all, a form of social recognition, no matter how attenuated. Although he cannot disappear, the actor, like Bernhard, makes his effort toward the "art of being left alone." And the speech that issues from this effort to escape the social, while not exemplary of the "highest," nevertheless attains a kind of provisional freedom.

Bernhard is the one listener who does hear and understand the actor. But this is a strange kind of listening. He is able to hear the actor's meaning only because he has been thinking—and occasionally muttering aloud to himself—identical thoughts. Uncertainty as to the space in which it occurs characterizes this listening. Is the actor's voice inside Bernhard's head? Is the actor somehow giving voice to Bernhard's own thoughts? Or is the source of these thoughts the actor's interior? Does his interior—his thoughts and feelings—just happen to closely resemble Bernhard's?

We have all had the experience of reacting to something someone says with the thought: that's just what I think! There is an uncanniness to this kind of listening experience. Ordinarily, upon hearing another express ideas we hold, we feel drawn to the other. We feel that a bond has been established, that a friendship has begun. Our natural impulse is to get to know this mind that mysteriously, and in isolation from us, evolves thoughts so resonant with our own.

Nothing like this happens between the actor and Bernhard. Reflecting on how the actor's speech thrilled him, he writes, "But this does not mean that I should take to him now, were I to meet him again. He remains for me the unattractive and essentially superficial stage character he was from the start" (*Woodcutters*, 175).

The thrilling relation between the actor and the narrator can never occur in social space, where they confront each other as monsters. They are the same kind of monster. The narrator observes with disgust as the actor takes his leave while fulsomely praising the hosts whom he has just been castigating. Moments later, Bernhard himself takes his leave, observing with the same disgust his own false assurances to the hostess that he has had a wonderful time.

Bernhard does not take the uncanny communion between him and the actor as evidence of the possibility of establishing a good social relationship, a friendship. Rather, he speaks of the actor as having been, for a time, "transformed." The actor underwent "a truly philosophical metamorphosis" (172). The actor became the "completely different person" he wanted to be. When he became this person, he communed with Bernhard, not in social space, but in a space interior to this transformed "person." His speech took on the qualities of Bernhard's own internal speech; it carried the conviction and power of internal speech.[20] This transformation, the "absurd" prospect of which tantalizes the actor, represents the attainment of the highest. Bernhard affirms that—for a brief time—the actor attained this ultimate freedom. "He underwent a truly philosophical metamorphosis." Does this mean Bernhard has also undergone this sea change? The answer to this question depends on how we understand their relation.

The identity of the actor's thoughts with Bernhard's puts the relation between the actor and Bernhard—affectively marked by Bernhard's alternating repulsion and fascination—into question. This uncanny symmetry between two beings distributed between two halves of a darkly comic first-person narration also describes *Molloy*, the first novel of Beckett's trilogy.[21] The actor/Bernhard escapes from others, not by leaving them behind, but by somehow expanding to include them. And he accomplishes this feat though artistic means. "We don't attain the highest just by wanting it." The profound mechanisms of the metamorphosis attempted by *Woodcutters* exploit the artistic method developed by Beckett in *Molloy*. Briefly examining the transformed persons of that novel will clear the way for understanding Bernhard's.

Molloy is a key work in the development of what Anthony Uhlmann has recently called "Beckett's art of nonrelation."[22] Beckett explores the contours of this art through the form of first-person narration, a form that dominates his prose writing from 1946 to 1964.[23] Hugh Kenner, in one of the earliest accounts of the trilogy that occupies the center of this period, shows how the first-person form gives rise to nonrelation. Beckett "carries the Cartesian process backwards, beginning with a bodily je suis and ending with a bare cogito."[24] The novels are inhabited by a subjectivity that cannot fix itself to any object and, through this lack of objecthood, encounters no firm boundaries between itself and everything it perceives.

Molloy/Moran is continually trying to place himself; trying to determine and delimit what is inside by trying, unsuccessfully, to find an object that is unambiguously outside. A few sentences will give the flavor of his experience:

> I must have been on the top, or on the slopes, of some considerable eminence, for otherwise how could I have seen, so far away, so near at hand, so far underneath, so many things, fixed and moving. But what was an eminence doing in this land with hardly a ripple? And I, what was I doing there, and why come? These are things that we shall try and discover. But these are things we must not take seriously. There is a little of everything, apparently, in nature. . . . And I am perhaps confusing several different occasions, and different times, deep down, and deep down in my dwelling.[25]

Molloy cannot position himself in relation to things. He is constantly unsure whether a given apparition is next to him, far from him, imagined, or remembered. In part, this condition is thematized through the speaker's famous trouble with objects, from his bicycle to his "sucking stones." In part, it is thematized through the complete failure of the social recognitions that serve, as the Hegelian tradition tells us, to delimit us as isolate and integral selves.[26] If I become myself by identifying with the object you recognize when you see me, Molloy's "I" cannot be recognized. "I was becoming unrecognizable," Moran says, summing up his dealings with others (*Molloy*, 233). Encountering him, others see nothing solid, nothing real, and so Moran's sense of his own phantom objecthood gradually melts utterly into air. Molloy's encounters—knocking on his mother's teeth or trying unsuccessfully to explain himself to a policeman—similarly fail to yield recognition.

And yet there are a number of examples of successful communication in the novel. Every instance involves Molloy/Moran talking to *himself*: "And the voice I listen to needs no Gaber to make it heard. For it is within me. . . . Yes, it is an ambiguous voice and not always easy to follow, in its reasonings and decrees. But I follow it more or less, I follow it in this sense, that I know what it means, and in this sense, that I do what it tells me" (180–81).

Intrasubjectivity replaces intersubjectivity as the space of successful communication. Since this self cannot be fixed by reference to an object, the very meaning of "self" is transformed. The voice Moran hears is an "ambiguous" voice. It is not quite his own, but neither does it come from without. Without any determinate boundary to the subject, voices inhabit Molloy's experience like a world. This "I" becomes a hive of voices.

Daniel Katz notes that Beckett creates Molloy's condition in part by radicalizing formal features of first-person discourse. "Anyone can say 'I'—'I' refers only to the person saying 'I' at a particular moment. . . . Subjectivity, then, comes to depend on enunciation—if 'I' refers only to the person saying 'I' at a particular moment, then the moment and the utterance both make possible and are logically prior to any subjective designation, rather than simply being the expression of a moment at which the subject already happened to find itself."[27] First-person discourse produces subjectivity without regard for psychological consistency, and Beckett exploits this effect to create the illusion of an infinitely capacious subject.

For Katz, the point of noticing the dependence of Molloy's subjectivity on the curious properties of first-person discourse is to argue, in familiar poststructuralist terms, that subjectivity is the effect of the operation of a system. "I" compulsively personifies Molloy as a side effect of its workings. The objectivity of the system comes to seem in such analyses the determining factor.

But what is so remarkable about *Molloy* is the extent to which this subjectivity, created by language, itself causes the materiality of language to vanish. Molloy's discourse makes the materiality of its support disappear. Granted, it disappears only for *him*. But the novel is a record of Molloy/Moran's experience and of the process by which Molloy/Moran composes his experience as discourse. This is a novel that thematizes writing. Molloy begins by telling us he is writing, and Moran ends the same way. Thus, his condition is identified as a condition of writing. For this author, the process of composition, so far from revealing the resistant materiality underneath subjectivity, annihilates it.

The deconstructive reading accurately registers the structure that enables the curious experience embodied by the novel. To do this, it must approach the text distantly, as a reader who can distance himself from instances of another's written "I." But if we ask how things are for Molloy, how things are for the writer of the "I," a quite different perspective emerges. To move from an interpretive position dominated by the reader's relation to the text to an interpretive position dominated by the writer's relation to the text is here to switch the basic question we are asking. The question no longer is, How can subjectivity be unmasked as objectivity? Now the question is, What kind of subjectivity dissolves all objects? Viewed from the perspective of the writer Molloy, the space of a written first-person narrative is a space in which subjectivity becomes boundless.

From within this narrative, Molloy reaches fruitlessly for objects, for something or someone outside his own consciousness. "To restore silence is the function of objects," he writes (*Molloy*, 16). He equates the discovery of a firm boundary between self and not-self with the cessation of language. This quixotic quest to discover objectivity within the world of the first-person text generates a bizarre fantasy. Molloy imagines blackening his sheet of paper. He imagines "fill[ing] in the holes of words till all is blank and flat" (16). This desire for writing to become an object makes vividly clear the fact that writing here is *not* an object. Writing—first-person writing, writing that says "I"— is the medium of a total, object-devouring subjectivity. The writer cannot tell whether he is perceiving, remembering, or imagining.

He cannot tell whether a given object is inside or outside him. The writing makes the identification of a boundary or limit to his experience impossible.

And yet this seemingly total subjectivity has a seam. Molloy did not, after all, write *Molloy*. Brian McHale has located the fissure caused by the nonidentity of actual and fictional author in the trilogy's frequent references to god. Molloy, Malone, and the Unnamable know they must have come from somewhere; they must have a creator, and they pursue this creator, with increasing urgency, across the trilogy. The nameless narrator of the trilogy's final novel, for example, knows "he can never get outside his own imaginings to the reality of his ultimate creator. . . . The god whom the unnamable can never reach, is of course Samuel Beckett himself, and the retreating ceiling is the unbreachable barrier between the fictional world of the unnamable and the real world which Samuel Beckett shares with us, his readers."[28]

Thomas Bernhard's revision of Beckett's first-person narration is simple. He erases this barrier between the "I" that comes to consciousness in the text and "I" of the author.[29] We have seen how the features of Beckett's first-person narration supply for the consciousness it enshrines all the criteria of Bernhard's "highest art." This consciousness has passed beyond all social relations. Bernhard, in writing *Woodcutters*, seizes the true satisfaction this consciousness represents.

This withdrawal from relation totally transforms the "I." The nonrelational "I," the "I" of radical first-person narration, has nothing in common with the "I" in relation, the "recognizable" I, the "gargoyle" I. It has undergone what Bernhard calls a "philosophical metamorphosis." In *Molloy*, a character who is not Samuel Beckett undergoes this metamorphosis. This character's strange condition is an object of interest for readers, who have for sixty years explored the manifold relations his condition obtains with "the real world."

In *Woodcutters*, the subject that has undergone the transformation is the creator, the author. If the form of first-person narration supplies the mechanism of this transformation, the themes of the novel articulate the desirability of the transformed state as the only "real satisfaction" possible in art or life. This change, though small, is not minor. *To establish the identity of author and narrator is to transform the meaning of the post-Beckett novel.* It is to supply the motive, the desire for this kind of novel, the desire that this kind of novel uniquely satisfies. It is to place this desire—for freedom from social relations and from social being—and the satisfaction of this desire, at the heart of the meaning of the form. Molloy writes because he has found himself writing in a book called *Molloy*. Bernhard writes because he wants, in writing himself into a book like *Molloy*, to become free, to achieve the highest goal of art/life.

One way of capturing what is new in Bernhard's autobiographical project is by comparing it with Paul de Man's account of autobiography. "We assume," de Man writes, "that life produces the autobiography as an act produces its consequences, but can we not suggest, with equal justice, that the autobiographical project may itself produce and determine the life . . . by the resources of [the] medium?"[30] For Bernhard, the resources of first-person narration first revealed by Beckett do indeed determine the form of life, the "real satisfaction," of the referent of *Woodcutters'* first person. The point here, however, is not to expose, with de Man, the constructedness of a putatively extraliterary consciousness. It is rather to celebrate what that construction makes possible: a life free of recognition, an unrecognizable life.

Of course this celebration depends on bracketing the "undecidability" that the imbrication of sign and referent, trope and grammar, life and text, meaning and matter, create for de Man. But this bracketing, it turns out, is rather easy. As sophisticated literary readers, and against the Austrian courts, we will admit, for example, that to identify the Auersbergers with a particular couple from Bernhard's extratextual life is problematic for many reasons. The distortions introduced by the book's thematic identification of art with fraud, to take just one reason, introduce a fictional element into the representation of these particular artists and collectors. Further, we might imagine that in orchestrating the boundary-evading textual turns of his own "I," Bernhard is performing another artistic fraud.

And we might be right. But we must remember our place. We are only readers. Undecidability is a problem for readers. It is our problem, not Bernhard's. It does not mar the joy of the creator of *Woodcutters*. And the joy with which he greets the prospect of true artistic satisfaction at the very end of the novel he has just written certainly means that this is the joy of satisfaction achieved.

Bernhard's belief that authorship entails a transformation of the writer derives much of its plausibility from the testimony of centuries of authors who declare themselves transformed by writing, along with the conventions associating artistic speech with a quasi-divine apotheosis of the voice.[31] *Woodcutters'* innovation lies in specifying the mode of the transformation, articulating a form adequate to that mode, and declaring this transformation of the author the sole and highest value of the work. This value is the result of what modernism learns from postmodernism.

Bernhard thus endows the first-person narrative with an entirely new meaning and value. That meaning and value utterly exhausts itself in the experience of its creator. What is verifiable from our readers' perspective is the following sequence:

1 Bernhard thinks, in good postmodern fashion, that the problem of art is a social problem.
2 He thinks through this postmodern problem to conclude that the ideal form of art will not be dependent on social relations.
3 Logically, such a form can give satisfaction only to its creator, never to its audience.
4 In freeing life from recognition, such a form will "transform" its creator and give him the only "real satisfaction" possible in art or life.
5 The end of *Woodcutters* suggests that Bernhard sees in his novel just such a form.
6 *Woodcutters'* exploitation of the first-person narrative techniques of Beckett's *Molloy* provides limited evidence that the joy expressed at the end of the novel is the joy of real satisfaction at total transformation.[32]

*

I want to conclude by briefly facing a possible objection to my reading of Bernhard's transformed modernism. The objection is that Molloy is unhappy, that *Molloy* is an unhappy book, and that to transform oneself into someone like Molloy inhabiting a book like *Molloy* is to suffer a misfortune, not to be satisfied. The objection, in other words, is that Bernhard must be ironic when he speaks of the satisfaction of anti-relational art, that the joy he expresses at the prospect of beginning to write must have a more pedestrian source.

"I'll write about this *artistic dinner* in the Gentzgasse *at once, now. Now*, I thought—*at once.*" Bernhard is excited, perhaps, by the prospect of composing a work that thousands of readers and dozens of critics will adore. He is excited by the prospect of cementing his reputation as the greatest living writer in the German language. Or maybe he is excited simply by the idea of working off some nervous energy. In any case, no one could be excited by the prospect of transforming oneself into a boundaryless "I." No one could want to be Molloy. Unless, that is, one wants to become immortal. Molloy represents one of the great immortal figures of world literature, perhaps the most powerful evocation of immortality in postwar writing. And Molloy is not immortal in the sense that generations of readers continue to read him; this audience-oriented immortality through fame is something Molloy has no sense of. How could you imagine being recognized through the ages when you can't get your own mother to recognize you? Rather, Molloy is immortal in a more immediate sense. To become a subject with no boundaries and no objecthood is to exist in a state in which the question of one's death is without meaning. Molloy endlessly refers to "my life without end," to his "interminable life" (*Molloy*, 18). "At the same time it is over and it goes on, is there a tense for that?" (47)

Yet the mere fact of endlessness does not of course guarantee happiness. Far from it. Certain images of endlessness have long furnished hell, and Molloy can be seen as a close cousin to Sisyphus, the figure so beloved of the existentialists. But unlike Sisyphus, Molloy's experience is one not of mere repetition but of constant laughter and surprise. Wolfgang Iser has noted Molloy's unlimited vitality. Sentence after incredible sentence is generated out of a condition lacking suspense, lacking teleology, lacking relationships. For Iser, Molloy is a "self set free to pursue a course of endless self-discovery . . . a supercritical chain reaction."[33]

Finally, a case can be made that much of Molloy/Moran's experience is best described as a species of mystical vision: "And I note here the little beat my heart once missed, in my home, when a fly, flying low above my ash-tray, raised a little ash, with the breath of its wings" (*Molloy*, 223). In this single moment of intensely observed particularity, the expansion of the subject's feeling ("the little beat my heart once missed") blots out the difference between observed and observer. The timeless quality of this moment lies in its utter severing from before and after; it obeys, as do so many sentences here, the logic of the fragment. Of course one might see in the fly an image of dirt and decay. Or one might see it—like the image of the fly that interrupts Shenryu Suzuki's *Zen Mind, Beginner's Mind* or the image of the fly that serves Emily Dickinson as emblem for eternity—as an image whose nature repels the clichés that cling to winged things.

These brief reflections on the affective dimensions of Beckettian first-person narration might give us some grounds for supposing that Bernhard need not be ironic when he describes the condition of the narrator of such a work as the only "real satisfaction." But these reflections may be quite beside the point. When Bernhard talks about satisfaction, and when he expresses joy at the prospect of writing himself into this *Molloy*-esque work, he's not addressing us. Of course the fact that he's writing to himself doesn't mean he's *not* being ironic. One can be ironic in addressing oneself. But if Bernhard's own irony makes him laugh, then he is in the Molloy position and enjoying it. And if Bernhard is not being ironic at all, then he is in the Molloy position and enjoying it.[34]

* 7 *

Race Makes Class Visible

What would we see in a world where race had become invisible? For a number of critics, a world purged of the legacies of racism is one where our most pressing problems—our economic problems—would become starkly visible. Economic injustice, the concentration of a large share of the national wealth in a tiny minority of wealthy families, which writers like Walter Benn Michaels, Kenneth Warren, and Adolph Reed have identified as the primary source of *current* injustice, has gotten steadily worse over the past decades.[1] Government policies designed to ameliorate the effects of economic injustice have dwindled, while policies that exacerbate inequality and its effects have proliferated.

Why has this happened? We have a form of government in which public opinion plays a major role. Of course certain legal and constitutional structures supporting inequity may well prove resistant to democratic change. But why haven't we even begun to test the limits of democratic change? Voters harmed by the current distribution of wealth vastly outnumber those who benefit. Why hasn't public opinion forced our representatives to create more progressive policies?

Several kinds of forces are blocking public response to economic injustice. The first consists of political actions taken by the wealthy or by those representing their interests. Though a distinct minority, the rich shape the democratic process through campaign donations and through a legislative process allowing minority interests to block legislation.[2] The second force consists of beliefs that lead people to interpret injustice in such a way as to reduce the impulse for systematic change. For example, some people believe that wealth is the just reward for hard work.[3] Others think that each generation rises; if they themselves are relatively poorly off, their children will do better.[4] Finally, the critique of dogmatic equality, which we explored in the second chapter of this book, shows how egalitarianism at one level—the level of labor contracts and property rights—supports inequality at another level—the level of distribution.[5]

Still others believe that racial identity, not class position, is what's most important in social relations. Sometimes—as in Nixon's "southern strategy"—the effect is to cause poor whites to vote according to their sense of their racial interests and against their economic interests.[6] But racial thinking can also blind people on the Left to economic injustice. Progressives who see the world in racial terms may try to apply the remedy for racism—recognition—to class, which requires a very different kind of remedy—redistribution.[7]

The insistence on seeing society in terms of race has been ubiquitous in American literary and cultural studies, and this tendency is the target of Michaels's and Warren's call to transform our cultural politics. Not only does antiracism not address economic injustice, these critics claim, but our tendency to view politics in terms of race renders invisible the most pressing contemporary form of injustice. Corporate America loves the focus on race; corporations embrace all forms of diversity and celebrate a progressive racial politics that systematically deflects focus from a class politics that would be far harder for the ruling class to swallow. Only when our politics become race-blind, argue the critics of antiracism, can progressives become effectively class conscious.

The racial thinking targeted by Warren and Michaels, like the individualism targeted by Timothy Noah or the "family values" targeted by Thomas Frank, exemplify beliefs preventing Americans from addressing economic injustice.[8] And if we think that such beliefs are the only reason Americans don't vote for redistributive policies, our debate about this issue will take a certain form, the form it has in fact taken. We argue about whether racial thinking, for instance, actually performs the ideological work the critics allege.[9]

But there is a third kind of blockage. This other force that prevents the public from rising up against economic injustice is perceptual and cognitive in nature. Beliefs like those surveyed above give people ways to interpret the injustice we *see*. As I will show, the nature of human perception, combined with the postwar transformation of the American class structure, causes people simply not to *see* injustice at all, and to fail to connect the instances of deprivation they do encounter with systematic trends.

Gwendolyn Brooks's 1949 poetic experiment with post-racial seeing illuminates the operation of this third perceptual-cognitive force in our attitudes about injustice. While Brooks's poetry explores Black experience in an astonishing variety of dimensions, I wish here to focus on a pair of poems that rigorously explore one peculiarly complex aspect—the relation of race to class—by creating a poetic world that resists racial sight. "I love those little booths at Benvenuti's" and "Beverly Hills, Chicago" inhabit a perceptual matrix that has yet to exist in the United States. Brooks creates a new way of seeing in these works, a way of seeing in which race simply doesn't show up.

One word for the post-racial vision Brooks develops in the linked poems is *imaginary*. Another word is *ideal*. One doesn't have to believe that an ideal triangle exists somewhere in reality in order to make use of it in calculating the measurements of an actual triangle. Similarly, Brooks's ideal way of seeing helps us understand a key facet of our actual social and political problem. She shows us that we possess a flawed but potent perceptual-cognitive resource for identifying economic injustice. Racial marking provides an index of social structure that also enables people to perceive economic injustice. In America, race makes class visible. Brooks shows us racial seeing as a paradoxically progressive economic resource by imagining a world without it.

*

"I love those little booths at Benvenuti's" begins with a description of people who are expecting to see race. The poem follows a group of slumming whites on their trip to the South Side of Chicago, to a restaurant frequented by working-class Blacks:

> They get to Benvenuti's. There are booths
> To hide in while observing tropical truths
> About this—dusky folk, so clamorous!
> So colorfully incorrect,
> So amorous,
> So flatly brave!

Boothed-in, one can detect,
Dissect.[10]

The restaurant booth becomes a theater booth, and the slummers anticipate a theatrical display of Blackness:

What antics, knives, what lurching dirt; what ditty—
Dirty, rich, carmine, hot, not bottled up,
Straining in sexual soprano . . . (*Blacks*, 126)

Even early in the poem, Brooks's evocative rendering of the *content* of the vision the whites expect to exercise in the restaurant—lurid images of Black people—shouldn't blind us to her characterization of the *form* of that vision. "Observing tropical truths . . . one can detect, / dissect." The whites come equipped with a kind of seeing that reveals knowledge. For the racist whites, to see a Black body is instantly to know all kinds of invisible things about it. Racial seeing is incisive; it penetrates surfaces to reveal information not ordinarily accessible to vision.

Halfway through the next stanza is the line "They lean back in the half-light, stab their stares." The word *stab* combines two aspects of racial vision that Brooks will soon separate. First, the "stabbing stare" threatens violence against the people exposed to it. In entering a field defined by racial vision, Black people find their skin, hair, and movements transformed into signs marking them as hypersexualized, barely socialized creatures of the "tropics." Racial seeing, in other words, formats Blacks for oppressive treatment. Even if these particular whites aren't present agents of material oppression, they are the agents of a form of vision that supports Jim Crow.

The second sense of *stab* is difficult at this point in the poem to fully disentangle from the first. Brooks writes that the whites expect they'll be "observing . . . truths." The knifelike vision cuts cleanly from surface to essence. I think the following formula captures the epistemological movement here: racial vision proceeds from *example* to *pattern*. At first, this formula can seem to describe the cognitive process involved in seeing anything. But racial vision is not, as we will shortly see, the kind of movement from example to pattern that occurs whenever we recognize something, as when we see a wooden object as a chair. The pattern here involves a systematic distribution of social value. Racial seeing in this poem associates Black bodies with a pattern of social deprivation. *Antics, tropical, dirty, hot, sexual*: individually, these words might carry a variety of values. Taken together, as racial seeing binds them together, these terms signify low status and are implicitly contrasted with the high status possessed by the white slummers.

So analysis precipitates two kinds of "truth" from these lines. The first—that which assigns specific predicates to Blackness—is ideological or, more simply, false. It is not true that Blacks can be accurately characterized as racial vision presents them, as quasi-human jungle creatures. But the second piece of information—that which reveals Blacks to be the subjects of systematic deprivation in the United States—is not ideological. It is simply true.

Now, it is difficult to disassociate this latter meaning (Blacks are deprived) from the former (Blacks are "dirty," "hot," "tropical"). Further, there is a causal connection between these two meanings. At least part of the reason Blacks are deprived is because whites see them as a "dirty," "sexual," "tropical" "dusky folk." Racial seeing gives access to two entangled but conceptually distinct kinds of information—one false, one true. The false information conveyed by race might be described as *stereotype*; the true information might be described as *position in a social system*. But type and position are mixed. The value of racial vision's capacity to see directly into abstract social patterns is compromised by its malign contribution to those patterns.

Having explored what the whites expect to see, we turn now to what Brooks gives them to see:

> They lean back in the half-light, stab their stares
> At: walls, panels of imitation oak
> With would-be marbly look; linoleum squares
> Of dusty rose and brown with little white splashes,
> White curls; a vendor tidily encased;
> Young yellow waiter moving with straight haste,
> Old oaken waiter, lolling and amused;
> Some paper napkins in a water glass;
> Table, initialed, rubbed, as a desk at school. (*Blacks*, 126–27)

The slummers' stares are blunted on surfaces that refuse to yield social information. There's lots of color here, but not the kind that racial vision can work with. Color is the ground of racial seeing. The properties of racial vision reveal themselves in the way racial color vibrates between the abstract and the concrete. White people are not white; Black people are not black. But there is that in the tones and hues of skin color which yields to stabbing stares, and enables instant passage from actual pink-tan to abstract white, from actual red-brown to abstract black. In Brooks's "Benvenuti's," that passage is blocked.[11]

To create an American space in which race doesn't appear is no easy task. Brooks's creation of this fictional space constitutes an achievement of this pair of poems and suggests criteria by which we should judge them. We should attend to the aesthetic means by which Brooks realizes the fiction of a space resistant to racial vision, and to the kinds of knowledge this experiment both depends on and yields. These criteria are logically distinct, but in practice they are entangled.

For example, Brooks realizes the fictional space of "I love those little booths" through the brilliant decision to describe the coloration of bodies in terms of the coloration of furniture. She describes the inhabitants of the restaurant as "colored," but as these colors melt into the colors of furniture, they refuse to cohere along racial lines. "Dusty rose and brown . . . young yellow . . . old oaken . . . white curls." Color bleeds from furnishing to body without seam, and in this process the ground of racial vision leaks away. Earlier, I contrasted how racial seeing moves from example to pattern with how our seeing of furniture moves from example to type. Here we see this shift dramatized. It is not that the slummers aren't recognizing what they're seeing— "paper napkins in a water glass," "linoleum squares / Of dusty rose and brown"—the images are clearly recognizable. But this recognition stops well short of the abstract social patterning racial vision provides. These images could exist anywhere—in a diner in Nebraska, for example, or a family restaurant on the North Side. They fail to position this space in relation to all other spaces in the way the expected sight of Blackness would instantly accomplish.

The poem's images fail to establish the social location of the restaurant precisely because those images cannot be detached from their place in their immediate context. Brooks makes this *adhesion to context* the organizing principle of the space, one that applies indifferently to people and to furniture:

The colored people arrive, sit firmly down
Eat their express spaghetti, their t-bone steak
Handling their steel and crockery with no clatter,
Laugh punily, rise, go firmly out the door. (*Blacks*, 127)

The repetition of *firmly* signals something of the effort required to elude racial vision. Here Brooks attributes this effort to her subjects, as she shows them hanging on to their material environment as if for dear life. This adhesion to environment proclaims that the proper context for interpreting the individual is the context of the room that individual happens to inhabit. Such an attachment blunts any attempt of vision to penetrate *through* that material context to the abstract context of social structure.[12]

Brooks describes the slummers' reaction to entering this uncanny space with words that bring out the epistemological significance of the vision they have lost:

They stare. They tire. They feel refused,
Feel overwhelmed by subtle treasons!
. . . .
The absolute stutters, and the rationale
Stoops off in astonishment.
But not gaily
And not with their consent. (*Blacks*, 127)

What has been defeated here is the idea that vision yields knowledge, that to see something is to know more about it than appears to the eye. The sliding from the concrete to the abstract characteristic of racial color is arrested in the space of this poem. And to the antiracist readers in the poem's audience, this feels like a victory. We're happy that the racists didn't get what they wanted; we're glad they didn't see what they expected. At the end of the poem, it's easy to forget that good information has been lost along with the bad. It's easy to forget that what has disappeared along with Blackness is the ghost of social deprivation, made visible with racial seeing the way heat is made visible with infrared goggles. Easy to forget—if the poem that immediately follows "I love those little booths at Benvenuti's" didn't force us to remember.

"Beverly Hills, Chicago" reverses the situation of the companion poem preceding it. Instead of rich whites ("Whose friends, if not themselves, arrange / To rent in Venice 'a very large cabana . . .'") visiting a working-class Black area, now working-class Blacks drive through a wealthy white area. The two poems' visual dynamics, however, are identical.

Again, the people observed in the poem are described as adhering to their environment. The color white appears here but as a description of the color of old people's hair—a color possible for all races— and thus highlights the absence of racial color. As before, a close description of environment replaces racial marking. But the materials of the environment of "Beverly Hills" differ from the "imitation oak" and "linoleum" of "Benvenuti's":

> It is only natural that we should look and look
> At their wood and brick and stone
> And think, while a breath of pine blows
> How different these are from our own.

The working-class Black inhabitants of the car, driving through the wealthy white neighborhood, notice the difference of the materials in this environment compared with their own. They identify these materials as preferable to their own; seeing the neat gardens and clean brick walkways makes them reflect on the relative shoddiness of their own spaces. The Sunday drivers register the difference between rich and poor, but, crucially, they are unable to *place* this difference. They cannot connect their own deprivation with this display of luxury. These concrete images of wealth do not fit into an abstract social system showing that the deprivation of one group is directly related to the wealth of the other:

> We do not want them to have less.
> But it is only natural that we should think we have not enough.
> We drive on, we drive on.
> When we speak to each other our voices are a little gruff.

Just like the white slummers in "Benvenuti's," the drivers in "Beverly Hills, Chicago" suffer disappointment. Their gaze fails to satisfy their desire for knowledge. What they see when they drive through the wealthy district is just what Americans always see when they drive through such areas. They see the difference between rich and not-rich, between the very top of the income distribution and the rest. But this difference in wealth is not visible as a difference in class, if we understand "class" as the product of systematic inequality in production and exchange.[13]

The perceptual-cognitive structure of seeing the difference between rich and poor is profoundly *unlike* the structure of racial vision. In America, Black people are deprived in relation to white people, and the deprivation of Blacks depends on the ascent of whites. As analysts have long seen, this is simply what the Black-white racial structure is.[14] *And this structure is instantly visible.* To see a Black body in a racially coded space is instantly to understand a sign of deprivation *in relation* to white bodies. Blackness has *less* social value *because* whiteness has *more.*

On the other hand, to see a rich person's house is simply to see something one doesn't have but wants. Brooks's Sunday drivers manifest no sense that their own deprivation is connected to the luxury before them. In racial vision, an abstract map of social conflict unfolds from the immediate sight of racial difference. The sight of the fruits of inequality, however, produces nothing but unease, repressed resentment. "We do not want them to have less . . ."

The observers of "Benvenuti's" and "Beverly Hills, Chicago" both suffer from the absence of racial vision. Because they inhabit a race-blind space, the whites in the first poem fail to see the source of their power in the Blacks' abjection. The Blacks in the second poem fail to see the source of their deprivation in the whites' luxury. Both are disappointed: the whites are refused the comforting evidence of their superiority; the Blacks are refused the motivating evidence of their oppression. Both sets of observers feel that their epistemological gaze has been "blunted" on material surfaces that refuse to yield social meaning.

Our response to the different poems is asymmetrical, mirroring the complexity of racial vision. In the first poem, the progressive reader is glad that the racist expectations of the slummers have been frustrated. In the second, she's upset that the working-class Blacks are deprived of a kind of vision that might lead to social and political action.

Gwendolyn Brooks has presented us with an idealized poetic space, an imaginary space in which race does what it never does in

America: not show up. If my description of the poems' dynamics has been accurate, we can agree that these poems are not mimetic and have little or no value in the enterprise to which such poems are typically put: revealing features of an actual historical context.

So what value do they have? Read as I read them, the linked poems make a series of claims, which, if not entirely unique, have never to my knowledge been made together in quite the same way:

1 In a space where Americans can't see race, they have a hard time seeing class.
2 Race, as a kind of vision revelatory of social structure, also makes class visible.

The progressive reader's asymmetrical response to the poems' identical fictions implies a third claim:

3 *Racial* vision might play a progressive role in the response to *economic* inequality.[15]

Read as I read them, the aesthetic work of Brooks's two poems has been to realize an imaginary world. Imaginary worlds are a dime a dozen; a judgment about the importance of *this* world rests on whether we leave it knowing something we didn't before we entered. The aesthetic value of Brooks's two poems thus depends on how we assess the claims enumerated above.

*

There are several sources of evidence we can adduce in support of Brooks's implicit claims. Perhaps the easiest way to defend the logic of the poems is to point out that race and class do in fact coincide, and they coincide nearly to the same extent now as in the early civil rights era. Black unemployment was double that of whites in 1960 and was still double that of whites in 2012. The poverty rate for Blacks has come down since the early 1960s, but it was still double that of whites in 2010. Graduation rates are far higher for whites than for Blacks.[16] Data on income and net worth present an even starker—and worsening—disparity: "between 2000 and 2011, Black median household income fell from 64% to 58% of the white figure." By 2009, white households' net worth was twenty times than of Blacks.[17] To see race today, then, is still largely to see class.

But of course this defense fails to answer the serious objections to the claims I understand Brooks's poems to make. I think few would deny the relative economic deprivation of Blacks in America. But the focus on race seems not to help in addressing this economic deprivation. If the problem with racism is discrimination, then a certain set of tools—those used successfully by the civil rights movement—is indicated. But these tools are insufficient for dealing with class. Here the problem is not discrimination but a system that produces inequality under conditions of formal equality. This economic deprivation is prosecuted without violation of civil rights. It is prosecuted by the normal operation of capitalism, which reliably concentrates wealth in the hands of the few, even if those few manifest complete commitment to diversity and equal opportunity.

The critics of antiracism may admit that the commitment to formal equality among the ruling class is not yet complete; racial discrimination does still exist, and some of the economic deprivation of minorities may well be produced by ongoing discrimination. Even progressives skeptical of the capacity of antiracism to address our most pressing social problems will agree that we must be vigilant in continuing to enforce civil rights laws so as to root out discrimination in employment, housing, and education.

But they may nevertheless claim that economic deprivation resulting from *historical* discrimination is not best addressed in the way we address *active* discrimination. For proof, we need only consult the statistics alluded to above, which show that despite huge gains in reducing discrimination in employment, housing, and education, the economic inequality of Blacks persists, and persists nearly unchanged by some key measures. Countering class inequality requires a different set of tools. Therefore, an increasing number of critics argue that it is time to clearly distinguish the goals and means of a politics aimed at reducing economic inequality from the goals and means of a politics aimed at reducing racial injustice.

I can see nothing wrong with these arguments, which have been powerfully advanced by Warren, Michaels, and others. They seem to me entirely logical. Class is different from race. The problem Brooks's poems help us with, however, is not *logical* but *practical*. Warren's and Michaels's work has put class back in the center of conversations about the politics of American literature. The next step is to begin to think about the practical problems a cultural politics of class confronts. And the most pressing of these is that Americans simply have a hard time seeing class as a problem. Logic doesn't help. Or rather, our understanding of the difference between class and race must be supplemented with an understanding of the cognitive and perceptual mechanisms that enable or disable a population's recognition of social logics. And paradoxically, once we focus on the practical problem of raising class consciousness, we see that a clean distinction between class and race becomes harder to maintain.

Social scientists have long puzzled over the fact that Americans tend not to recognize income inequality as a serious problem. According to models of voting behavior, writes political scientist Frederick Solt, "democracies should be expected to respond to greater economic inequality by increasing redistribution . . . the evidence indicates, however, that higher levels of inequality are not associated with more redistributive spending."[18] A widely cited 2011 study by Michael Norton and Dan Ariely sought to understand why "Americans, especially those with low income, are not advocating for greater redistribution of wealth."[19] The authors found that "respondents dramatically underestimated the current level of income inequality."[20] People simply tend not to see economic injustice for the systematic problem it is.

This incapacity to understand the level of unequal distribution is borne out by studies of voters' attitudes toward economic issues more generally. Summarizing those studies, Paul Krugman writes, "The political science evidence on economics and elections is unambiguous: what matters is the rate of change, not the level."[21] While writers such as Thomas Frank have stressed the role of ideological factors in causing voters to downplay economic issues in favor of "cultural" issues, it is not the case that people don't care about their economic well-being. When one's own situation, and that of one's family and friends, is getting *worse*, then one is motivated to vote on economic issues. However, people seem to have a limited capacity to recognize and vote on more abstract, long-range economic trends. While a jump in the unemployment rate from 4 to 10% will motivate action, voters will tend to respond to a static unemployment rate of 10% in much the same way they respond to a static unemployment rate of

4%: not very much. The environmental cues that trigger recognition and action in the first case are missing in the second case.

As Norton and Ariely's study suggests, the long-term skewing of income distribution also appears to lack the kind of concrete cues that enable people to link their own economic situation with broad, systematic trends. Working people occasionally see rich people in real life; they see expensive cars and mansions on television, but—unless race enters into the picture—they tend to respond to these signs of the one percent in much the same way as the people in "Beverly Hills, Chicago": with desire, and perhaps resentment.

Seeing a Bentley pass by, we may think, "We do not want them to have less. / But it is only natural that we should think we have not enough." But the evidence suggests that voters tend *not* to think, "These people have more *because* we have less." And while certain beliefs surely play a role in Americans' inaction on economic injustice—the belief that if you work hard in America you'll be rewarded, for example, or that "family values" trump economic values—a large part of the problem is simply that people have a hard time recognizing differences in wealth for the systematic effects of capitalism that they are.[22] What is hard for people to see in differences of wealth—an abstract, conflictual social pattern—is easy for them to see in differences of color. Racial vision reveals various kinds of additional information about a person in addition to what is visible. One word for what seeing race has and seeing wealth doesn't is *essentialism*. We can understand *essentialism* to mean the capacity to associate visible cues with invisible properties. Humans are born essentialists; essentialism is just how we're wired to understand our environment. As the psychologist Paul Bloom writes, "We are far from a complete theory of the origin of essentialism. But I think the evidence is now abundant that much of essentialism does not have cultural origins. It is a human universal. . . . We know that even babies infer invisible properties based on what things look like."[23]

By showing that humans are born essentialists, Bloom and other scientists hardly mean to endorse all the judgments that essentialism produces. Many of these judgments—and race is an obvious example—are demonstrably false. Consider, for instance, the false "tropical truths" the racial vision of Brooks's slummers find in Black bodies: "dirty . . . carmine, hot, not bottled up."

And yet, as I intimated early in this chapter, demonstrably false contents like these do not exhaust the work that racial seeing performs. Irene Tucker has recently helped us understand this work. In *The Moment of Racial Sight*, Tucker focuses not on the content of racial judgments but on their form. She describes how race "renders people instantly knowable."[24] And this cognitive, epistemological function is conceptually distinct from the particular contents that function may accumulate over the course of racial history. With racial vision, to see is to know. Furthermore, in the modern American racial vision that concerns us here, race gives access to two different kinds of social knowledge. First are the specific characteristics of the kind voiced by Brooks's white slummers. But second, racial vision also enables us to instantly see individuals in terms of abstract social patterns. And class is one of these patterns. A passage in Tao Lin's 2013 novel *Taipei* strikingly illustrates this capacity of racial vision. *Taipei* performs a vision test similar to that of Brooks's 1949 poems, but instead of creating an imaginary nonracial America, *Taipei*'s protagonist travels to a country where American racial divisions don't apply.

The protagonist, Paul, who lives in New York, goes to Taipei to visit his Taiwanese parents. While walking in a shopping district with his girlfriend, he reflects on the differences between the two cities. Being in Taipei makes him realize how loud New York is. It also enables him to see something else he doesn't like about the American city: "I don't like places . . . where everyone working is a minority."

Paul's girlfriend naturally presses him on this statement. "Like, visually?"

"Um, no," he says. He continues, hesitantly: "Just that . . . here, when you see someone, you don't know . . . that . . . they live like two hours away and are um . . . poor, or whatever."[25]

The United States, like Taiwan, has increasingly become a service economy, and this has helped depress the visibility of class. The visual cues that once signified class—the style of dress and comportment associated with blue collar work—have given way to company-provided uniforms and strict rules on behavior and speech. Employers, in effect, force workers to imitate the middle-class patrons they serve. Like the waiters in Brooks's "Benvenuti's," the service workers of the novel's Taipei betray no signs of deprivation. The workers' occupation is visible, their class isn't.

But in New York, Paul realizes, one factor resists the erasure of class: race. Service positions in New York tend to be staffed disproportionately by members of racial minorities. The information conveyed by race—that racially marked bodies are deprived relative to white bodies—reacts on the worker's occupation.

Examining this process closely, we can distinguish several distinct moments Paul experiences as simultaneous. First, he identifies the workers as racial minorities. That identification includes the knowledge that racial minorities are systematically *worse off* than whites. Now, at this initial level, "worse off" signifies a deficit in status, in positive social recognition. The struggle against this deficit takes place at the level of appreciation. This is the level literary studies has tended to inhabit, by providing recognition to the works of Black authors, for example.[26] Logically, there is no route from the struggle for social justice at this level, in which appreciation effectively counters deprivation, to the economic level, in which redistribution is the weapon of choice.

But in practice there is such a route. When Paul notices that all or most of the service workers are minorities, his awareness of the deprivation of minorities in terms of *recognition* transfers to an awareness of the deprivation of service workers in terms of *income*. All this happens without reflection, without the kind of calculation and access to statistical income distributions that social science has shown American voters are so bad at. The worker's race instantly transforms occupation into class.

Paul *sees* that workers at a Manhattan McDonald's "live like two hours away and are um . . . poor." This upsets him in exactly the way that advocates of reducing income inequality wish Americans would get upset. Race makes the systematic inequity of the service economy visible to everyone, accessible to everyone. Trying to make statistics into a slogan—"We are the ninety-nine percent"—has had mixed success at best. Turning statistics into direct visual experience—the kind of experience Paul reports—is clearly better.

And yet the visibility with which race endows class is hardly an unmixed blessing. The linkage of race and class constitutes a bitter paradox, and is perhaps the knottiest problem confronting the struggle against injustice today. But experiments like Brooks's and observations like *Taipei*'s suggest that this knot cannot simply be cut without depriving America's embryonic (or, more darkly, vestigial) class consciousness of one of its chief supports.

We can bring out the paradox of racial vision by asking what would happen if the poems, counterfactually, belonged to the historical world rather than the fictional world Brooks creates. What would happen if racial vision were available in her two poems? The slummers wouldn't be as disappointed as they are, and the working-class Blacks would go home with something more than mute resentment. The slummers would see "tropical" essences lurking beneath Black skin, and the Sunday drivers would see that the rich whites have more *because* the working-class Blacks have less.

At first glance, the outcome seems symmetrical. The slummers activate the virus of racism, which may lead to further discrimination, which may further impoverish urban Blacks. The impoverished Blacks, on the other hand, see their deprivation as a consequence of the accumulation of whites' wealth, which may lead them to vote for politicians promising an end to racism *and* the implementation of economic policies designed to address material inequality.

But in fact, the two situations are asymmetrical. The kind of knowledge revealed by racial seeing is not equivalent in the two poems. The specific content of the slummers' racial vision does not receive support from the behavior of the Black restaurant's inhabitants:

> What antics, knives, what lurching dirt; what ditty—
> Dirty, rich, carmine, hot, not bottled up,
> Straining in sexual soprano . . .

Even if racial vision were available in this space, the slummers wouldn't see any of the activities listed above:

> The colored people arrive, sit firmly down
> Eat their express spaghetti, their t-bone steak
> Handling their steel and crockery with no clatter,
> Laugh punily, rise, go firmly out the door.

The slummers would see these people in terms of Blackness, would see them as deprived of a social value their whiteness possesses. But the whites would nevertheless go home disappointed at these people who refuse to "clown" (*Blacks*, 127). The behavior of the Blacks would give the lie to the specific characteristics racial vision purports to reveal.

But the judgments produced by a racial vision wielded by the Sunday drivers would be different. These judgments would in fact receive support from reality; the information racial vision would grant them would constitute direct insight into American social structure. The whites' wealth is directly related to the Black workers' deprivation.

It is true that racial vision reveals class position only by entangling it with race. And it is also true that, as Michaels and Warren argue, redressing racial inequality requires different tools from those useful for redressing class inequality. But the addition of racial vision to the world of this poem would have the practical effect of keying the display of wealth to social structure. In other words, race would turn the display of wealth into the display of something like class. Brooks's workers would drive away with justified anger, not repressed resentment.

We are now in a position to evaluate the three claims I listed as the fruit of Brooks's vision test. I think there are good grounds for believing that for both cognitive reasons (we tend to understand the world through essentializing vision) and historical reasons (the service economy provides fewer cues for our essentialism), Americans have a hard time seeing class on its own.

I also think that there are good grounds for at least exploring the idea that race sometimes works to make class visible. In describing these grounds, I should not be taken to mean that we would have been able to see this peculiar link between race and class without Brooks's poems. It would be more accurate to say that Brooks's two poems provide a lens through which these different concepts become assimilable. This is their major achievement, and a basis for the judgment of their value.

The third claim, suggested but not, for reasons we shall see, expressed by Brooks's poems—that racial vision may play a progressive role in relation to income inequality—is harder to judge. In confining ourselves to the situation of Brooks's poems, we may well conclude that if the Sunday drivers were to gain access to racial seeing, the focus on white/Black could subvert the focus on rich/poor. And this subversion, we might think, may have been a good thing in 1949 but is counterproductive in the post–civil rights era. It also seems possible to conclude, however, that the dynamic may work in the opposite direction, by linking our weak concern for economic justice with our strong concern for racial justice.

The question may be academic. Brooks, by leaving the poems side by side without commentary, refuses to disentangle progressive from oppressive features of racial sight or to evade the paradoxes of the relation of race to class. These paradoxes seem dissolvable only from an abstract, austerely logical perspective. Her poems are cunning traps for such perspectives, snaring them in the complexities of embodied cognition and perception. The final claim issuing from Brooks's imaginative effort to think outside American reality may, ironically, be bitterly realistic. Americans can't seem to help seeing race, and they can't seem to be helped to see class. Given our cognitive and historical limitations, perhaps there is no practical, democratic way to class consciousness in America except the one that passes through race consciousness.

*

Having made a preliminary case for the value of Brooks's vision test, I want to conclude by sketching the historical context of her counterfactual experiment. As I have argued elsewhere, the effort to understand the relation of literature to history confronts a basic dilemma.[27] While the significance of the work depends in part on the nature of the historical context, we cannot specify the relevant aspects of that context in advance of a specification of the qualities of the work. Each work engages—and transforms—particular dimensions of its period. We must try to see the world from the perspective of the work, a perspective which in turn reveals features of history often rendered invisible without it. The danger of beginning with the historical context is illustrated by those otherwise astute critics who miss the strongly anti-mimetic color imagery in "I love those little booths at Benvenuti's" and "Beverly Hills, Chicago," finding the expression of historical dynamics with which they are already familiar.[28] By beginning with a formal description of Brooks's vision test, we are now equipped to track the affinities and resistances that bind her poems to contemporary discourses while keeping them distinct.

We have seen how Brooks imagines a way of seeing that is blind to racial difference. We have also seen how she mourns the social knowledge lost when we stop seeing race. While I hope I have made clear the logic which associates racial seeing with social knowledge, until now the positive features of Brooks's poetic style of vision may have seemed somewhat mysterious. It isn't just that race is invisible in these poems, it's that the world's visible order is rearranged. *Annie Allen's* curious imagery, which so deforms the sociological legibility of Brooks's scenes, is driven by more than a simple concern to imagine the world without race. Indeed, the significance of Brooks's effort to show what is lost with racial vision only emerges fully when we probe the historical roots of the poetry's visual order. A way of seeing in which *adhesion to context* blocks abstract social knowledge is not pure fantasy, nor is it Brooks's private invention. Rather, it is a response to several of the period's social and intellectual currents.

In the early postwar period, Gwendolyn Brooks was not alone in imagining new ways of seeing or in taking the city as the site of a transformed visual mode. We will see that the poet's experimentation with urban vision manifests a complex relation to the postwar attack on the modernist image of the city and its alignment of the visual order with an abstract social order. On the one hand, Brooks crafts a poetics of urban immersion and adhesion to context attuned to exactly those social dynamics the modernist planners would be castigated for ignoring. But she does not share the free market bias of the urban antimodernist movement; her poetry is consistently sensitive to the problem of economic inequity. "I love those little booths at Benvenuti's" and "Beverly Hills, Chicago" make a case for retaining awareness of racial difference in the representation of urban immersion. The role of race in Brooks's subsequent career suggests that she increasingly found that case convincing. Placing the poet's claims for racial seeing in the context of the urban debate illuminates her representation of race in relation to the central problem of urban life. How can people gain knowledge about social arrangements characterized by unprecedented complexity, uncertainty, and rapid change?

Jane Jacobs, with the publication of *The Death and Life of Great American Cities* in 1961, became the most influential critic of urban modernism. Jacobs argues that the modernist image of the city, ruthlessly applied to actual cities during postwar urban renewal projects, is above all designed to enable a certain kind of seeing. She writes of Le Corbusier's influential city plans that they "said everything in a flash." The modernist city is characterized by "clarity, simplicity, harmony"; the application of modernist planning renders cities "so orderly, so visible, so understandable."[29]

Modernist city space is arranged so that to see is to understand. The various functions of city space are clearly marked for the viewer; commercial, residential, and industrial uses are carefully separated and consigned to different, clearly delimited districts. Planning replaces the confused and confusing tangle of the premodern city; planning begins by razing the excrescence of history. Individuals in the city imagined by Le Corbusier and his American disciples will have no difficulty locating themselves; the city's grid will stretch out before them in straight lines and right angles.

The made environment envisioned by modernist designers will perform functions that individuals once had to struggle with alone. In a block in the old city, perceiving shapes and understanding social functions constituted two separate operations. One often had to work to understand where this street led or what that building was for. The visible appearance of the premodern city concealed social function and social identity. In the clean modern shapes of urban renewal, social order and social meaning will be visible to the naked eye.

An urban environment arranged so as to enable its inhabitants to easily locate themselves with respect to the social whole seems like a good thing. But the problem, Jacobs argues, is that the modernists' way of aligning seeing with understanding distorts the social order it is designed to illuminate. In their mania for clarity, the planners turn the city "into an ideal of order and gentility so simple it could be engraved on the head of a pin" (*Death and Life*, 9). This modernist effort to map the city finds its echo and heir in the valorization by contemporaneous literary and cultural studies of "cognitive mapping," and the arguments that Jacobs advances against the modernist mappers continue to tell against their postmodern descendants.

Jacobs suggests that maps of the city often conceal as much as they reveal, in that what one can understand is subordinated to what one can see. "There is a quality meaner than outright ugliness or disorder, and this meaner quality is the dishonest mask of pretended order, achieved by ignoring or suppressing the real order that exists and is struggling to be served" (14–15). In a celebrated passage, she compares the urban renewers to the bloodletters of the nineteenth century (12). In both cases, thinkers are seduced by an overly simple, misleadingly elegant theory and wreak havoc on biological and social bodies. The city, like the human body—to which Jacobs constantly compares it—is the proper subject of a science sensitive to its complexity, as it lacks the kind of clarity and simplicity that would make it easily transmissible. The idea that urban social logics can be rendered as clean, readily grasped maps is for Jacobs the result of substituting visual for epistemological values.

The mania for mapping—whether by modernist designers or postmodern critics—undermines the effort to understand the complex workings of social space in service of an effort to make social space understandable to those without specialized knowledge. The proponents of urban renewal neglect the close study of urban life, while postmodern cognitive-mapping proponents like Fredric Jameson admit they are "tourists" among the social scientific disciplines engaged with analyzing modern society.[30] We have seen evidence for the difficulty people encounter in understanding even large-scale patterns of economic inequality; Jacobs suggests that it is simply impossible to create an accurate map of a complex social space that will possess the kind of "clarity, simplicity, harmony" necessary to make the data easily comprehensible to anyone.

Jacobs criticized the modernist imaging of city space in two ways that are particularly relevant for Brooks's approach to these issues. First, insofar as the maps became templates for razing and rebuilding cities, Jacobs attacks them as imposing an artificial social order on the city. While she implies that these plans can be the tools of racist agendas, Brooks and other Black writers—to say nothing of historians of urban renewal—are painfully aware of the extent to which modernist planning served to segregate and disempower minorities and the poor.[31]

Second, Jacobs believed that modernist planners misunderstood the nature of capitalist society, which is driven by the market. This perception meshes broadly with Brooks's, though with an important difference. While Brooks's analysis of capitalism functions in the service of critique, Jacobs's is presented in the context of a celebration of markets freed from plans. Brooks's experiment with racial vision constitutes a critical intervention in the kind of social space Jacobs describes. Her poetry fashions an answer to the problem of critique in a space where accurate maps are hard to transmit in a form that will motivate mass political action. On the other hand, Jacobs's discussion of the economic dimension of the city is critically oriented against planning and leaves no room for a discussion of systematic inequality. She understands the complex "organic" urban order distorted by the modernists of the city above all in terms of commerce and exchange. Often, her language is identical to that of free market economists like Milton Friedman, as when she contrasts the big plan of government order with the "small plans" of free individuals. Cities, she writes, are "ground for the plans of thousands of people" (*Death and Life*, 14). Recalling Adam Smith's "invisible hand," she imagines these thousands of plans organizing themselves into a harmonious order. In sum, Jacobs's vision of the postmodern, unplanned city is of a space where regulations imposed from above dissolve, and a free market order comes into being.

But once planning was finally eliminated, two different "natural" human tendencies appeared to Jacobs to threaten her free urban market. She believed that people's ability to focus on the opportunities for consumption and exchange on a city block saturated by commerce would be disrupted by long, wide views. While enjoying the "big picture" afforded by large squares or broad, unbroken avenues, one might forget to gaze into the shop window. Not only is awareness of the big picture epistemologically distorting, it also impedes economic function. People should not even try to map their environment, Jacobs thought; they should not be seduced into trying to understand their social position in terms of the whole. Urban dwellers should attend to their immediate context and focus on making the exchanges that accumulate to form an unmappable free market order. Therefore, one of the only planned interventions Jacobs advocates is to break up long streets permitting views far into the distance with corners, walls, and awnings (*Death and Life*, 375–90).

The other tendency that could block free exchange is people's attitudes toward race and class. Racial prejudice threatens conflict as well as diminishes and restricts exchanges between people. In addition, borrowing models from the biological sciences, Jacobs sees diversity as crucial to the health of an organic urban environment (143). Free economic exchange both thrives on and serves to multiply difference; any brake on this process is malign. Jacobs's other planned intervention into her spontaneous order, therefore, is the advocacy of appreciation for racial difference. And what works for race, she implies, will also work for class. The main problem confronting the poor is the prejudice they suffer at the hands of the well-to-do (31). Therefore, the poor are included with racial and ethnic minorities as the target of appreciation and positive recognition.

Brooks's thinking about the city responds to many of the same pressures as Jacobs does. Like Jacobs, she is opposed—aesthetically, epistemologically, and politically—to the modernist vision and to the urban renewal projects designed to realize it. She is suspicious of the kind of knowledge offered by the map or the bird's-eye view, and she realizes the tendency of these devices to distort or to misrepresent the social order. But unlike Jacobs, Brooks does not want to neutralize class and racial difference. Instead, as we've explored, she sees racial vision as a means of obtaining insight into the economic injustice produced by market orders. Further, Brooks values race as a means of knowledge that one can access from *within* the space of the city street. Race operates as a simple index of the systematic deprivation produced by capitalism. What is striking is how *little* one needs to know to access this social knowledge.[32] The racial seeing Brooks isolates is perfectly calibrated to the problem of critiquing the kinds of spaces Jacobs describes. How can we transmit knowledge of economic injustice in a context of unparalleled social complexity?

We've seen how Brooks isolates the social value of racial vision in the two linked poems of 1949. But these poems should be understood in the context of her career-spanning interest in the problem of how individuals gain access to knowledge of their social position from within a complex urban environment. Criticism of Brooks has tended to divide her career into two phases: an early phase, in which she downplayed race, and her work after the mid-1960s, when, influenced by the Black Arts movement, she embraced racial themes in her poetry. And yet by comparing poems from before and after this break, I think we can see the consistency of her approach to race. On the other hand, our awareness of how the early poems formulate the desirability of racial vision enriches our understanding of her unique place among the Black Arts writers.

The Death and Life of Great American Cities traces the trajectory of American cities, from spontaneous order to the deathly, mechanical regularity of the modernist vision. Like "I love those little booths at Benvenuti's" and "Beverly Hills, Chicago," Brooks's 1968 poem "In the Mecca" imagines a counter-historical space.[33] The poem is set in

a structure erected in 1891 as an elegant Chicago apartment building. By the 1920s, the wealthy white residents of the Mecca have been
replaced by working-class African American families, who are in turn
replaced by impoverished African Americans arriving from the Deep
South. In 1952, the building is purchased by the Illinois Institute of
Technology, which demolishes it, replacing the baroque, labyrinthine
wood-and-stone monster with the "clarity, simplicity, harmony" of
a new building designed by Ludwig Mies van der Rohe. The story
of the Mecca's rise and fall is reproduced across the country during
the urban transformations of the 1950s and 1960s. Yet Brooks's poem
inverts this chronology. This is how "In the Mecca" begins:

> Now the way of the Mecca was on this wise
> Mies Van der Rohe retires from grace
> and the fair fables fall. (*Blacks*, 406–7)

Here modernism lies in the past; the present tense of the poem
belongs to the confusion and complexity of the Mecca, rising on the
ruins of clean modern forms. The poem explores a different kind of
city space, keyed to a different kind of seeing. Brooks's chronological
inversion, imagining that the Mies van der Rohe structure predates
the Mecca, suggests that the aesthetic space of her poems cannot simply be understood as mimetic of actual urban conditions.

Why, in 1968, does Brooks choose to set a poem about inner-city
African American life in a turn-of-the-century building destroyed
in 1952? Why isn't this poem set in one of the many Le Corbusier-
derived housing projects that dominate the inner city from the mid-
1950s on? Gwendolyn Brooks has deliberately chosen to set her representation of contemporary African American life in an antimodernist
space. I think the key to her choice lies in how this space inverts the
modern relation between seeing and understanding.

Brooks's poems build a space where vision and cognition split
off. She sees and foresees a time when the racist effects of city planning will crumble—as they are and have been crumbling with the
dismantling of urban renewal–era housing projects. The problem of
the Mecca—the problem of the organic city—is the problem Brooks
faces in her poems. In this space—a space not *entirely* defined by racism, a space *also* defined by class inequality—the perception of race

takes on critical social value. The primary difference between 1949's "Beverly Hills, Chicago" and the 1968 poem from the collection *After the Mecca* titled "The Wall" is that the racial seeing unavailable to the Sunday drivers is now made robustly available. "The Wall" bristles with Blackness:

> black boy-men.
> Black
> Boy-men on roofs fist out . . .
> A little black stampede . . .
> On Forty-Third and Langley
> Black furnaces resent ancient
> Legislatures
> Of ploy and scruple and practical gelatin. (*Blacks*, 444–45)

If much criticism of Brooks has focused on a sharp break between her early (universalist) and late (race-conscious) poetry, reading "Beverly Hills, Chicago" next to "The Wall" allows us to see the earlier poem *formulating the rationale* the later poem will execute. "Beverly Hills, Chicago" suggests why a focus on race might be valuable; "The Wall" puts that focus into poetic practice. Part of my point is that Brooks's earlier poems are not universalist—if we take that term to describe a vision of social harmony—but are acutely aware of deprivation and inequality. Instead of seeing her career divided by race, I want to suggest that we understand it as unified by a rigorous exploration of the problem of social critique in a context where access to social knowledge is severely limited.

A comment by George Kent in 1971 illuminates these dynamics. "Brooks' poems," he writes, "tend not to represent a reach for some preexisting universal to be arrived at by reducing the tensions inherent in black experience. Their universalism derives, instead, from complete projection of a situation or experience's *space* and *vibrations*, going down deep, not transcending."[34] Like Jane Jacobs's, Brooks's vision is lodged in the midst of city; she peers at the world from within, without the epistemological transcendence imagined by the mappers. The poet is vividly aware that the aesthetic spaces she constructs block this desire to see the big picture, and her poems carefully register the frustration this blockage elicits. In *Annie Allen's*

"The Womanhood," Brooks's speaker addresses a bird and expresses her longing for the bird's-eye view that would disclose a sense of her position. She desires a perspective that would make sense of the city she lives in. She longs for the bird's "open apostolic height," and writes that the bird can

> Afford to pity me
> whose hours at best are wheats or beiges
> lashed with riot-red and black
> tabasco. (*Blacks*, 123)

Perhaps the bird can see rich and poor, center and periphery; the speaker's vision is lost in the mottled shades that form the background of her daily movements. We note the absence of racial Black and white in these lines, and the coloration's resemblance to the world of "I love those little booths at Benvenuti's" and "Beverly Hills, Chicago." While Brooks's poems will never occupy the bird's-eye view, will never map the city, she *will* allow her characters to see the world in terms of race. The knowledge desired by speakers of this poem and of "Beverly Hills, Chicago" will be partially fulfilled by the race consciousness of "The Wall" and "The Mecca." The significance of Brooks's midcareer decision to more emphatically include racial markers in her verse is blurred unless we see how the desire that fuels that decision is present in the poetry from the outset of her career.

To take another example, consider one of Brooks's most frequently anthologized poems, "kitchenette building," from her first book, *A Street in Bronzeville*. Like "In the Mecca," the poem is set in the kind of aging urban structure targeted by modernist city planning. The speaker of this poem also imagines a kind of vision that rises above her daily movements. She calls this vision a "dream" and asks:

> Could a dream send up through onion fumes
> its white and violet, fight with fried potatoes
> and yesterday's garbage ripening in the hall. . . .

> We wonder. But not well, not for a minute
> since number five is out of the bathroom now
> we think of lukewarm water, hope to get in it. (*Blacks*, 20)

Critics have seen this poem as organized around a tension between the "violet" dream and the "greyed in" life of the people.[35] And yet, to suggest that Brooks is sympathetic to the desire for the "dream" is to miss a crucial dimension of the poem's work. When she writes, "dream makes a giddy sound, not strong," the poet is making a statement of aesthetic values (*Blacks*, 20). Brooks likes strong words; she wants the hard surfaces and extreme closeups of urban daily life in her poems; she rejects the giddy heights, the bird's-eye view, the fantasy map.

Here the dream that rises up from the slum as the avatar of transcendent vision is a weak, foolish fancy. Escape from the urban prison doesn't pass through the unreal tones of the dream. It comes in stronger colors. Across Brooks's career, the aesthetic of urban immersion interacts with the desire to understand urban injustice. The problem is that the people who most need to know have no time for learning. Insight for those deprived of money, of decent work, of time, must come in an instant or not at all. Brooks's answer—flawed, paradoxical, but still serviceable—arrives not in "white and violet" but in Black and white.

Conclusion

Artistic judgment has the structure of a skill. It is something everyone does and everyone can learn to do better. The analysis I have undertaken in this book begins with judgment as a process of disclosing values rather than with the values judgment discloses. This constitutes a novelty of my approach.

Writers from Kant to Ruskin to Shklovsky to Cleanth Brooks to Adorno to Rancière believe that art yields a specific kind of good. Their accounts of judgment are determined by their conception of the beautiful, the organic, defamiliarization, formal complexity, critical power, or equality. The benefit of this traditional approach is that it provides a clear and simple answer to the question, Why is it good to study art or literature? Or, What human benefits flow from the practice of judgment? For Kant, disinterested judgment secures the special pleasure of the beautiful and intimates a source of human community beyond the empirical. For Adorno, the appreciation of artworks that withdraw from the social world yields special insight into the structure of that world. The cost of the traditional approach is that it inevitably excludes many actual and possible artistic values. Thus, these theorists tend to become associated with certain styles or movements; their models lose explanatory power beyond certain limits. It is as difficult to imagine a Kantian account of science fiction, a genre maximally driven by concepts, as it is to imagine an Adornian account of the rap lyric.

Judgment, as these thinkers have understood it, thus begins to look less like a skill and more like advocacy for a particular kind of art or aesthetic response. Perhaps here we have an additional reason for the contemporary suspicion of judgment. We distrust it in part because existing accounts stack the deck in favor of a particular style, period, movement, or tradition. By circumscribing what counts as aesthetic, traditional accounts are often vulnerable to the charge that their judgments amount to little more than a preference for one kind of artistic experience over another. This preference isn't so much defended by the prevailing accounts of judgment as it is their prerequisite.

By contrast, the benefit of describing and exemplifying the evaluative process in terms of a specific set of features and practices, and a specific set of checks and balances, is to demonstrate that expert artistic judgment has a claim on us beyond that of mere preference. Yet there is a cost to this approach in that it sacrifices a simple, delimited set of criteria for judging value. If someone asks me what the value of studying literature is, I can point to specific examples. I can show them how Dickinson successfully imagines what it's like to die, how Bernhard creates a template for the perfect novel, how Brooks reveals new dimensions of vision. Judgment is a process of disclosing and verifying values. It shows us works that are worth our time. But it doesn't operate on a single scale, it doesn't reveal greater or lesser quantities of a single widely acknowledged value. Artistic judgment requires that we place our existing values in suspension. Aesthetic education promises us values we may not yet know how to value.

The principle I discuss in chapter 4, that the right criteria for judging a work cannot be determined before the encounter with that work, is perhaps the most radical consequence of the approach to judgment I have developed in this book. On the one hand, I have come to believe this principle necessary for sustaining the trans-subjective dimension of judgment, for reasons I give in that chapter. On the other hand, it places an open, or blank, space just where advocates of literary education might want most to be emphatic. I can see that it would be desirable if, at the end of a book such as this, I could say: Literary education gives us *x* valuable thing. Of course I can without deception say that it gives us many valuable things—beauty, insight, critical distance, empathy, escape, strangeness, humor—in unimaginably refined and powerful forms. But ultimately, the list of the goods supplied by aesthetic education is open. The nature of artistic judgment as an expert discipline means that we cannot fully define the benefits of its practice in advance. This is a consequence of the rigor of judgment.

It is, however, possible to define the benefits of this evaluative process itself. First, it counters the malign tendency to reduce all value to existing consumer preference—an artifact of capitalism ultimately ruinous for individual and collective life. Second, in taking our orienting principles from the object, the practice of judgment engages a kind of negative capability. There is self-transcendence in submitting one's values, concepts, and perceptions to reorganization by the work. The expert undergoes the same self-alienating process, the same cultivation, she urges on her students. The claim of expertise is thus partially based on the way expert skills give experts an intensified sense of skepticism about their own values and preconceptions. Third, the combination of tacit skills and knowledges with the means for both peers and nonexperts to test a given value ensures that this model of artistic judgment provides public evaluations without forcing its objects through distorting modes of quantification, objectification, or measurement.

In the process of answering the several objections to judgment enumerated in my introduction—that judgment is subjective, primarily expressive of social status, not a fit subject of expertise, without a vital political dimension, and so on—I have provided detailed arguments for the benefits just listed. The final three chapters provided detailed examples of the practice of judgment, showing the various elements of expertise in operation, yielding particular values, and submitting them to testing by the reader. I wish to conclude by very briefly sketching several additional, institutional benefits we might expect from the adoption of this model. Fuller arguments in support of these institutional changes lie outside the scope of this study, not least because they depend on a widespread acceptance of the fact that judgment is at the heart of our professional work—an acceptance that has not yet occurred, and may never. Therefore, I offer these speculations in the spirit of a concluding thought experiment. I will refer to my home discipline of English, but I think there may be analogous benefits for other literature departments as well as such cognate disciplines as art history and music.

First, as I have emphasized throughout, my model is largely descriptive of current practices. These practices have, through the ideological suppression of judgment, often operated underground and in disguised forms. But aesthetic education—and the literature syllabus—is difficult if not impossible without judgment. So we find it everywhere even as it's foresworn. Similarly, the various skills I have shown to comprise literary expertise are without exception products of the development of the discipline and widely, if not unanimously, practiced by its professors, even when these skills are not understood in relation to the project of judgment.

It is true that in several important respects, my model is normative rather than descriptive—in its approach to criteria, for instance. But by and large, my intervention has been to unify a set of dispersed practices, operating under various kinds of subterfuge and misapprehension, and to give them a rationale, a form, and a defense. I hope this will enable the profession to be more intentional about its practices and to replace the current muddled understandings of literary expertise with a precise and capacious model. Literature professors are experts in judgment; aesthetic education transforms people's relation to culture, makes them better judges, and gives them values, perceptions, and insights they couldn't have imagined previously.

Therefore, one consequence of adopting, or admitting, this model of judgment might be to provide the academic study of literature and the arts with the clear human and social value which is presently obscured. Compare, for example, the recent effort of the president of Pomona, a prominent liberal arts college, who also happens to be an English professor, to enumerate the value of an English degree without admitting judgment. English, we hear, helps students value what they already value. It enhances critical thinking. It helps them appreciate difference. And it gives them "aesthetic empathy," which means not an appreciation for works of art, exactly, but an appreciation of other people's appreciation of works of art. (The Pomona students' example of the object of their aesthetic empathy: the fans of Celine Dion.) This education, the college president believes, helps students in the "marketplace of ideas": "When Silicon Valley types say they want to hire humanities majors, it's not because they want coders who know Gwendolyn Brooks poems."[1]

The confused and even contradictory quality of this brief for English without judgment—note that the penultimate item actually does require judgment—is not, I think, unrepresentative of the crisis of legitimization facing our profession. I think it would be better to embrace our role as experts at both selecting powerful works of art and teaching our students how to learn from them. It is possible, indeed likely, that the proponents of strictly vocational education will continue to object. But these enemies are hardly neutralized by the kind of rhetoric deployed by Pomona's president. The drawbacks of another popular understanding of literary study without literary judgment—English as quasi-history, pretend economics, imaginary biology, or amateur political science—have been increasingly evident since the Sokal hoax. As I described in chapter 4, there is room in the process of judgment to pursue with integrity the inevitably inter-disciplinary questions that literature raises.

A second possible institutional consequence of embracing the centrality of judgment to our enterprise concerns the relationships aesthetic expertise makes possible with two of the main components of the English department—creative writing and composition. Both have famously tense relationships with literary study. In the case of creative writing, this has often been because the disavowal of judg-ment on the part of literature PhDs places them at odds with the focus on craft and on evaluation in the workshop. In the case of composi-tion, something like the reverse dynamic operates, as composition-ists protest the implicit preference for some kinds of writing—great literature—over others, such as academic papers, blog posts, or mis-sion statements. The clarification of the nature and process of expert literary judgment won't erase the tensions with these departmental companions, but it may make our connections and differences explicit as well as suggest new modes of collaboration. The simple principle that one can't become a good writer without becoming a good reader offers an obvious path for collaboration. With a viable model of judg-ment, we have now a deep and nuanced way of describing exactly how we help students become good readers.

Finally, I come to a more ambivalent potential institutional con-sequence of adopting the proposed model of judgment. The norma-tive, rather than descriptive, dimensions of my model come into focus when we consider the various practices that, from this perspective, we should *stop* doing. Chief among these are the various kinds of faux-interdisciplinary projects characteristic of the bizarro world of literary studies—from computational literary criticism to biological, economic, psychological, or historical claims that can't sustain peer review by actual biologists, economists, psychologists, or historians.

It's hard to see that anything meaningful would be lost by adopting appropriate professional standards with respect to interdisciplinary work. Similarly, the fantasy that we study not valuable literature but literature in general is also something we should give up. But since no one except some computational literary critics has ever imagined a means of actually taking the whole of literature as an object of study, and since those critics' projects tend to be excellent examples of faux interdisciplinarity, this, too, is a loss that no one needs to mourn.[2]

But there is another practice, which I believe to be in tension with the practice of literary judgment and which has a more robust claim on us. If I have presented the study of literature as a form of aesthetic education, there is an equally powerful, equally venerable way of seeing literary study as a form of *moral* education. There are of course many ways in which one can discover moral values in works of art or gain moral insights from them. My model's openness with respect to criteria opens the way for appreciating such moral values alongside philosophical, political, historical, or formal ones.

But when I speak here of moral education, I refer to the practice of taking works of literature as means of inculcating good moral attitudes in students. The content of those attitudes changes over time—think of the differences, for example, between the appropriate attitudes toward sexual behavior urged in a nineteenth- versus a twenty-first-century literature classroom—and the right attitudes are today described as "political," "social," or "ethical" as often as they are "moral." But institutional literary study has functioned as moral training just as often as aesthetic education, if not more so.

I side with Plato on the ultimate incompatibility of aesthetic and moral education—if by the latter we mean the practice of using literary works to illustrate and propagate positive moral attitudes. The very openness to values that is a hallmark of expert artistic judgment offers a challenge to the project of moral education. And here at the end of this book we may have discovered the final objection to artistic judgment. Certainly, there are many literature professors who object to saying that one book is better than another as a work of art, yet they have no trouble declaring one work morally superior to another.[3]

This objection lies beyond the scope of this book, however. Here I have tried to answer the question, What qualifies an English professor to say that one work of literature is better—more worth one's time— than another? Put differently, what skills or knowledges underlie our claim to artistic judgment? As to what qualifies a literature professor to be a moral judge, I cannot say. My final speculation—or hope—for this book is that it will inspire someone to make the case for literature professors as moral experts, to describe the skills and knowledges underlying this expertise, to show what moral expertise can teach us that we don't already know, and to exemplify moral approaches to literary works. Then, faced with these alternative models of expertise, perhaps those dedicated to the professional study of literature will finally be able to decide what we are.

Acknowledgments

This book owes its existence to two events that occurred in 2015. The first was a small rebellion in my spring seminar on American poetry, in which my students asked me why they had to read Sylvia Plath. Their tenacity and acuity over the ensuing discussions forced me to abandon the vacuous platitudes with which I had previously concealed my inability to both say how judgment works in practice and define literary expertise. This book is a belated response to their questions.

The second event was the publication and reception of the *Nonsite* article by Aaron Kunin discussed in my first chapter; in it, he makes the case for the aesthetic, as opposed to moral, evaluation of poetry. Aaron's essay—and the willfully obtuse misreadings of his lucid argument that greeted its publication—awakened me to a vital sense of the paralysis of judgment in contemporary literary culture. His own judgment, together with his intellectual grace and extraordinary learning, has illuminated each page of this book, which he graciously read in draft.

Many others assisted me with their criticism, their knowledge, and their questions. I am especially grateful to Maggie Vinter, Jason Gladstone, Kerry Larson, Soren Forsberg, Evan Kindley, Kate Marshall, Herbert Tucker, Brad Pasenek, Nan Da, Patrick Fessenbecker, Francis Ferguson, Lauren Berlant, Walter Michaels, Todd Cronan, Kate Stanley, Nick Gaskill, Charles Palermo, Sharon Cameron, Len Gutkin, and the two readers for the University of Chicago Press. I'd also like to thank perceptive and challenging audiences at Columbia University, Carnegie Mellon University, the University of Western

Ontario, the University of Chicago, the University of Virginia, Rutgers University, Christopher Newport University, Yale University, and Case Western Reserve University. All the arguments in the second half of the book had their origin in the classroom, and I gratefully acknowledge the crucial role played by my fabulous students, who held me to Hume's test. At the press, Alan Thomas has been a wonderful and supportive editor, and Randolph Petilos, Erin DeWitt, and Sandra Hazel offered invaluable assistance. Case Western Reserve University provided research support throughout this project, and a Guggenheim Fellowship supported its conclusion.

Finally, I wish to thank my wife, Lauren Voss, for many hours spent discussing the topics addressed in the book, for her aesthetic acuity, and for her love and support. This book is dedicated to her and to our amazing daughter, Aislin.

*

Early versions of parts of the first chapter appeared in *Critical Inquiry* 45, no. 4 (Summer), Copyright © 2019 by The University of Chicago, all rights reserved, and in the *Chronicle Review, The Chronicle of Higher Education* (Summer 2019). An early version of the fifth chapter appeared in *ELH* 83, no. 2 (Summer): 633–54, Copyright © 2016 Johns Hopkins University Press. Chapter 6 first appeared in *Nonsite* (Spring 2013). Several paragraphs of chapter 4 first appeared in *PMLA* 132, no. 4 (October 2017), and are reprinted by permission of the copyright owner, The Modern Language Association of America (www.mla.org).

Notes

INTRODUCTION

1. The repression of judgment has, however, given perverse incentives for the development of genuinely value-free projects of literary study. Andrew Piper, for example, justifies his project by arguing that only computational methods are adequate for exploring all a period's literature. Piper says, quite correctly, that all previous scholars making claims about literary periods base their investigation only on a "selection" of that period's literature (Piper, "The Select"). Computational methods are needed to explore *all* a period's literature, which no one could ever read. And it is necessary to consider the totality of a period's writing in order to make any literary claim that doesn't entail a value judgment. Piper's argument is of interest because it neatly shows how those historicists who imagine they are working without judgment are in fact committed to quite robust forms of judgment in their—often implicit—criteria for selecting from the unmanageably large total body of novels published, say, in the nineteenth century. By its nature, Piper's project of course involves importing into literary study not just the concepts but the disciplinary procedures of statistics and computer science—procedures that, as Nan Z. Da has carefully demonstrated, he doesn't understand and is unable to use (Da, "Computational Case"). Da's analysis of this most rigorously judgment-free project thus suggests that to the extent a literary project lacks value judgments, it also lacks value.

2. See, for example, Guillory, *Cultural Capital*, xiv, 41, 124. In some ways, this problem is an artifact of Guillory's taking a sociological critique of aesthetic value—Bourdieu's—as the basis for his own defense. Value terms describing the status of literary works within a community from a critical sociological perspective may be inadequate when making the positive case for the study of literature. See chapter 1 for an extended discussion of Guillory's argument.

CHAPTER ONE

1. The problem is not so much that critics and professors don't practice aesthetic judgment; while efforts to justify syllabi on non-aesthetic grounds have gained momen-

tum in recent decades, my sense is that such judgments are still, as John Guillory put it twenty-five years ago, "inevitable" in literary and artistic education (Guillory, *Cultural Capital*, xiv; I take up his larger argument at length below). The indefensibility of judgment means, however, that judgment is cut off from reflections about the aims and values of the profession as a whole and in particular is cordoned off from reflection about the political aims of that practice. This tends to consign aesthetic judgment to a kind of conservative politics by default. (See, for instance, Harold Bloom's *The Western Canon* for an influential argument that aesthetic judgment is incompatible with progressive politics.)

2. There are many kinds of aesthetic judgment that don't seem to make an evaluative claim. In the following, I will argue that the judgment that a given work represents a more rewarding use of scarce attentional resources than others is necessary to the project of aesthetic *education*. While some judgments meet this criterion in an obvious way—"beautiful," "complex," "important"—I will also briefly explore the sense in which some judgments that don't seem obviously evaluative nevertheless meet this minimal criterion.

3. Two recent examples of literary journalism, drawn from opposite ends of the political spectrum, illustrate this dynamic. Sarah Ruden, writing for the conservative *National Review*, argues that Longfellow is better than Whitman, proved by the greater popularity of the former. Whitman has been kept alive only through the efforts of elitist teachers: "*Leaves of Grass* would have fallen away had not professors . . . championed it" (Ruden, "Walt Whitman"). Gabrielle Starr and Kevin Dettmar, two English professors writing in the *Chronicle of Higher Education*, respond to the idea that Gwendolyn Brooks is worth teaching because she is a great poet by arguing, on the one hand, that professors shouldn't try to foist their own tastes on students and, on the other, that "when Silicon Valley types say they want to hire humanities majors, it's not because they want coders who know Gwendolyn Brooks poems" (Starr and Dettmar, "Who Decides?").

4. Rancière, *Aesthetics and Its Discontents*, 35–36. Subsequent references are given in the text.

5. See Rancière, *The Ignorant Schoolmaster*. For a detailed consideration (and defense) of Rancière's rejection of judgment in the name of equality, see Davide Panagia's *Rancière's Sentiments*.

6. In an important respect, Rancière transfers this ambivalence about judgment to his account of art-making. He describes an oscillation between works that try to close themselves off from the social world in order to shelter a space of new values—in familiar modernist fashion—and works that seek to transform the social world itself at the cost of their autonomy. These questions are related but not identical to the question raised by the passage I discuss, where the problem of educational standards—as distinct from artists' own orientation to society—is the explicit focus. My view is that in describing this oscillation, Rancière simply recapitulates the impasse I identify, but demonstrating this would take me beyond the scope of the present discussion.

7. Guillory, *Cultural Capital*, 288–323. Subsequent references are given in the text. Guillory is responding to Barbara Herrnstein Smith's *Contingencies of Value*.

8. Ross, *Communal Luxury*, 57–58. The passages Ross cites from the Communards suggest a more nuanced outlook than the total rejection of aesthetic criteria she

describes. (See for instance the animus they direct against "the pretended works of our time" [59].)

9. Rancière, *Aesthetics and Its Discontents*, 42.

10. Guillory, *Cultural Capital*, xiv.

11. Guillory, xiv.

12. Kaufman, "Adorno's Social Lyric," 359.

13. Kaufman, 368.

14. Hullot-Kentor, "Right Listening," 185–86. Hullot-Kentor's description of Adorno's opposition to the radio broadcast of classics, motivated by the belief that Americans are simply too degraded to benefit from high art, points to Adorno's limited value as a source of inspiration for the project of aesthetic education that most directly concerns me here (191–93).

15. Adorno, *Aesthetic Theory*, 230. Ironically, in their resistance to aesthetic judgment, many of the applications of Adorno's work today function in a context captured by this quotation from his essay "On the Fetish Character": "The representatives of the opposition to the authoritarian schema become witnesses to the authority of commercial success" (32). As I will discuss in detail in the next chapter, Adorno's mid-twentieth-century diagnosis of the knot that ties antifascism to capitalist triumphalism reflects a dynamic already visible a century before he wrote, one that operates today with unprecedented force.

16. Rose, "Fear of the Aesthetic," 231.

17. Rose, 226, 232.

18. *Princeton Encyclopedia of Poetry and Poetics*.

19. Frye, "Polemical Introduction," 18. Subsequent references are given in the text.

20. Kuhn, *Structure of Scientific Revolutions*, 94. I am grateful to Chris Haufe for conversations about consensus formation in the natural sciences.

21. While it lies beyond the scope of this chapter, it would be worth comparing the assault on aesthetic judgment with the contemporary assault on scientific judgment in this respect. Flat-earth claims, for instance, or climate science denialism demonstrates a suspicion of expertise consonant with what I will call dogmatic equality.

22. See for instance Genette, *Essays in Aesthetics*. Genette opposes aesthetic judgments to judgments that can be "submitted to a factual proof" (30).

23. Dowling, *The Vulgarization of Art*, 15. Recent developments in psychology illuminate this persistent tendency in the history of aesthetic theory to undervalue the role of education in taste. Lisa Feldman Barrett, summarizing the past two decades' research into emotion—including "aesthetic" emotions—in *How Emotions Are Made*, describes a consensus that "emotions are not reactions to the world"; they are "constructed" (31). Our concepts, education, personal histories, and values determine how given sensory and physical information is assembled into a feeling. Emotions are not universal; there is no area of the brain associated with wonder or with fear. An abstract painting encountered by someone with the relevant education is quite literally not the same object as that to which a person without that background responds. Yet while emotions are constructed, "the entire process of construction is invisible to you" (26). Nothing in your experience of the painting reveals the contribution of your cognitive background. Therefore it is easy, as demonstrated by the generations of aesthetic theorists Dowling investigates, to imagine that taste is "natural" and that the work of aes-

thetic education should be to clear away the barnacles that prevent the worker from having the kinds of responses to art that William Morris or John Ruskin have.

24. Dowling, *The Vulgarization of Art*, 11.

25. Bourdieu, *Distinction*.

26. Hume, "Of the Standard of Taste," 136. Subsequent references are given in the text.

27. Yet critics continue to try to evade judgment by imagining that the valuable qualities of an artwork can be described in purely objective terms. The preferred objective term, since the New Criticism, has tended to be *complexity*. Elaine Auyoung, to take a recent example, regards literary works as objects that are "complex enough" to "hold our attention" by enabling us "to discover in them new patterns and structures" ("What We Mean by Reading," 107). Such formulations explain less than they appear to, given that an objective understanding of complexity is insufficient to discriminate between the works that hold professors' attention and those that don't. (Is Austen's *Emma*, to take Auyoung's primary example, simply more complex than the many works that don't hold our attention from that period? Would it be even better if it were even more complex—by adding more characters, for example? What concept of complexity determines that a poem by Keats is a more complicated artifact than an article in a journal of advanced physics?) Judgments about particular *kinds* of complexity or pattern determine critics' selection of literary works, and their selective readings within those works. The fact that in our practice we often blur the fact/value distinction shouldn't lead us to imagine that we can construct a theory of literary reading based solely on objective features like complexity. As I will argue in chapter 3, the conflation of fact and value in our practice derives from peculiar features of expert judgment itself.

28. If one common reaction to a work in an unfamiliar tradition is to see in it only perceptual noise, another common reaction is to see it only in terms of familiar categories. Hence the cliché verdict on abstract painting—"that's just a bunch of scribbles—my four-year-old can do the same thing better." As I will explore in subsequent chapters, the capacity to see something one *doesn't* recognize—the capacity to be surprised by a work—is a skill, an outcome of aesthetic education. In *Writing against Time*, I describe artists' efforts to discover a perceptual sweet spot between familiarity and noise, a spot characteristic of our first experience of objects. I've subsequently come to appreciate the kinds of backgrounds needed to perceive an artistic work "as if for the first time," and to understand the often concealed role of aesthetic education in furnishing audiences with these backgrounds.

29. Jones, "Hume's Literary and Aesthetic Theory," 438.

30. Jones, 433.

31. Kant, *Critique*, 104. The commentary I have found most useful is Henry Allison's classic study, *Kant's Theory of Taste*.

32. Ferguson, "Canons, Poetics, Social Value," 1157.

33. For a cogent recent effort to show how "aesthetic enjoyment" fuses with the delimitation of aesthetic objects in the New Criticism, see Gaskill, "Close and the Concrete." For a spirited defense of the New Critics' effort to pit literary expertise against the culture industry, see Eric Bennett's "Dear Humanities Profs."

34. North, *Literary Criticism*, x. Subsequent references are given in the text.

35. Richards, *Principles of Literary Criticism*, 31. Subsequent references are given in the text.

36. Bruce Robbins notes this confusion with considerable understatement when he writes, "It's not self-evident, for example, where he stands, finally, on the universality of aesthetic experience." Robbins offers a qualified, "old-fashioned" defense of judgment as the gesture of the professor holding a work he finds beautiful up to students as an "appeal" they may accept or reject ("Discipline and Parse"). Presenting the professor's judgment in terms of an "appeal" sidesteps the egalitarian objection and avoids grappling with the idea—crucial to education and explored by Ferguson and Frye—of the sources of the professional judgments structuring educational experience.

37. For a detailed argument about the potential, and the limits, of neuropsychological research in literary studies, see my *Writing against Time*. The primitive nature of current research doesn't preclude the detection of potentially fruitful lines of inquiry. See, for example, this investigation of how physical expertise plays a role in the aesthetic appreciation of dance: Kirsch, Urgesi, and Cross, "Shaping and Reshaping."

38. Ngai, *Our Aesthetic Categories*, 128. Subsequent references are given in the text.

39. Muller, *Tyranny of Metrics*, 40. Subsequent references are given in the text.

40. Muller's arguments with respect to academia have been anticipated by Stefan Collini, who writes of the British effort to introduce metrics into academia in the 1980s: "Public debate in modern liberal democracies has come to combine utilitarian valuations with a distrust of procedures that are not mechanically universalizable. It is a curious feature of such debate that where 'understanding' and still more 'cultivation' can be pilloried as 'elitist,' 'research' retains an open and ostensibly democratic character: the stock of 'knowledge,' it suggests, is accessible to all, and anyone can replicate the experiment . . . 'results' are seen as something objective, and so the role of the exercise of judgment is usurped by the kind of totting-up of 'items published' that can be made intelligible to the average accountant on the street" (Collini, "Against Prodspeak," 239).

41. Kuhn, *Structure of Scientific Revolutions*, 94.

42. Moran, *The Philosophical Imagination*, 66; italics in the original. Subsequent references are given in the text.

43. A recurrent objection to Rawls's theory from the Left has been that it "leaves the market intact" (Peffer, *Marxism, Morality, and Social Justice*, 377). See Cohen, *Rescuing Justice and Equality*, for an extensive critique of Rawls on this basis.

CHAPTER TWO

1. Tocqueville, *Democracy in America*, 584.

2. Maguire, *The Conversion of Imagination*, 191.

3. Kunin, "Vanessa Place."

4. Larson, *Imagining Equality*, 155.

5. Maguire, *The Conversion of Imagination*, 192.

6. Kaledin, *Tocqueville and His America*, 371.

7. Tucker, headnote to Marx, "Gotha Program," 525.

8. Marx, "Gotha Program," 525.

9. Marx, *Capital*, quoted in Reiman, "Moral Philosophy," 165. Reiman sees pas-

sages like this as "examples of how moral beliefs may function as ideological supports for capitalism because they have been unconsciously modeled on the relations that characterize capitalism" (165).

10. Marx, "Gotha Program," 525. Subsequent references are given in the text.

11. See Allen Wood's classic article, "Marxian Critique of Justice." See Reiman, "Moral Philosophy," for a general overview of the reception of "Gotha."

12. Cohen, "Alan Wood's *Karl Marx*," quoted in Reiman, "Moral Philosophy," 152.

13. Peffer, *Marxism, Morality, and Social Justice*, 319. Peffer follows Cohen in trying to show that Marx's reasons for rejecting equality "are not sound" (319).

14. North, *Literary Criticism*, 8.

15. For the history of the ideological effort to describe market choice as a form of voting, see my *American Literature and the Free Market*.

16. Zamora, "Should We Care?"

17. Leiter, "Marxism," 28n30.

18. Leiter, 29n30.

19. Henry, *Marx*.

20. Postone, *Time, Labor, and Social Domination*, 163.

21. Postone, 164.

22. Beggs, "Zombie Marx."

23. Bhardwaj, "Higher and Lower Pleasures," 127.

24. Riley, "Mill's Political Economy," 295–96.

25. Riley, 297.

26. Riley, 314.

27. Raffaelli, *Marshall's Evolutionary Economics*, 100.

28. Mirowski, *More Heat Than Light*, 233.

29. Mirowski, 219.

30. Raffaelli, *Marshall's Evolutionary Economics*, 100.

31. John Gray's *Hayek on Liberty* provides an excellent overview of Hayek's vision of the market as an evolutionary, self-organizing system.

32. For a sympathetic discussion of the strengths and weaknesses of Mill's distinction between higher and lower pleasures, see Small, *Value of the Humanities*, 115–24. Recently, economists have begun to question the equation of utility with happiness, exploring the possibility that consumer choices and consumer satisfaction diverge in ways that may lend support to a broadly Millian distinction between kinds of pleasures. Social media has furnished a rich object for such studies. See especially Allcott et al., "Welfare Effects of Social Media." See also Smith, "What We Want."

33. Many of the neoclassicals, it is true, disavowed any philosophical position in assuming the equality of preferences. But there is a subtle link between the purely scientistic neoclassical understanding of equality of preferences, which presents as philosophically neutral and simply an assumption designed to enable the construction of demand curves, etc., and the more robust psychological and philosophical position—voiced by Marshall—that viewing all preferences as equal is socially beneficial. Both positions tend in practice to regard interference with demand by "outside authorities" with suspicion, and such later writers as F. A. Hayek would give philosophical heft to the thin neoclassical understanding of equalization. While a full exploration of this point lies outside the scope of the present study, I think a case can be made that main-

stream modern economics—which exercised unparalleled influence on policy, education, and the media—disseminated a commitment to the equality, in terms of values, of individual consumer market choices and a hostility to the project of criticizing consumer choice that ranges across a spectrum, from the scientistic to the philosophical to the ideological.

34. Kahneman, *Thinking Fast and Slow*, 378.

35. Kahneman, 413–14.

36. Marx and Engels, *The Communist Manifesto*, 9.

37. Callard, "Liberal Education," 14.

38. Callard, *Aspiration*, 10. Subsequent references are given in the text.

39. Philosophical aesthetics has developed a variety of arguments against evaluative skepticism. In "Aesthetic Rationality," to take a recent example, Keren Gorodeisky and Eric Marcus approach the problem within a broadly Kantian framework. They seek to resolve what has been called Kant's Problem, the tension between aesthetic judgment's first-person character—I can't judge an object to be beautiful without seeing that beauty for myself—and the fact that one can rationally come to doubt one's judgment in the face of expert disagreement, for example, or by learning that others don't see the feature on which one's judgment is based. Gorodeisky and Marcus resolve this problem by distinguishing between aesthetic judgments—which refer to an affective response to an object—and aesthetic beliefs, which refer to beliefs about an object's features that may merit certain affective responses. Since both aesthetic judgments and aesthetic beliefs are at stake in aesthetic experience, one can accept judgment's irreducibly first-person character while understanding how one might be led to doubt one's judgments and become motivated to improve one's taste.

40. Many of the efforts to distinguish between artworks and commodities depart from Adorno's argument that artworks possess formal features distinguishing them from commodities. I have argued elsewhere that Adorno's account depends on the labor theory of value, which posits that value is placed in the work at the time of production. This theory is demonstrably false as an economic claim; the frequent passage of works from various pop cultural ghettos into canons and vice versa suggests that it is also false as an empirical claim about art. But more important, this theory imagines that we can define the nature of judgment, the status of the object as art or culture industry trash, and the source of value in advance of the particular encounter of particular audiences with particular works in particular contexts. In my view, there is no shortcut to judgment, as I will argue at length in the next chapter. Nicholas Brown's *Autonomy* represents a recent example of the effort to distinguish between artworks and commodities, and between judgment and preference, on the basis of the kind of general properties a Humean approach to aesthetic eschews. Brown argues, for example, that for a commodity, "the only intention embodied in its form is the intention to exchange"; therefore, it doesn't have the kind of autonomous form that insulates artworks from the market and makes them rewarding artifacts to interpret (8). Yet in practice, distinguishing between an artist's interest in pleasing an audience and his "suspension" of that interest in favor of various formal or semantic intentions is a difficult matter of judgment and cannot be easily read off formal features of the work. Audiences are not pleased simply by the intention to please, and the actual process of creating a work designed for the market often consists in the effort to achieve some formal quality or

innovation. Insofar as Brown proposes a clear formal distinction between artworks and commodities, it is easy to find many counterexamples. Insofar as this distinction is unclear, then it simply conceals the dynamics of expert judgment. The search for an ultimately market-resistant object terminates in the vision of a completely inaccessible object, a fantasy toward which Adorno sometimes, especially in *Aesthetic Theory*, tends. Aesthetic judgment can be distinguished from consumer preference only pragmatically, not a priori. This distinction depends on the cultivation of forms of attention and criteria of value with the capacity to transform, challenge, or enrich existing values. This cultivation describes a complex process, a discipline, not a simple discrimination between different formal categories. The difference between consumer preference and cultivated judgment involves the transformations of subjectivity that form the subject of the next chapter.

41. John Frow ("The Practice of Value") writes, "The central point I want to make about the culture industries is that there is no necessary connection, either positive or negative, between the fact of industrialized commodity production and cultural value; the latter is determined within particular regimes of value" (73).

42. *Paraliterary*, Merve Emre's study of the range of extra-academic institutions that shaped midcentury reading, suggests several questions about the contemporary climate, questions I don't pretend to know the answer to and that would serve as an interesting topic for a successor to Emre's study. What are the most robust extra-academic institutions of literary instruction today? Have these institutions been transformed by the market egalitarian impulses that Lorentzen and *n + 1* (below) find in the publishing and reviewing industries? To what extent do current paraliterary organizations interrupt the algorithmic techniques by which cultural consumption takes the form of a more or less direct relation between consumer and content producer? Do the internationalist and political orientations of Emre's institutions have contemporary successors? Where do we class books like Thomas Foster's excellent and popular *How to Read Literature Like a Professor*, which provide a form of critical reading—in his case, a symbolic approach derived from Northrop Frye—once prevalent in the academy but now seemingly anomalous? Does the paraliterary partially consist in an archive of abandoned academic methods? Of previous academic canons? In my next chapter I will briefly discuss, in relation to the question of criteria, Emre's description of some of the key literary values and criteria cultivated by the midcentury institutions. Here I simply want to pose some questions about the wider ecology of judgment suggested by Emre's useful concept of the paraliterary institution. A related and even more important question, suggested by Foster's discussion of his book's audience among teachers, involves the relation between college and university literary judgment and primary and secondary literary education. These questions lie outside the scope of the present book but are clearly crucial for any democratic vision of the role of judgment in contemporary society.

43. "Too Much Sociology."

44. Lorentzen, "Like This or Die."

45. Indeed, the restoration of aesthetic judgment's place in literary education will, in my view, serve to expand and transform a canon that has essentially been frozen in time, passed on inert from an increasingly distant era when aesthetic judgment formed a central part of critical practice. None of this implies of course that there are no power-

ful sociological and aesthetic lessons to be gleaned from studying differences between art designed for mass audiences versus art that intentionally restricts its accessibility. Such considerations, however, lie beyond the scope of this book. In terms of the structure of critical practice I am advocating, nothing whatever about *value* can be determined simply from a work's popularity or lack thereof, nor is it possible to predetermine the criteria of judgment simply from a work's sociological status. (I will discuss the problem of criteria in chapter 4.)

46. Cowen, *In Praise of Commercial Culture*, 7.

47. Cowen, 7.

48. Cowen, 24.

49. My personal experience has been that literary editors at some presses are still willing and able to make acquisition decisions largely on the basis of aesthetic criteria. (My editor at Farrar, Straus and Giroux, for example, shared with me her decision to reject a certain novel, even though she felt—correctly—that it would be a big seller, because she thought the style was bad.) But from speaking with other editors, my sense is that this capacity is becoming more of a luxury.

50. Cowen, *In Praise of Commercial Culture*, 28.

51. See the final chapter of my *American Literature and the Free Market*.

52. The fullest exposition of this idea is in chapter 4 of Adorno and Horkheimer's *Dialectic of Enlightenment*. But see also this similar reflection from Adorno's essay "Free Time": "In a system where full employment itself has become the ideal, free time is nothing more than a shadowy continuation of labor" (194). It might be worthwhile pointing out here that one of my differences from Adorno is that I don't see art as something that promises, and will disappear into, a fully liberated society but rather as a realm in which various forms of human happiness and liberation are themselves investigated and realized. This requires an account of judgment that is more than an account of critique. Thus, while central aspects of Adorno's critique of the culture industry remain inspirational, his positive conception of powerful art—especially in *Aesthetic Theory*—is limited in its commitment to a narrow form of critique.

53. Graeber, *Bullshit Jobs*.

54. See Maraniss, *Once in a Great City*.

55. This is perhaps a good place to indicate what should be obvious: I don't think aesthetic education in itself will eradicate the ills of capitalism—the conditions and quality of work, the environmental crisis, and poverty must all be addressed through different means. Aesthetic education is important in its own right as one of the sources of human cultivation repressed by the dominance of markets. It is also the area of political struggle in which the expertise of professors of the humanities is most relevant. But it is also important—as I hope this chapter will show—in raising the possibility of forms of value that go beyond consumer preferences. All the other forms of struggle against capitalist conditions depend on this possibility. I believe that the aesthetic sphere raises the question of value in a more intense and focused way than perhaps any other sphere, and in a way in which the challenges to a form of value beyond market value are raised in their strongest form.

56. Hagglund, *This Life*, 11.

57. Hagglund, 258.

58. Keen, *Debunking Economics*.

59. Harvey, "Marx's Refusal."

60. Hagglund, *This Life*, 305.

61. Hagglund, 300.

CHAPTER THREE

1. Polanyi, *The Tacit Dimension*, 4. Subsequent references are given in the text.

2. Ben Knights comments perceptively on the relation of Polanyi's model to Poulet and the Geneva school, for whom "reading experiences recapitulate, mime, or shadow the deep structures of the author's mind" (*Pedagogic Criticism*, 90). Knights's book provides a fascinating, fine-grained history of twentieth-century British literary pedagogy complementary to Joseph North's more polemical, wide-scope *Literary Criticism*.

3. Heidegger, "Origin of the Work."

4. See chapters 1 and 2 of my *Writing against Time*.

5. So for example Bourdieu, in *Distinction*, grasps the importance of something like tacit knowledge, but he fails to understand it in terms of the structure of expertise. He speaks of taste as depending on "implicit learning analogous to that which makes it possible to recognize familiar faces without explicit rules or criteria" (xxvii). He would be closer to the mark if he described this implicit learning as analogous to—indeed, as exemplifying—the kind of training his own sociological expertise manifests.

6. Selinger and Crease, "Dreyfus on Expertise," 223.

7. Selinger and Crease, 223.

8. Selinger and Crease, 229.

9. Buchenwald, afterword to Holmes, *Investigative Pathways*, 193.

10. Barrett, *How Emotions Are Made*, 283.

11. I owe this formulation to the poet Li Young Lee, who after a reading at my university in 2016 described close reading as a means of "defeating our projections."

12. See, for example, the attack on my position by Gabrielle Starr and Kevin Dettmar, "Who Decides?," and my response, "The Hypocrisy of Experts."

13. Turner, "What Is the Problem?," 181.

14. Selinger and Crease, introduction to *Philosophy of Expertise*, 3.

15. Turner, "What Is the Problem?," 181.

16. In early April 2020 while making the final revisions to this book, I was watching the COVID-19 pandemic and the government responses to it unfold, events likely to shape attitudes toward expertise for some time to come. The crisis has been exposing many facets of the conflict between expertise and democracy: the status of expert knowledge in the face of radically incomplete information; the tendency to present fundamentally political decisions as expert decisions; the tension between different fields of expertise (public health versus economics, epidemiology versus research on the health consequences of poverty and unemployment); and the increasing assimilation of attitudes toward expertise into the terms of America's political polarization.

17. Clune, "Bizarro World."

18. Among the most efficient descriptions of the problems with Jameson's influential historical theory—expressed, for example, in *The Political Unconscious*—is Patrick Fessenbecker's "Critique" in the colloquy "We, Reading, Now." Fessenbecker observes that Jameson's effort to tie literary forms to particular historical periods is hobbled by a

very basic problem: his description of the historical conditions that gave rise to a given form also pertain to many periods that didn't give rise to it. The historical part of the maxim "always historicize" thus can't stand up to the most basic historical scrutiny. Fessenbecker offers an intriguing speculation as to the historical conditions that made this kind of claim seem compelling in literary studies in the early 1980s.

19. Edmundson, *Why Read?*, 106.

20. See, for example, C. Thi Nguyen's "Autonomy and Aesthetic Engagement." I note also that this essay suffers from a misunderstanding as to the nature of aesthetic expertise not uncommon in philosophical aesthetics. (Compare Nguyen's account of expertise here with the one I develop in this and the succeeding chapters.) One of the limitations of philosophical aesthetics lies in the fact that its exponents, due to their disciplinary position, frequently have little or no direct experience of practical criticism and thus tend to base their concept of aesthetic expertise on such caricatures as the museum audio tour or the jazz critic as Nguyen presents them.

21. Edmundson, *Why Read?*, 122.

22. Edmundson, 122.

23. Bromwich, *Politics by Other Means*, 202. Subsequent references are given in the text.

24. Hume, "Of the Standard of Taste," 143–44.

25. Soni, "Crisis in Judgment," 276.

26. Soni, 267.

27. There are ways of appreciating the role of expertise from within a broadly Kantian framework, however, as Gorodeisky and Marcus demonstrate in "Aesthetic Rationality," the essay referenced in the previous chapter.

28. Soni, "Crisis in Judgment," 280.

29. Soni, 264.

30. Soni, 266.

CHAPTER FOUR

1. Frow, "The Practice of Value": "All acts of judgment of any complexity involve interpretation; that is, an assessment not only of the fit between the particular and the universal but of the constitution of the universal itself as it operates in this context" (71). Frow's conception of judgment has similarities with the model of tacit judgment I derive from Polanyi: "All complex judgements, I want to argue, are to some extent indeterminate, in that the codes we bring to them are in such a state of continuous development" (71).

2. Polanyi, *The Tacit Dimension*, 23.

3. Sibley, "Aesthetic Concepts," 1.

4. Sibley, 2.

5. Sibley, 4.

6. It may perhaps be possible, using neural net techniques, to train computers to recognize aesthetic concepts. But such techniques are entirely parasitic on people's capacity to recognize "cute" or "delicate" or "beautiful" forms, as the computer's training involves exposing it to thousands of images that humans have described as "cute," etc., in order to enable successful predictions. This technique is quite different from the

process of programming a computer with rules for recognizing, for example, a circle, and it is compatible with Sibley's thesis. See chapter 6 of Patrick Fessenbecker's excellent *Reading Ideas in Victorian Literature* for a rich discussion of Sibley's aesthetics.

7. Sibley, "Aesthetic Concepts," 5.

8. Sibley, 16.

9. Nabokov, *Nikolai Gogol*.

10. Harding, *Regulated Hatred*; on a new approach to the aesthetics of the slave narrative, see Daniel Lutrull's essay on Harriet Jacobs (unpublished manuscript).

11. Sibley, "Aesthetic Concepts," 18.

12. Sibley, 19.

13. An important objection to my discussion of the benign role of scholarship is that various national and university systems—in the United Kingdom, most notoriously—have adopted metrics which provide perverse incentives to scholars to produce, for example, many low-quality publications. Insofar as administrations attempt to replace professional judgment of a scholar's work with quantifiable "objective" measures, academic publications increasingly share the problems Jerry Muller has identified in the "metrics fixation" of higher education (*The Tyranny of Metrics*). To be clear, my argument for the value of professional publication in relation to the project of aesthetic education is predicated on such publications being assessed at every level through expert judgment and the processes of peer review.

14. Graff, *Professing Literature*, 124.

15. See especially Felski's excellent *Uses of Literature*.

16. Felski, *The Limits of Critique*, 128.

17. Felski, 179.

18. Aubry, *Guilty Aesthetic Pleasures*, 12.

19. Hartman, *Criticism in the Wilderness*.

20. Nelson, *The Argonauts*; Kunin, *Love Three*.

21. Aubry, *Guilty Aesthetic Pleasures*, 43.

22. Aubry, 60.

23. Graff, *Professing Literature*, 230.

24. Graff, 238.

25. Borges, *Selected Nonfictions*, 365.

26. Wall, "On Freedom," 286.

27. Wall, 287.

28. Emre, *Paraliterary*, 7.

29. For a wonderful example of this underused method, see Graham Harman's *Weird Realism*. While I find myself in almost total disagreement with the philosophical lessons Harman draws from H. P. Lovecraft, his analysis of Lovecraftian style is the most illuminating I know.

30. See John Frow's *On Interpretive Conflict*, 207–14, for a perceptive treatment of the perennial problem of the relation between cognition and aesthetic judgment in Kant. Henry Allison's study *Kant's Theory of Taste* is another excellent resource on this complex topic. My point here is simply that the influence of Kant's aesthetics has been most felt in literary studies as a preference for form over concepts—although undoubtedly the positions taken in the third critique itself are more nuanced. See *Writing against Time* for my own perspective—indebted to Allison—on this question.

31. Levine, *Forms*, 23. Subsequent references are given in the text.

32. See the philosopher of science Alex Rosenberg's "Cura Te Ipsum" for a critique along these lines; see also my response to Rosenberg, "What Does Literature Know?"

33. Gleik, *Time Travel.*

34. Dickinson, *Poems of Emily Dickinson*, 194.

35. Clune, Sarneki, and Traynor, "Cue Fascination."

36. Adorno, *Aesthetic Theory*, 228.

37. Adorno, 228.

38. As I argued in the second chapter, the selection of objects of study is a principal task of expert judgment, and it is impossible to delimit the set of these objects—literature, in this case—outside the practice of judgment. The question of whether rap lyrics, tweets, or romance novels constitute literature for the purposes of literary studies is decided not by taxonomy but by judgment, and it is thus ultimately involved with the more relevant question of *which* objects within a genre or medium justify a claim on the public.

CHAPTER FIVE

1. Rosenberg, "Cura Te Ipsum." The position I will develop here departs from the emphases of my reply to Rosenberg in "What Does Literature Know?," in which I contest his view of the relation between literature and science. The tendency to describe literature's value in terms of its emotional effects is an old one; its most forceful contemporary proponents typically describe these effects using models derived from cognitive science. See, for example, Goldman, *Simulating Minds*, and Vermule, *Why Do We Care?*

2. Dickinson, *Poems of Emily Dickinson*, 465.

3. Freud, "Thoughts for the Times," 14:289, summarized in Gordon, *Imagining the End*, 3.

4. Yvor Winters understood that judging this poem's aesthetic success depends on its capacity to provide an experiential analogue to death. Winters argues that the poem is "fraudulent" because it presents the experience of death only "as an idea, not as something experienced" (*In Defense of Reason*, 16). While I disagree with Winters in that I believe Dickinson does indeed present death in terms of "something experienced," I think he asks precisely the right kind of question about the poem. Subsequent readers of the death poems have tended to follow David Porter, who argues that Dickinson takes the unfathomability of death as an occasion for the display of poetic style, entirely unmoored from any mimetic function. "Death," he writes, "is the occasion for her language performance" (*The Modern Idiom*, 188). For such readers, the poem is aesthetic in the sense of being entirely sealed off from any claim about the way the world is. See also Cameron, *Lyric Time*, 120–21, and Deppman, *Trying to Think*, 189–192, 203.

5. For a recent example of this venerable critical trend, see Michaels, "Forgetting Auschwitz."

6. I begin to explore contemporary first-person writing along these lines in "Pop Disappears."

7. Hume, "Of Personal Identity," 33.

8. Parfit, *Reasons and Persons*, 225. Sharon Cameron's account of Dickinson also expresses a sense of impersonality, though one quite different from the model I develop

here. Cameron's sense depends on seeing the poems not as records of a single experience but as assemblages of different experiences by different subjects. Her later work on Eliot and Emerson similarly sees impersonality in terms of multiple perspectives. But if she tends to read Dickinson, as I have shown, in an intensely anti-mimetic manner, her later work is more ambiguous regarding the status of the impersonal. She adduces the claims of Levinas, Parfit, and Buddhist psychologists to characterize the literary texts, which suggests that she believes the writing to have a mimetic dimension (Cameron, *Impersonality*, chaps. 4, 6). In her chapter on Emerson, she cites a passage from Buddhist scripture that might serve as a description for what Dickinson's depiction of death in terms of absorbed listening reveals about the latter state: "In the heard, there will be merely the heard, in the sensed, there will be merely the sensed" (6). In any case, my argument about selfless experience in Dickinson is indebted to Cameron's work, which has placed the question of the relation of experience to personhood at the center of the study of nineteenth-century American literature.

    9. Shakespeare, *Macbeth*, act 3, scene 2, line 23.

    10. Shakespeare, *Hamlet*, act 3, scene 1, line 60. The other famous descriptions of death in the play—the "unknown country," "what dreams may come," etc.—thematize the ineluctable fact that we lack sure knowledge of death. That it remains an impenetrable mystery does not of course prevent the effort to create aesthetically convincing experiential analogues, as indeed Shakespeare's own comparison of death to sleep demonstrates. Shakespeare is one obvious touchstone for the nineteenth-century poetic images of death I explore here. For a discussion of the problem of representing death in Enlightenment aesthetics, see Adam Wasson's "Dying between the Lines." Wasson's essay is particularly interesting in its detailed analysis of the representational paradoxes Lessing becomes involved in when trying to think of death in terms of the cessation of experience. Masson thus explores in an Enlightenment context the "unimaginability thesis" regarding death, a thesis of which Freud is perhaps the most famous modern exponent.

    11. Any reading of the poem that emphasizes the sense of hearing in the crucial experience of passing from life to death must account for Dickinson's use of the word *blue* to describe the buzz. Greg Johnson suggests that the color blue serves as Dickinson's emblem—repeated elsewhere in her poetry—of disembedded, inhuman forms of perception. He notes, for example, a similar use of the color in "Three times—we parted—Breath—and I" (*Emily Dickinson*, 158). On this reading, blue often serves Dickinson to describe the extraordinary status of a perception rather than its visual content.

    12. Peterson, "Surround Sound," 76.

    13. Gallagher and Zahavi, *The Phenomenological Mind*, 3.

    14. See Hubert Dreyfus's lucid discussion of Heidegger's account of "availableness" and "occurrantness" in *Being in the World*, 60–87. It's important to note that in Heidegger, the interruption throws the person out of absorption, while in Dickinson the interruption throws the person into absorption. The philosophical implications of this difference are complex and various, and their exploration lies beyond the scope of this chapter. I will note here that Heidegger's own analysis of death culminates in an insight into Dasein's "nothingness" (310). His analogue to the experience of death is not absorbed listening but anxiety; the key feature of the experience of anxiety is that "the world has nothing more to say to us" (311). Anxiety can serve as an experiential ana-

logue to death, for the Heidegger of *Being in Time*, insofar as it is an experience of the meaninglessness or absurdity of our existence. This presentation of meaninglessness is quite different from the subjectless experience that the poetic tradition explored here presents as an analogue to death.

15. Fried, *Absorption and Theatricality*.

16. Parfit, *Reasons and Persons*, 216.

17. Kane, *Sound Unseen*, 159. Kane's book provides a rich history of the nineteenth-century interest in acousmatic sound that is broadly relevant to my nineteenth-century poetic examples.

18. Absorbed listening can be aided by a muted awareness of one's body, but this doesn't depend on a panpsychic idea that experience can happen outside bodies. What is crucial is the absence of the sense of psychological continuity through absorption in immediate experience. While awareness of our body may tend to recall us to our identity, nothing about bodily awareness as such triggers this, and it is possible to sever the connection—as, for example, in the meditative practice cited by Cameron in *Impersonality*, 5–6.

19. Keats, "Ode to a Nightingale."

20. O'Hara, "The Day Lady Died."

21. My position has affinities with what John Gibson identifies as an emerging perspective on the relation between art and knowledge. This perspective suggests that "art, rather than offering us knowledge of the world, is of value because of how it transforms the knowledge we *already* possess." Gibson, "Cognitivism and the Arts," 585.

22. Arsić, "What Music Shall We Have?," 177.

23. Here I follow Kane, who focuses not on the type of sound—musical or otherwise—but on the "acousmatic situation," the orientation of the subject to the sound (*Sound Unseen*, 225). He argues that in analyzing acousmatic sound, the distinctions between music studies and sound studies vanish (226).

24. Arsić, "What Music Shall We Have?," 188.

25. Arsić, 178.

26. Keats, "Ode to a Nightingale."

27. Jackson, "Thinking Dickinson Thinking Poetry," 210.

28. Jackson's philosophical fuzziness hardly ends here. The purpose of her essay is to show how, in a letter, Dickinson critiques the "romantic obsession with the relation between perception and knowledge . . . by attaching a flower to her lines about a flower" (211). Quite apart from Jackson's striking admission that she has no evidence that the poem was ever included in such a letter, this claim is absurd on many levels. A desiccated flower attached to a letter would hardly instantiate the living flower of the lines in question; in such a context, the dried flower stands in referential relation to the living one. The dynamics of this reference would differ importantly from the relation of word to signified, but the dried flower couldn't serve as an occasion for the reader's unmediated experience of a living flower in the way that Jackson imagines. But pretend that Jackson did have some evidence that Dickinson sent the poem in a letter with a flower, and pretend the flower reached the recipient in full health and was just that flower which Dickinson saw when she composed her lines. Even admitting all this, which we can't, Jackson's idea that problems about "the relation between perception and knowledge" can be solved simply by giving the reader an occasion for perception

reveals an extraordinary ignorance about the philosophical and literary history of those problems.

29. Bate, "Negative Capability," 332, 341. For a brilliant recent exploration of this dynamic, which concludes with a fascinating reading of Dickinson's "A Bird, came down the Walk," see Nathanson, "'The Birds Swim through the Air.'"

30. Pfahl, "Ethics of Negative Capability," 454.

31. Gallagher and Zahavi, *The Phenomenological Mind*, 102.

32. Gallagher and Zahavi, 221.

33. Vendler, *Odes of John Keats*, 86.

34. Diehl, *Dickinson and the Romantic Imagination*, 119.

35. Grob, "Noumenal Inferences," 309.

36. Vendler, *Odes of John Keats*, 102.

37. Vendler, 85.

38. Keats, "Why did I laugh to-night?," 333.

39. Keats, "Ode to a Nightingale."

40. At such moments, Keats appears superficially to resemble certain well-known Romantic and Post-Romantic equations of death and music. Nietzsche, for example, exclaims in *The Birth of Tragedy* that "it is only through the spirit of music that we can understand the joy involved in the annihilation of the individual" (104). This joy derives from Nietzsche's idea, itself derived from Schopenhauer, that "music gives expression to the will in its omnipotence." Yet what Nietzsche calls the "metaphysical comfort" that music imparts by intimating a primal unity beyond the individual and that is characterized in terms of will is alien to Keats, for whom absorption in music reveals the selfless dimension of experience itself. Nietzsche constantly refers to this collective world of will existing "behind" phenomenal experience, an invisible world to which music provides access. But for Keats, there is nothing "behind" phenomena; the experience beyond individuality is the experience of the phenomena itself.

CHAPTER SIX

1. Baudelaire, *Paris Spleen*, 16.

2. Bourdieu, *Distinction*. The social critique of aesthetics was not of course confined to Bourdieu-style sociological accounts. For two particularly influential literary critical examples, see Armstrong, *Desire and Domestic Fiction*, and Eagleton, *Ideology of the Aesthetic*.

3. There are three distinct ways of treating affect and experience in recent criticism. One mode, inflected by neuroscientific and cognitive scientific approaches, is exemplified by critics like Blakey Vermule (*Why Do We Care?*) and Alan Richardson (*The Neural Sublime*). Another mode, inflected by philosophical and sociological approaches, is exemplified by critics like Sianne Ngai (*Ugly Feelings*) and Phillip Fisher (*Wonder, the Rainbow, and the Aesthetics*). Finally, Gérard Genette (*The Aesthetic Relation*) and Charles Altieri (*Painterly Abstraction*) extend and develop the Kantian account of aesthetic experience.

4. See Kaufman, "Red Kant."

5. Rancière, *Aesthetics and Its Discontents*, 13.

6. See Dimock, *Through Other Continents*, and Kunin, "Artifact, Poetry As."

7. Guillory, "Sokal Affair"; Latour, "Why Has Critique Run Out of Steam?"

8. Fried, *Art and Objecthood*; Felski, *Uses of Literature*.

9. For an influential discussion of postmodern art as the critique of art, see Owens, *Beyond Recognition*.

10. Bernhard, *Woodcutters*. Subsequent references are given in the text. This is the central novel in a trilogy of works about art and artists—it is preceded by *The Loser* and followed by *Old Masters*. My decision to focus on *Woodcutters* is dictated partly by the clarity and intensity with which Bernhard's view of art is presented thematically in this book and partly by the fact that several features—which I explore below—of the form of its first-person narration make it a particularly compelling site for exploring Bernhard's commitment to that mode.

11. Matthias Konzett draws from Bernhard's acute sense of Austria's Nazi past in describing him as an "early postmodernist in postwar Austrian literature" ("National Iconoclasm," 15). Bernhard turned his back on the avant-garde of his youth as part of what Konzett cites Geoffrey Hartman as calling the post-Holocaust reckoning that led art to become "suspicious of itself" (12). This suspicion, as we shall see, comes to bear a close resemblance to Bourdieu's critique of aesthetics. The resemblance is especially striking when both writers focus on the same object: Bourdieu and Bernhard offer nearly identical critiques of Heidegger's obscurity as a tactic for gaining recognition. Bernhard's critique is developed in his novel *Old Masters*, Bourdieu's in *Political Ontology of Martin Heidegger*.

12. Bernhard is not alone in accepting Bourdieu's analysis of the social role of aesthetic judgment while rejecting his solution. As we saw in chapter 1, John Guillory has argued that to simply erase the social claims of the aesthetic would be to deliver the social field entirely over to economic stratification (Guillory, *Cultural Capital*). I should also note here something that will become clear over the course of my discussion. Bernhard, in rejecting the idea that the elimination of the aesthetic will rehabilitate the social, also rejects the idea that a robust aesthetic realm can play a redemptive social role. See Leo Bersani's *The Culture of Redemption* for an account of literary history relevant to Bernhard's position in this respect.

13. On the libel suit that greeted publication of *Woodcutters* and the subsequent banning of the novel in Austria, see Honegger, *Thomas Bernhard*, 239–42. I take up the implications of identifying *Woodcutters'* first-person speaker with Bernhard in detail below.

14. See especially Gellen and Norberg, "The Unconscionable Critic": "The narrator, silent and immobile in his armchair, assumes the role of the spectator who sits in the darkened theater and remains invisible to the actors" (58). The authors also describe the hostility to the social as such in the novel. But where they take this to mean that the narrator's critique is unreasonable—in the sense that he expresses no reason for his hostility to the social—I will argue that it is in fact animated by both a reasonable rejection of recognition and a reasoned commitment to a mode of collective being outside recognition. For a reading of Bernhard's critical position that attends to its properties as "second order observation which observes observations and distinguishes distinctions," see Theisen, "Art of Erasing Art," 552.

15. *Old Masters*, which takes place entirely in a well-lit museum, provides an extended version of the critique concentrated in these few pithy statements in *Woodcutters*.

16. For the classic account of Diderot's antitheatrical aesthetics, see Fried, *Absorption and Theatricality*. On the ubiquity of the theme of art's failure in Bernhard, see Sharp, "Thomas Bernhard," 206. For a reading of Bernhard's sense of the failure of art that links it to Benjamin's concept of the loss of aura, see Harrison, "Social(ist) Construction of Art."

17. A number of critics have noticed the negativity with which Bernhard views the social as such. George Steiner objects to the novels' "obsessive, indiscriminate misanthropy," which he sees as motivated by "mere hatred" ("Black Danube," 127). Rudiger Gorner notes Bernhard's similarity, in his rejection of social relations, to Sartre, for whom the Other represents hell ("The Broken Window Handle," 92).

18. This phrase comes from Bernhard's *Old Masters* (34) and expresses his sense that scrutiny will expose the fatal theatricality of even the greatest works.

19. Mill, "Thoughts on Poetry."

20. This transformation, in which another person begins to utter the narrator's private thoughts, is most fully developed with respect to the figure of the actor. But this transformation is not restricted to the actor. It actually happens to *every* character in the novel, even Auersberger, who at one point declares, "Society ought to be abolished" (*Woodcutters*, 141). This ubiquity gives another twist to Bernhard's insistence that the actor's "philosophical metamorphosis" has nothing to do with the actor as a person he might meet outside the space of this particular dinner party (and the novel which encloses it). In fact, as we will see, formal properties of first-person narration make what happens between Bernhard and the actor a possibility for every other character. The possibility of relation sliding into identity is briefly realized for figures like Auersberger and Joana, and it is sustained throughout the second half of the novel for the actor.

21. "Moran both is and is not identical with Molloy." McHale, *Postmodernist Fiction*, 13.

22. Uhlmann, *Beckett and the Philosophical Image*, 36. See also Leo Bersani, who describes the "figure of nonrelationality" in Beckett's fiction ("Sociality and Sexuality," 103–4).

23. Uhlmann, *Beckett and the Philosophical Image*, 49.

24. Kenner, "The Cartesian Centaur," 62.

25. Beckett, *Molloy*, 17. Subsequent references are given in the text.

26. For the classic sociological account of subject formation—an account informed by Hegel—see Mead, *Mind, Self, and Society*. For an account of the centrality of the recognition dynamic to post–World War II politics, see Fraser, "From Redistribution to Recognition?"

27. Katz, *Saying I No More*, 20, 21.

28. McHale, *Postmodernist Fiction*, 13.

29. J. J. Long in *The Novels of Thomas Bernhard* argues that *Woodcutters* is "the most autobiographical of all Bernhard's novels . . . at the same time, it foregrounds fictional devices to a greater extent than Bernhard's other fictional works" (146). This is a good way of describing how Bernhard's "I" is transformed, rather than simply mimetic, first person. Mark Anderson notes the "metonymic" rather than "metaphoric" relations that bind different persons in the novel into an uncanny unity ("Fragments of a

Deluge," 125). Anderson describes this effort "to break down the barrier between self and other" as "the impossible, insane project behind Bernhard's texts" (126). He reads this "absolutist desire to merge with one's writing," however, as a quasi-suicidal effort to destroy subjectivity itself. His reading thus parallels Katz's reading of Beckett as a deconstructively inflected analysis of key features of Bernhard's project that nonetheless misreads, in my view, the nature of the prospect of "real satisfaction" and of the subjectivity that animates it.

30. De Man, "Autobiography as De-Facement," 920.

31. On the transformation of the lyric "I" in Western poetic traditions, see Grossman and Halliday, *The Sighted Singer*. For an account of this process in prose fiction, see Miller, *The Disappearance of God*. Writing of Emily Brontë, Miller argues that "the author herself has disappeared in her creation" (161). Brontë's own sense of the value of her creation is as a private enrichment of her own experience; the reader is needed only to "make it real" (162).

32. Michael Fried has identified a similar strategy in Courbet, whom he sees as attempting an "all but literal merger of himself as painter-beholder with the painting on which he was working" (Fried, *Courbet's Realism*, 224). Of course the difference in medium, which enables Bernhard to exploit the grammatical properties of the first person, means that the parallel between these figures remains distant.

33. Iser, "Subjectivity as the Autogenous Cancellation," 83.

34. The dramatic expansion of creative writing programs in the United States—one of the great transformations of higher education in the past half century—provides the ideal conditions for the democratization and generalization of Bernhard's way of disappearing from the social world. This offers a new perspective on the salience of the creative writing program to the project of aesthetic education. It has often been said that there are now more writers than readers of serious literature. What has not been noticed until now is that this condition approximates modernism's highest goal. The generation of audienceless writers now under training are Bernhard's ideal readers.

I want to stress the word *ideal*. The creative writing program as it currently exists—and as it has been described by Mark McGurl—is often hostile to Bernhardian transformation. As McGurl argues, the program is oriented toward *excellence*, the current preferred word for "valuable recognition." Furthermore, he makes a good case for why the preferred model for first-person narration in creative writing workshops—Raymond Carver—operates in a regime of recognition (McGurl, *Program Era*). Carver's minimalism provides a mechanism for lower-middle-class students to transform their lives in a process that McGurl calls "shame management." These workshops train the writer to create out of the materials of his life a less embarrassing surface.

There are good reasons why actually existing creative writing programs are oriented toward recognition at every level. These programs are, after all, embedded in the social world. But they don't have to be. The materials of their ideal existence have already been assembled: (1) the infrastructure and staff for training millions of Americans to write; (2) the desire on the part of undergraduates to write about their own lives; (3) the absence of an audience for most of this writing. In addition, there exists (4) a sense that the value of literature lies in its exteriority with respect to the social world of work, ambition, and utility.

All that remains to start up the machine that will enable millions to definitively solve the social problem is (5) the replacement of the old writing-program model, Raymond Carver, with the new writing-program model: Thomas Bernhard.

CHAPTER SEVEN

1. See Michaels, *The Trouble with Diversity*; Reed, *Class Notes*; Warren, *What Was African American Literature?*

2. Bonica et al., "Hasn't Democracy Slowed Rising Inequality?"

3. See Michaels, *The Trouble with Diversity*, 111–40.

4. See Noah, *The Great Divergence*, 43.

5. As we have seen, Marx doesn't think the principle of equality itself provides a means of overcoming economic injustice.

6. For an influential account of the Republican Party's capture of the white working class, see Kazin, *The Populist Persuasion*, 195–268.

7. For a classic account, see Fraser, "Rethinking Recognition."

8. See Thomas Frank's *What's the Matter with Kansas?* for an influential argument that the Right mobilized "cultural" values to entice voters to vote against their economic interests.

9. See Carpio et al., "What Was African American Literature?" Kenneth Warren's critics contest his argument that continuing to view Black writing through the lens of race has outlived its usefulness and now unwittingly serves anti-progressive interests. Gene Andrew Jarrett argues that racism extends beyond Jim Crow and continues to provide a focal point for African American literature's political efficacy. R. Baxter Miller points to the living memory of African American struggle as a principle of cohesion. Xiomara Santamarina argues that success in the struggle for redistribution is so unlikely that we should accept victories in the struggle for recognition as the best possible outcome. Only Sonnet Retman suggests that race and capitalism may be connected in such a way that the focus on race can contribute to a progressive response to our class problem. I take Gwendolyn Brooks to provide a model for how this might work.

10. Brooks, *Blacks*, 126. Subsequent references are given in the text.

11. One of the few critical studies to take up this poem at any length is Marsha Bryant's "Gwendolyn Brooks." Bryant sees Brooks as part of a generation of postwar writers that "sought to counter exotic images from the Harlem Renaissance and to resist negative stereotypes in contemporary media" (116). "I love those little booths at Benvenuti's" is clearly exemplary of this effort, and Bryant nicely contextualizes its appearance at "a pivotal point in the nascent civil rights movement. . . . Truman's desegregation of the armed forces in 1948" (123). I differ from her reading of the poem in two significant respects. First, she reads "Benvenuti's" as dramatizing the impossibility of contact between the races, whereas I point to the representation of color in the poem to argue that Brooks dramatizes the dissolution of racial difference in order to subject the prospect of this dissolution to scrutiny (124–25). Second, Bryant sees its companion poem, "Beverly Hills, Chicago," as stimulating "reflection on racial inequality," whereas I argue that it does the very opposite, thereby developing the visual logic of "Benvenuti's" rather than overturning it (127).

12. Critics have long seen the curiously transformed visual world of the poems of

Annie Allen as a "puzzle" (Spillers, "Gwendolyn the Terrible," 227). Claudia Tate, in "Anger So Flat," contrasts the "peculiarly abstract and extremely esoteric" style of this book with the "realistic depictions of urban setting" characteristic of Brooks's earlier work (140). Similarly, Spillers argues that "the literal situation is carefully disguised" ("Gwendolyn the Terrible," 231).

Most critics have understood the erosion of racial visual cues in *Annie Allen* in terms of Brooks's assimilationist tendencies, tendencies they saw as rewarded when the book won the Pulitzer Prize. For example, in "Sonnets of Satin-Legs Brooks," Karen Jackson Ford describes Brooks's "integrationist views" (346) and cites Don Allen's comment that *Annie Allen* was "written for whites" (368).

Evie Shockley, in *Renegade Poetics*, interprets the book in another way. She detects the presence of a Black aesthetic "different from—indeed, invisible to—the black aesthetic that began influencing [Brooks's] work in the late 1960's" (28). Like Shockley, I don't see the poems of *Annie Allen* as "integrationist," but unlike her, I do think there is a real continuity between these poems and the Black Arts–era Brooks of the late 1960s and beyond, in that the result of her experimental testing of the possibility of post-racial vision leads her to conclude that racial vision remains indispensable to a progressive American cultural politics.

13. What class is and how it is produced are famously fraught questions, which have divided the Left for decades. Marxists, post-Marxists, and liberal economists and political scientists all have distinct answers. I do not wish to enter these debates here (though for an indication of my views, interested readers should see my "What Was Neoliberalism?"). To understand the significance of Brooks's distinction between the display of wealth and the awareness of class, we need only believe that the economic deprivation of lower-class persons is causally related to the enrichment of the upper class. I think this is a "big tent" claim that nearly everyone on the Left can agree with, whether one thinks the cause is ultimately best explained as globalization, malign government policies, the nature of capitalism, the structure of the relations of production, the legacies of racism or sexism, technology, or some mix of all these factors.

This claim, however, should be distinguished from the economic politics that would follow from an unironic reading of the lines "We do not want them to have less / But it is only natural that we should think we have not enough." Such a reading might suggest that Brooks's politics are broadly consistent with the postwar transformation of the New Deal into a vision of the "affluent society," where a rising tide lifts all boats. In this vision, the enrichment of the top does not come at the expense of the deprivation of the bottom. (I am grateful to Adrienne Brown and Mary Esteve for this suggestion.) However, the affective tone of the passage—expressive of mingled anger, shame, and resentment—as well as Brooks's acute sensitivity to the exclusion of many Blacks from postwar prosperity, leads me to believe that the poet does not share this benign economic vision, one that under neoliberalism would come to seem like sheer fantasy.

14. For an influential example, see Henry Louis Gates Jr.'s introduction to Gates and Kwame Appiah's *"Race," Writing, and Difference*.

15. My claim for the distinctiveness of the position I associate with Brooks should be seen in the context of critical race studies on the one hand and the burgeoning field of "intersectionality" on the other. At least since Stuart Hall's famous argument that class is lived through race ("Race, Articulation, and Societies"), theorists have attended to

the imbrication of race and class in the production of subjectivity. But Brooks's thought experiment enables us to test the proposition that race makes class position visible. This has nothing to do with subjectivity and everything to do with epistemology. In other words, these poems will not help us with the question of the shared role of class and race in producing inequality. Assuming that we are interested only in the *outcome* that most Americans are economically deprived, Brooks's poems suggest that we *still* be interested in race as a politically useful index of economic injustice. This position can be described as "intersectionalist" if we accept Devon W. Carbado's recent argument that "intersectionality reflects a commitment neither to subjects nor to identities per se, but, rather, to marking and mapping the production and contingency of both" ("Colorblind Intersectionality," 815). But I would still want to note that Brooks, as I read her, is interested not in the *production* of subject position but in its *legibility*, which gives the implicit argument I take her to make an emphasis different from most work traveling under the intersectionality rubric.

16. "Inequality."

17. "Race Relations in America."

18. Solt, "Economic Inequality and Democratic Political Engagement."

19. Norton and Ariely, "Building a Better America," 12.

20. Norton and Ariely, 9.

21. Krugman, "Defining Prosperity Down."

22. See, for example, Fredric Jameson's argument that postmodern culture frustrates our ability to place ourselves relative to the social whole (*Postmodernism*, 1–54). See also Timothy Noah's argument that "Americans' overconfidence in upward mobility . . . has become the rationale for indifference toward income inequality—a rationale built on a demonstrably false basis" (*The Great Divergence*, 43).

23. Bloom, *How Pleasure Works*, 15.

24. Tucker, *Moment of Racial Sight*, 11. While I am indebted to Irene Tucker's argument about the capacity of race to convey social knowledge *immediately*, I should note that I develop this idea in a way rather different from her approach in her book. Whereas Tucker historicizes the cognitive dimension of race in eighteenth- and nineteenth-century contexts in which race paradoxically communicates something like the nature of the human as such, I focus on how race, in the twentieth-century American context, comes to carry a specific kind social information, that of class position.

25. Lin, *Taipei*, 187.

26. See Taylor, "The Politics of Recognition."

27. See my *American Literature and the Free Market*, 1–26.

28. See, for example, Shockley, who disagrees with earlier critics regarding the value of these "reportorial" poems but not their status as realistic portrayals of "racial and class dynamics at the intersections of white and black Chicago" (*Renegade Poetics*, 52–53).

29. Jacobs, *Death and Life of Great American Cities*, 23. Subsequent references are given in the text.

30. Jameson, *Postmodernism*, 267. If the economic structure of the United States were simple enough to understand with the kind of tools Jameson brings to bear, the population would hardly need his help.

31. For a good account of how urban renewal served segregationist aims in Brooks's Chicago, see Cohen and Taylor, *America Pharaoh*.

32. My way of describing how race communicates knowledge intentionally echoes how F. A. Hayek describes price in his seminal 1949 essay, "Use of Knowledge in Society." In my view, Brooks's world is one in which race—as an index readily legible to embodied observers—provides the crucial corrective information otherwise invisible in the price system: knowledge of the systematic inequity that that system generates.

33. Several critics have read "In the Mecca" in relation to Jacobs's concerns. Daniela Kukrechtova, in "Death and Life of a Chicago Edifice," associates the Mecca with the housing projects erected during urban renewal in a process "parodied among blacks as 'negro removal'" (458). But while she aptly articulates Black resistance to urban renewal, she misreads the status of the Mecca both in Brooks's poem and in history. John Lowney, in "'A Material Collapse That Is Construction,'" shows that in fact the building represented the state of the city that urban renewal was designed to eliminate. "Perhaps no other building symbolized post WW2 urban decline more starkly than the Mecca building," he writes, noting that it was built in 1891 and demolished by the Illinois Institute of Technology to make way for Mies van der Rohe's modernist icons on its campus (3–4). Lowney points out the extent to which urban renewal served racist aims, and he argues that Brooks's poem "interrogates the dystopian discourse of urban decline" in ways similar to Jacobs's critique of modernist city planning (4). But unlike Jacobs, who contrasts racist planning with a utopian free market, racism *also* infects the pre–urban renewal world of Brooks's Mecca.

34. Kent, "Poetry of Gwendolyn Brooks," 73.

35. Kent, 41.

CONCLUSION

1. Starr and Dettmar, "Who Decides?"

2. See Da, "Computational Case."

3. See John Guillory's characteristically acute statement of the problem in *Cultural Capital*. As in my extended engagement with Guillory in my first chapter, I think he diagnoses the problem here accurately, but the distance of twenty-five years has revealed the limits of his sense of the causes and remedies. Guillory writes, "The overturning of Kant's autonomous aesthetic is brought up short before Nietzsche's critique of morality" (25). He thus adopts in this instance a stance curiously similar to that expressed by Harold Bloom in his contemporaneous reaction against emerging trends in literary studies. At the time, Bloom famously described moral critics as "the school of resentment." But this linking of the narrow question of focus in literary study with a critique of morality as such seems wrongheaded to me. Whether the moral causes animating critics are the product of resentment is the wrong question to ask. The right question is, In what spheres do the training, talents, and practice of literature professors give them authority in the guidance of students? One can, as I do, embrace many of the moral attitudes urged by moral critics without thinking that the literature classroom is best viewed as a scene of moral instruction, or that literature professors are especially qualified to serve as moral guides.

Bibliography

Adorno, Theodor W. *Aesthetic Theory*. Translated by Robert Hullot-Kentor. Minneapolis: University of Minnesota Press, 1997.

Adorno, Theodor W. "Free Time." In Bernstein, *The Culture Industry*, 187–97.

Adorno, Theodor W. "On the Fetish Character in Music and the Regression of Listening." In Bernstein, *The Culture Industry*, 29–60.

Adorno, Theodor W., and Max Horkheimer. *Dialectic of Enlightenment*. Stanford, CA: Stanford University Press, 2002.

Allcott, Hunt, Luca Braghhieri, Sarah Eichmeyer, and Matthew Gentzkow. "The Welfare Effects of Social Media." *American Economic Review* 110, no. 3 (March 2020): 629–76.

Allison, Henry. *Kant's Theory of Taste*. Cambridge: Cambridge University Press, 2001.

Altieri, Charles. *Painterly Abstraction in Modernist American Poetry*. Cambridge: Cambridge University Press, 2009.

Anderson, Mark. "Fragments of a Deluge: The Theater of Thomas Bernhard's Prose." In Konzett, *A Companion to the Works of Thomas Bernhard*, 119–36.

Armstrong, Nancy. *Desire and Domestic Fiction: A Political History of the Novel*. Oxford: Oxford University Press, 1990.

Arsić, Branka. "What Music Shall We Have? Thoreau on the Aesthetics and Politics of Listening." In *American Impersonal: Essays with Sharon Cameron*, edited by Branka Arsić, 167–96. New York: Bloomsbury, 2014.

Aubry, Timothy. *Guilty Aesthetic Pleasures*. Cambridge, MA: Harvard University Press, 2018.

Auyoung, Elaine. "What We Mean by Reading." *New Literary History* 51, no. 1 (Winter 2020): 93–114.

Barrett, Lisa Feldman. *How Emotions Are Made: The Secret Life of the Brain*. Boston: Houghton Mifflin Harcourt, 2017.

Bate, Walter Jackson. "Negative Capability." In *Romanticism and Consciousness: Essays in Criticism*, edited by Harold Bloom, 326–42. New York: W. W. Norton, 1970.

Baudelaire, Charles. *Paris Spleen*. Translated by Louise Varese. San Francisco: New Directions, 1970.

Beckett, Samuel. *Molloy*. Translated by Patrick Bowles. New York: Grove Press, 1995.

Beggs, Mike. "Zombie Marx." *Jacobin*, July 14, 2011.

Bennett, Eric. "Dear Humanities Profs: We Are the Problem." *Chronicle of Higher Education*, April 13, 2018.

Bernhard, Thomas. *The Loser*. Translated by Jack Dawson. 1983. Reprint, New York: Alfred A. Knopf, 1991.

Bernhard, Thomas. *Old Masters*. Translated by Ewald Osers. 1985. Reprint, Chicago: University of Chicago Press, 1989.

Bernhard, Thomas. *Woodcutters*. Translated by David McLintock. 1984. Reprint, New York: Vintage Books, 1987.

Bernstein, J. M., ed. *The Culture Industry: Selected Essays on Mass Culture*. New York: Routledge, 1991.

Bersani, Leo. *The Culture of Redemption*. Cambridge MA: Harvard University Press, 1990.

Bersani, Leo. "Sociality and Sexuality." In *Is the Rectum a Grave? And Other Essays*, 102–19. Chicago: University of Chicago Press, 2010.

Bhardwaj, Kiran. "Higher and Lower Pleasures and Our Moral Psychology." *Res Cogitans* 1, no. 1 (2010): 126–31.

Bloom, Harold. *The Western Canon: The Books and School of the Ages*. New York: Riverhead, 1995.

Bloom, Paul. *How Pleasure Works: The New Science of Why We Like What We Like*. New York: W. W. Norton, 2011.

Bonica, Adam, Nolan McCarty, Keith T. Poole, and Howard Rosenthal. "Why Hasn't Democracy Slowed Rising Inequality?" *Journal of Economic Perspectives* 27, no. 3 (Summer 2013): 103–24.

Borges, Jorge Luis. *Borges: Selected Nonfictions*. Edited by Eliot Weinberger. New York: Penguin Books, 1999.

Bourdieu, Pierre. *Distinction: A Social Critique of the Judgement of Taste*. New York: Routledge, 1986.

Bourdieu, Pierre. *The Political Ontology of Martin Heidegger*. Cambridge: Polity, 1991.

Bromwich, David. *Politics by Other Means: Higher Education and Group Thinking*. New Haven, CT: Yale University Press, 1992.

Brooks, Gwendolyn. *Blacks*. Chicago: Third World Press, 1987.

Brown, Nicholas. *Autonomy: The Social Ontology of Art under Capitalism*. Durham, NC: Duke University Press, 2019.

Bryant, Marsha. "Gwendolyn Brooks, *Ebony*, and Postwar Race Relations." *American Literature* 79, no. 1 (March 2007): 113–41.

Buchenwald, Jed Z. "Afterword: F. L. Holmes and the History of Science." In *Investigative Pathways: Patterns and Stages in the Careers of Experimental Scientists*, by Fredric Lawrence Holmes, 193–202. New Haven, CT: Yale University Press, 2004.

Callard, Agnes. *Aspiration: The Agency of Becoming*. Oxford: Oxford University Press, 2018.

Callard, Agnes. "Liberal Education and the Possibility of Valuational Progress." *Social Philosophy and Policy* 34, no. 2 (Winter 2017): 1–22.

Cameron, Sharon. *Impersonality: Seven Essays*. Chicago: University of Chicago Press, 2007.

Cameron, Sharon. *Lyric Time: Dickinson and the Limits of Genre*. Baltimore: Johns Hopkins University Press, 1979.

Carbado, Devon W. "Colorblind Intersectionality." *Signs* 38, no. 4 (Summer 2013): 811–45.

Carpio, Glenda, Gene Andrew Jarrett, R. Baxter Miller, Sonnet Retman, Marlon B. Ross, Xiomara Santamarina, Rafia Zafar, and Kenneth Warren. "What Was African American Literature?" *PMLA* 128, no. 2 (March 2013): 386–408.

Clune, Michael W. *American Literature and the Free Market*. Cambridge: Cambridge University Press, 2010.

Clune, Michael W. "The Bizarro World of Literary Studies." *Chronicle of Higher Education*, October 26, 2018. https://www.chronicle.com/article/the-bizarro-world-of-literary-studies/.

Clune, Michael W. "The Hypocrisy of Experts." *Chronicle of Higher Education*, September 19, 2019. https://www.chronicle.com/article/the-hypocrisy-of-experts/.

Clune, Michael W. "Pop Disappears." *Los Angeles Review of Books*, July 28, 2013.

Clune, Michael W. "What Does Literature Know?" *3:AM Magazine*, January 24, 2014.

Clune, Michael W. "What Was Neoliberalism?" *Los Angeles Review of Books*, February 26, 2013.

Clune, Michael W. *Writing against Time*. Stanford, CA: Stanford University Press, 2013.

Clune, Michael W., John Sarneki, and Rebecca Traynor. "Cue Fascination: A New Vulnerability in Addiction." *Behavioral and Brain Sciences* 31, no. 4 (August 2008): 458–59.

Cohen, Adam, and Elizabeth Taylor. *American Pharaoh: Mayor Richard J. Daley—His Battle for Chicago and the Nation*. New York: Back Bay Books, 2001.

Cohen, G. A. "Review of Alan Wood's *Karl Marx*." *Mind* 92, no. 367 (July 1983): 44045; quotation is from p. 440. Quoted in Reiman, "Moral Philosophy," 152.

Cohen, G. A. *Rescuing Justice and Equality*. Cambridge, MA: Harvard University Press, 2008.

Collini, Stefan. "Against Prodspeak: 'Research' in the Humanities." In *English Pasts: Essays in History and Culture*, 233–41. Oxford: Oxford University Press, 1999.

Cowen, Tyler. *In Praise of Commercial Culture*. Cambridge, MA: Harvard University Press, 1998.

Da, Nan Z. "The Computational Case against Computational Literary Studies." *Critical Inquiry* 45, no. 3 (Spring 2019): 601–39.

de Man, Paul. "Autobiography as De-Facement." *MLN* 94, no. 5 (December 1979): 919–30.

Deppman, Jed. *Trying to Think with Emily Dickinson*. Amherst, MA: University of Massachusetts Press, 2008.

Dickinson, Emily. *The Poems of Emily Dickinson*, edited by Ralph W. Franklin. Cambridge, MA: Harvard University Press, 1998.

Diehl, Joanna. *Dickinson and the Romantic Imagination*. Princeton, NJ: Princeton University Press, 1981.

Dimock, Wai Chee. *Through Other Continents: American Literature across Deep Time*. Princeton, NJ: Princeton University Press, 2008.

Dowling, Linda. *The Vulgarization of Art: The Victorians and Aesthetic Democracy.* Charlottesville, VA: University of Virginia Press, 1996.

Dreyfus, Hubert. *Being-in-the-World: A Commentary on Heidegger's "Being and Time," Division I.* Cambridge, MA: MIT Press, 1991.

Eagleton, Terry. *The Ideology of the Aesthetic.* Oxford: Blackwell, 1991.

Edmundson, Mark. *Why Read?* London: Bloomsbury, 2004.

Emre, Merve. *Paraliterary: The Making of Bad Readers in Postwar America.* Chicago: University of Chicago Press, 2017.

Felski, Rita. *The Limits of Critique.* Chicago: University of Chicago Press, 2015.

Felski, Rita. *Uses of Literature.* Oxford: Wiley-Blackwell, 2008.

Ferguson, Frances. "Canons, Poetics, and Social Value: Jeremy Bentham and How to Do Things with People." *Modern Language Notes* 110, no. 5 (December 1995): 1148–64.

Fessenbecker, Patrick. "Critique: The History of a Premise." Essay published in the online colloquy "We, Reading, Now," Stanford Arcade, March 2015, https://arcade .stanford.edu/content/critique-history-premise.

Fessenbecker, Patrick. *Reading Ideas in Victorian Literature.* Edinburgh: University of Edinburgh Press, 2020.

Fisher, Phillip. *Wonder, the Rainbow, and the Aesthetics of Rare Experiences.* Cambridge, MA: Harvard University Press, 1998.

Ford, Karen Jackson. "The Sonnets of Satin-Legs Brooks." *Contemporary Literature* 48, no. 3 (Fall 2007): 345–73.

Foster, Thomas. *How to Read Literature Like a Professor.* New York: Harper Perennial, 2014.

Frank, Thomas. *What's the Matter with Kansas? How Conservatives Won the Heart of America.* New York: Henry Holt, 2005.

Fraser, Nancy. "From Redistribution to Recognition? Dilemmas of Justice in a Post-Socialist Age." *New Left Review* 1, no. 212 (July/August 1995). https://newleftreview .org/issues/I212/articles/nancy-fraser-from-redistribution-to-recognition -dilemmas-of-justice-in-a-post-socialist-age.

Fraser, Nancy. "Rethinking Recognition." *New Left Review* 3 (May/June 2000): 107–20.

Freud, Sigmund. "Thoughts for the Times on War and Death" (1915). In *Complete Psychological Works* (London: Hogarth Press, 1957), 14:289. Summarized in David J. Gordon, *Imagining the End of Life in Post Enlightenment Poetry*, 3. Gainesville: University Press of Florida, 2005.

Fried, Michael. *Absorption and Theatricality: Painting and Beholder in the Age of Diderot.* Chicago: University of Chicago Press, 1998.

Fried, Michael. *Art and Objecthood.* Chicago: University of Chicago Press, 1998.

Fried, Michael. *Courbet's Realism.* Chicago: University of Chicago Press, 1990.

Frow, John. *On Interpretive Conflict.* Chicago: University of Chicago Press, 2019.

Frow, John. "The Practice of Value." *Textual Cultures* 2, no. 2 (Autumn 2007): 61–76.

Frye, Northrop. "Polemical Introduction." In *The Anatomy of Criticism: Four Essays*, 3–29. Princeton, NJ: Princeton University Press, 2000.

Gallagher, Shaun, and Dan Zahavi. *The Phenomenological Mind.* New York: Routledge, 2012.

Gaskill, Nicholas. "The Close and the Concrete: Aesthetic Formalism in Context." *New Literary History* 47, no. 4 (Autumn 2016): 505–24.

Gates, Henry Louis, Jr. Introduction to *"Race," Writing, and Difference*, by Henry Louis Gates Jr. and Kwame Appiah, 1–20. Chicago: University of Chicago Press, 1992.

Gellen, Kata, and Jakob Norberg. "The Unconscionable Critic: Thomas Bernhard's *Holzfallen*." *Modern Austrian Literature* 44, no. 1/2 (2011): 57–75.

Genette, Gérard. *The Aesthetic Relation*. Ithaca, NY: Cornell University Press, 1999.

Genette, Gérard. *Essays in Aesthetics*. Lincoln: University of Nebraska Press, 2005.

Gibson, John. "Cognitivism and the Arts." *Philosophy Compass* 3, no. 4 (2008): 573–89.

Gleik, James. *Time Travel: A History*. New York: Pantheon Books, 2016.

Goldman, Alvin. *Simulating Minds: The Philosophy, Psychology, and Neuroscience of Mindreading*. Oxford: Oxford University Press, 2006.

Gordon, David J. *Imagining the End of Life in Post Enlightenment Poetry*. Gainesville: University Press of Florida, 2005.

Gorner, Rudiger. "The Broken Window Handle: Thomas Bernhard's Notion of Weltbezug." In Konzett, *A Companion to the Works of Thomas Bernhard*, 89–104.

Gorodeisky, Keren, and Eric Marcus. "Aesthetic Rationality." *Journal of Philosophy* 115, no. 3 (March 2018): 113–40.

Graeber, David. *Bullshit Jobs: A Theory*. New York: Simon and Schuster, 2018.

Graff, Gerald. *Professing Literature: An Institutional History*. 1987. Reprint, Chicago: University of Chicago Press, 2007.

Gray, John. *Hayek on Liberty*. New York: Routledge, 1998.

Grob, Alan. "Noumenal Inferences: Keats as Metaphysician." In *Critical Essays on John Keats*, edited by Hermione de Almeida, 308–30. Boston: G. K. Hall, 1990.

Grossman, Allen R., and Mark Halliday, *The Sighted Singer: Two Works on Poetry for Readers and Writers*. Baltimore: Johns Hopkins University Press, 1991.

Guillory, John. *Cultural Capital: The Problem of Literary Canon Formation*. Chicago: University of Chicago Press, 1993.

Guillory, John. "The Sokal Affair and the History of Criticism." *Critical Inquiry* 28, no. 2 (Winter 2002): 470–508.

Hagglund, Martin. *This Life: Secular Faith and Spiritual Freedom*. New York: Pantheon Books, 2019.

Hall, Stuart. "Race, Articulation, and Societies Structured in Dominance." In *Black British Cultural Studies: A Reader*, edited by Houston A. Baker Jr., Manthia Diawara, and Ruth H. Lindeborg, 16–60. Chicago: University of Chicago Press, 1996.

Harding, D. W. *Regulated Hatred, and Other Essays on Jane Austen*. 1940. Reprint, London: Athlone Press, 2001.

Harman, Graham. *Weird Realism: Lovecraft and Philosophy*. Alresford, Hants, UK: Zero Books, an imprint of John Hunt, 2012.

Harrison, Russel T. "The Social(ist) Construction of Art in Thomas Bernhard's *Alte Meister*." *Monatshefte* 101, no. 3 (Fall 2009): 382–402.

Hartman, Geoffrey. *Criticism in the Wilderness: The Study of Literature Today*. New Haven, CT: Yale University Press, 1980.

Harvey, David. "Marx's Refusal of the Labour Theory of Value." Reading Marx's Capital with David Harvey, David Harvey.org, March 14, 2018, http://davidharvey.org/2018/03/marxs-refusal-of-the-labour-theory-of-value-by-david-harvey/.

Hayek, F. A. "The Use of Knowledge in Society." In *Individualism and Economic Order*, 77–91. Chicago: University of Chicago Press, 1958.

Heidegger, Martin. "The Origin of the Work of Art." In *Martin Heidegger: Off the Beaten Path*, edited by Julian Young and Kenneth Haynes, 1–56. Cambridge: Cambridge University Press, 2002.

Henry, Michel. *Marx: A Philosophy of Human Reality*. Bloomington, IN: University of Indiana Press, 1983.

Honegger, Gritta. *Thomas Bernhard: The Making of an Austrian*. New Haven, CT: Yale University Press 2001.

Huhn, Tom, ed. *The Cambridge Companion to Adorno*. Cambridge: Cambridge University Press, 2004.

Hullot-Kentor, Robert. "Right Listening and a New Type of Human Being." In Huhn, *The Cambridge Companion to Adorno*, 181–97.

Hume, David. "Of Personal Identity." In *Immortality*, edited by Paul Edwards. Amherst, NY: Prometheus Books, 1997.

Hume, David. "Of the Standard of Taste." In *Selected Essays*, edited by Stephen Copley and Andrew Edgar, 133–53. Oxford: Oxford University Press, 2008.

"Inequality." *New York Times*, August 24, 2013.

Iser, Wolfgang. "Subjectivity as the Autogenous Cancellation of Its Own Manifestations." In *Samuel Beckett's "Molloy," "Malone Dies," "The Unnamable,"* edited by Harold Bloom, 82–91. New York: Chelsea House, 1988.

Jackson, Virginia. "Thinking Dickinson Thinking Poetry." In *A Companion to Emily Dickinson*, edited by Martha Nell Smith and Mary Loeffelholz, 205–21. Oxford: Wiley-Blackwell, 2008.

Jacobs, Jane. *The Death and Life of Great American Cities*. New York: Vintage Books, 1993.

Jameson, Fredric. *The Political Unconscious: Narrative as a Socially Symbolic Act*. Ithaca, NY: Cornell University Press, 1982.

Jameson, Fredric. *Postmodernism, or The Cultural Logic of Late Capitalism*. Durham, NC: Duke University Press, 1991.

Johnson, Greg. *Emily Dickinson: Perception and the Poet's Quest*. Tuscaloosa: University of Alabama Press, 1985.

Jones, Peter. "Hume on the Arts and the Standard of Taste: Texts and Context." In *The Cambridge Companion to Hume*, edited by David Fate Norton, 414–47. 2nd ed. Cambridge: Cambridge University Press, 2009

Kahneman, Daniel. *Thinking Fast and Slow*. New York: Farrar, Straus, and Giroux, 2013.

Kaledin, Arthur. *Tocqueville and His America: A Darker Horizon*. New Haven, CT: Yale University Press, 2011.

Kane, Brian. *Sound Unseen: Acousmatic Sound in Theory and Practice*. Oxford: Oxford University Press, 2014.

Kant, Immanuel. *The Critique of the Power of Judgment*. Cambridge: Cambridge University Press, 2001.

Katz, Daniel. *Saying I No More: Subjectivity and Consciousness in the Prose of Samuel Beckett*. Evanston, IL: Northwestern University Press, 1999.

Kaufman, Robert. "Adorno's Social Lyric and Literary Criticism Today." In Huhn, *The Cambridge Companion to Adorno*, 354–75.

Kaufman, Robert. "Red Kant, or The Persistence of the Third Critique in Adorno and Jameson." *Critical Inquiry* 26, no. 4 (Summer 2000): 682–724.

Kazin, Michael. *The Populist Persuasion: An American History*. Ithaca, NY: Cornell University Press, 1998.

Keats, John. "Ode to a Nightingale." In *Keats's Poetry and Prose*, edited by Jeffery N. Cox, 459. New York: W. W. Norton, 2009.

Keats, John. "Why did I laugh to-night? No voice will tell." In *Keats's Poetry and Prose*, 333.

Keen, Steve. *Debunking Economics: The Naked Emperor of the Social Sciences*. New York: Zed Books, 2011.

Kenner, Hugh. "The Cartesian Centaur." In *Critical Essays on Samuel Beckett*, edited by Patrick A. McCarthy, 59–66. Boston: G. K. Hall, 1989.

Kent, George E. "The Poetry of Gwendolyn Brooks." In *On Gwendolyn Brooks: Reliant Contemplation*, edited by Stephen Caldwell Wright, 66–80. Ann Arbor: University of Michigan Press, 1996.

Khlebnikov, Velemir. "The Lone Performer," trans. Gary Kern. In *Twentieth Century Russian Poetry*, ed. Yevgeny Yevtushenko, 121. New York: Anchor Books, 1994.

Kirsch, Louis P., Cosimo Urgesi, and Emily S. Cross. "Shaping and Reshaping the Aesthetic Brain: Emerging Perspectives on the Neurobiology of Embodied Aesthetics." *Neuroscience and Biobehavioral Reviews* 62 (March 2016): 56–68.

Knights, Ben. *Pedagogic Criticism: Reconfiguring University English Studies*. London: Palgrave Macmillan, 2017.

Konzett, Matthias. "Introduction: National Iconoclasm; Thomas Bernhard and the Austrian Avant-Garde." In Konzett, *A Companion to the Works of Thomas Bernhard*, 1–23.

Konzett, Matthias, ed. *A Companion to the Works of Thomas Bernhard*. Rochester, NY: Camden House, 2002.

Krugman, Paul. "Defining Prosperity Down." *New York Times*, July 7, 2013. http://www .nytimes.com/2013/07/08/opinion/krugman-defining-prosperity-down.html.

Kuhn, Thomas. *The Structure of Scientific Revolutions*. Chicago: University of Chicago Press, 1996.

Kukrechtova, Daniela. "The Death and Life of a Chicago Edifice: Gwendolyn Brooks' 'In the Mecca.'" *African American Review* 42, no. 2/3 (Summer/Fall 2009): 457–72.

Kunin, Aaron. "Artifact, Poetry As." In *The Princeton Encyclopedia of Poetry and Poetics*, edited by Roland Greene, Stephen Cushman, Clare Cavanaugh, Jahan Ramazani, Paul Rouzer, Harris Feinsod, David Marno, and Alexandra Slessarev, 87–89. 4th ed. Princeton, NJ: Princeton University Press, 2012.

Kunin, Aaron. *Love Three*. Seattle: Wave Books, 2019.

Kunin, Aaron. "Would Vanessa Place Be a Better Poet If She Had Better Opinions?" *Nonsite*, September 26, 2015.

Larson, Kerry. *Imagining Equality in Nineteenth Century American Literature*. Cambridge: Cambridge University Press, 2008.

Latour, Bruno. "Why Has Critique Run Out of Steam?" *Critical Inquiry* 30, no. 2 (Winter 2004): 225–48.

Leiter, Brian. "Why Marxism Still Does Not Need Normative Theory." *Analyse & Kritik* 37, no. 1/2 (November 2015): 23–50.

Levine, Caroline. *Forms: Rhythm, Hierarchy, Network*. Princeton, NJ: Princeton University Press, 2017.

Lin, Tao. *Taipei*. New York: Vintage Books, 2013.

Long, J. J. *The Novels of Thomas Bernhard*. Rochester, NY: Camden House, 2001.

Lorentzen, Christian. "Like This or Die: The Fate of the Book Review in the Age of the Algorithm." *Harper's*, April 2019. https://harpers.org/archive/2019/04/like-this-or-die/.

Lowney, John. "'A Material Collapse That Is Construction': History and Counter Memory in Gwendolyn Brooks' 'In the Mecca.'" *Melus* 23, no. 3 (Fall 1998): 3–21.

Lutrull, Daniel. "Jacobs: From Slavery to Solidarity." Unpublished manuscript, March 31, 2020, PDF.

Maguire, Matthew W. *The Conversion of Imagination: From Pascal through Rousseau to Tocqueville*. Cambridge, MA: Harvard University Press, 2006.

Maraniss, David. *Once in a Great City: A Detroit Story*. New York: Simon and Schuster, 2016.

Marx, Karl. "Critique of the Gotha Program." In Tucker, *The Marx-Engels Reader*, 541.

Marx, Karl. *Capital*, 1:280. London: Pelican Boks, 1976. Quoted in Reiman, "Moral Philosophy," 165.

Marx, Karl, and Friedrich Engels. *The Communist Manifesto*. Edited by Gareth Stedman Jones. New York: Penguin, 2006.

McGurl, Mark. *The Program Era: Postwar Fiction and the Rise of Creative Writing*. Cambridge, MA: Harvard University Press, 2009.

McHale, Brian. *Postmodernist Fiction*. London: Taylor and Francis, 1987.

Mead, George Herbert. *Mind, Self, and Society*. Chicago: University of Chicago Press, 1934.

Michaels, Walter Benn. "Forgetting Auschwitz: Jonathan Littell and the Death of a Beautiful Woman." *American Literary History* 25, no. 4 (Winter 2013): 915–30.

Michaels, Walter Benn. *The Trouble with Diversity: How We Learned to Love Identity and Ignore Inequality*. New York: Henry Holt, 2007.

Mill, J. S. "Thoughts on Poetry and Its Varieties." In *Dissertations and Discussions, Politics, Philosophy, and History*, 1:89–120. London: Henry Holt, 1859.

Miller, J. Hillis. *The Disappearance of God: Five Nineteenth Century Writers*. Cambridge, MA: Harvard University Press, 1963.

Mirowski, Philip. *More Heat Than Light: Economics as Social Physics, Physics as Nature's Economics*. Cambridge: Cambridge University Press, 1989.

Mootry, Maria K., and Gary Smith, eds. *A Life Distilled: Gwendolyn Brooks, Her Poetry and Fiction*. Champaign: University of Illinois Press.

Moran, Richard. *The Philosophical Imagination*. Oxford: Oxford University Press, 2017.

Muller, Jerry Z. *The Tyranny of Metrics*. Princeton, NJ: Princeton University Press, 2018.

Nabokov, Vladimir. *Nikolai Gogol*. New York: New Directions, 1961.

Nathanson, Tenney. "'The Birds Swim through the Air at Top Speed': Kinetic Identification in Keats, Whitman, Stevens, and Dickinson (Notes towards a Poetics)." *Critical Inquiry* 42, no. 2 (Winter 2016): 395–410.

Nelson, Maggie. *The Argonauts*. Minneapolis: Graywolf Press, 2016.

Ngai, Sianne. *Our Aesthetic Categories: Zany, Cute, Interesting*. Stanford, CA: Stanford University Press, 2013.

Ngai, Sianne. *Ugly Feelings*. Cambridge, MA: Harvard University Press, 2007.

Nguyen, C. Thi. "Autonomy and Aesthetic Engagement." *Mind*, September 24, 2019.

Nietzsche, Friedrich. *The Birth of Tragedy: Basic Writings of Nietzsche*. Translated by Walter Kaufman. New York: Modern Library, 2000.

Noah, Timothy. *The Great Divergence: America's Growing Inequality Crisis and What We Can Do about It*. London: Bloomsbury, 2013.

North, Joseph. *Literary Criticism: A Concise Political History*. Cambridge, MA: Harvard University Press, 2017.

Norton, Michael I., and Dan Ariely. "Building a Better America—One Wealth Quintile at a Time." *Perspectives on Psychological Science* 6, no. 1 (January 2011): 9–12.

O'Hara, Frank. "The Day Lady Died." In *Collected Poems*, edited by Donald Allen, 325. Berkeley: University of California Press, 2003.

Owens, Craig. *Beyond Recognition: Representation, Power, and Culture*. Berkeley: University of California Press, 1994.

Panagia, Davide. *Rancière's Sentiments*. Durham, NC: Duke University Press, 2018.

Parfit, Derek. *Reasons and Persons*. Oxford: Oxford University Press, 1996.

Peffer, R. G. *Marxism, Morality, and Social Justice*. Princeton, NJ: Princeton University Press, 1990.

Peterson, Katie. "Surround Sound: Dickinson's Self and the Hearable." *Emily Dickinson Journal* 14, no. 2 (2005): 76–88.

Pfahl, Linda von. "The Ethics of Negative Capability." *Nineteenth Century Contexts* 33, no. 5 (December 2011): 451–66.

Piper, Andrew. "The Select." In "Computational Literary Studies: A *Critical Inquiry* Online Forum." *Critical Inquiry*, April 1, 2019. https://critinq.wordpress.com/ 2019/03/31/computational-literary-studies-a-critical-inquiry-online-forum/.

Polanyi, Michael. *The Tacit Dimension*. Chicago: University of Chicago Press, 1999.

Porter, David. *Dickinson: The Modern Idiom*. Cambridge, MA: Harvard University Press, 1981.

Postone, Moishe. *Time, Labor, and Social Domination: A Reinterpretation of Marx's Critical Theory*. Cambridge: Cambridge University Press, 1996.

The Princeton Encyclopedia of Poetry and Poetics. Edited by Roland Greene, Stephen Cushman, Clare Cavanaugh, Jahan Ramazani, Paul Rouzer, Harris Feinsod, David Marno, and Alexandra Slessarev. Princeton, NJ: Princeton University Press, 2012.

"Race Relations in America: Chasing the Dream." *Economist*, August 24, 2013. https:// www.economist.com/leaders/2013/08/24/chasing-the-dream.

Raffaelli, Tiziano. *Marshall's Evolutionary Economics*. New York: Routledge, 2003.

Rancière, Jacques. *Aesthetics and Its Discontents*. Cambridge: Polity, 2009.

Rancière, Jacques. *The Ignorant Schoolmaster: Five Lessons in Intellectual Emancipation*. Stanford, CA: Stanford University Press, 1991.

Rawls, John. *A Theory of Justice*, rev. ed., 393. Cambridge, MA: Harvard University Press, 1999. Quoted in Richard Moran, *The Philosophical Imagination*. Oxford: Oxford University Press, 2017, 85.

Reed Jr., Adolph. *Class Notes: Posing as Politics and Other Thoughts on the American Scene*. New York: New Press, 2001.

Reiman, Jeffrey. "Moral Philosophy: The Critique of Capitalism and the Problem of Ideology." In *The Cambridge Companion to Marx*, edited by Terrell Carver, 143–67. Cambridge: Cambridge University Press, 1991.

Richards, I. A. *Principles of Literary Criticism*. New York: Routledge, 2002.

Richardson, Alan. *The Neural Sublime: Cognitive Theories and Romantic Texts*. Baltimore: John Hopkins University Press, 2010.

Riley, Jonathan. "Mill's Political Economy: Ricardian Science and Liberal Utilitarian Art." In *The Cambridge Companion to Mill*, edited by John Skorupski, 293–337. Cambridge: Cambridge University Press, 1998.

Robbins, Bruce. "Discipline and Parse: The Politics of Close Reading." *Los Angeles Review of Books*, May 14, 2017.

Rose, Sam. "The Fear of the Aesthetic in Art and Literary Theory." *New Literary History* 48, no. 2 (Spring 2017): 223–44.

Rosenberg, Alex. "Cura Te Ipsum." *3:AM Magazine*, January 2, 2014.

Ross, Kristin. *Communal Luxury: The Political Imaginary of the Paris Commune*. Brooklyn: Verso Books, 2015.

Ruden, Sarah. "Walt Whitman Isn't America's Greatest Poet." *National Review*, August 26, 2019.

Selinger, Evan, and Robert P. Crease. "Dreyfus on Expertise: The Limits of Phenomenological Analysis." In Selinger and Crease, *The Philosophy of Expertise*, 213–45.

Selinger, Evan, and Robert P. Crease. Introduction to *The Philosophy of Expertise*, 1–10.

Selinger, Evan, and Robert P. Crease, eds. *The Philosophy of Expertise*. New York: Columbia University Press, 2006.

Shakespeare, William. *Hamlet*. In Wells et al., *The Oxford Shakespeare*.

Shakespeare, William. *Macbeth*. In Wells et al., *The Oxford Shakespeare*.

Sharp, Francis Michael. "Thomas Bernhard: Literary Cryogenics or Art on Ice." *Modern Austrian Literature* 21, no. 3/4 (1988): 201–15.

Shockley, Evie. *Renegade Poetics: Black Aesthetics and Formal Innovation in African American Poetry*. Iowa City: University of Iowa Press, 2011.

Sibley, Frank. "Aesthetic Concepts." 1959. Reprint, in *Approaches to Aesthetics: Collected Papers on Philosophical Aesthetics*, edited by John Benson, Betty Redfern, and Jeremy Roxbee Cox, 1–24. Leicester, UK: Clarendon, 2006.

Small, Helen. *The Value of the Humanities*. Oxford: Oxford University Press, 2013.

Smith, Barbara Herrnstein. *Contingencies of Value*. Cambridge, MA: Harvard University Press, 1991.

Smith, Noah. "What We Want Doesn't Always Make Us Happy." *Bloomberg*, May 1, 2019.

Solt, Frederick. "Economic Inequality and Democratic Political Engagement." *American Journal of Political Science* 52, no. 1 (January 2008): 48–60.

Soni, Vivasvan. "Introduction: The Crisis in Judgment." *Eighteenth Century* 51, no. 3 (Fall 2010): 261–88.

Spillers, Hortense. "Gwendolyn the Terrible: Propositions on Eleven Poems." In Mootry and Smith, *A Life Distilled*, 224–38.

Starr, Gabrielle, and Kevin Dettmar. "Who Decides What's Good and Bad in the Humanities?" *Chronicle of Higher Education*, September 17, 2019. https://www.chronicle.com/article/who-decides-whats-good-and-whats-bad-in-the-humanities/.

Steiner, George. "Black Danube." In *George Steiner at the "New Yorker,"* 117–27. New York: New Directions, 2009.

Tate, Claudia. "Anger So Flat: Gwendolyn Brooks' *Annie Allen.*" In Mootry and Smith, *A Life Distilled,* 140–52.

Taylor, Charles. "The Politics of Recognition." In *Multiculturalism,* edited by Amy Guttman, 25–74. Princeton, NJ: Princeton University Press, 1994.

Theisen, Bianca. "The Art of Erasing Art: Thomas Bernhard." *MLN* 121 (2006): 551–62.

Tocqueville, Alexis de. *Democracy in America.* New York: Library of America, 2004.

"Too Much Sociology." Editorial, *n + 1* 16 (Spring 2013).

Tucker, Irene. *The Moment of Racial Sight: A History.* Chicago: University of Chicago Press, 2012.

Tucker, Robert C. Headnote to "The Critique of the Gotha Program," by Karl Marx. In Tucker, *The Marx-Engels Reader,* 525.

Tucker, Robert C., ed. *The Marx-Engels Reader.* 2nd ed. New York: W. W. Norton, 1978.

Turner, Stephen. "What Is the Problem with Experts?" In Selinger and Crease, *The Philosophy of Expertise,* 159–86.

Uhlmann, Anthony. *Samuel Beckett and the Philosophical Image.* Cambridge: Cambridge University Press, 2006.

Vendler, Helen. *The Odes of John Keats.* Cambridge, MA: Harvard University Press, 1985.

Vermule, Blakey. *Why Do We Care about Literary Characters?* Baltimore: Johns Hopkins University Press, 2010.

Wall, Cheryl. "On Freedom and the Will to Adorn: Debating Aesthetics and/as Ideology in African American Literature." In *Aesthetics and Ideology,* edited by George Levine, 283–303. New Brunswick, NJ: Rutgers University Press, 1994.

Warren, Kenneth. *What Was African American Literature?* Cambridge, MA: Harvard University Press, 2012.

Wasson, Adam. "Dying between the Lines: Infinite Blindness in Lessing's *Laokoon* and Burke's *Enquiry.*" *Poetics Today* 20, no. 2 (Summer 1999): 175–95.

Wells, Stanley, Gary Taylor, John Jowett, and William Montgomery, eds. *The Oxford Shakespeare.* Oxford: Oxford University Press, 2005.

Winters, Yvor. *In Defense of Reason.* Athens, OH: Swallow Press, 1987.

Wood, Allen. "The Marxian Critique of Justice." *Philosophy and Public Affairs* 1, no. 3 (Spring 1972): 244–82.

Zamora, Daniel. "Should We Care about Inequality?" *Jacobin,* November 1, 2018. https://jacobinmag.com/2018/11/inequality-capitalism-markets-marx-political -economy.

Index

absorbed listening: absence of self experienced in, 117, 118, 119, 123, 125, 126–27, 129; as analogue to experience of dying in Dickinson's "I heard a Fly buzz—when I died—," 112, 115–16, 117–18, 121–22, 123, 124, 129; as analogue to experience of dying in O'Hara's "The Day the Lady Died," 121; and desire for death in Keats's "Ode to a Nightingale," 121, 123, 124, 127–30; "losing ourselves" in sound, 111, 113, 118, 120; perspective of, 117; precipitation out of, 120, 129, 130; psychological continuity and, 205n18; as state in which we don't have experiences, 113; subject/object distinction dissolves in, 125; Thoreau on, 122–23; vision threatens, 120–21; what could make the music more intense, 123; without being returned to yourself, 121

acousmatic sound, 121, 127, 128, 205n21

Adorno, Theodor: aesthetic education and, 193n14; on aesthetic hierarchy, 14–15; *Aesthetic Theory*, 14–15, 199n52; on artworks that withdraw from social world, 181; on artworks vs. commodities, 197n40; criteria of, 67; on culture industry, 55–56; "The Culture Industry," 14; *Dialectic of Enlightenment*, 199n52; "Free Time," 199n52; Hume's model of judgment vs., 5; on judgment and progressive politics, 14; on literary ideas as opinions, 106; "On the Fetish Character," 193n15

advertising, 10, 47, 51, 52–53, 56

aesthetic concepts, 88–92; challenging identifications of, 91–92; evaluation without, 105; Sibley on, 88, 91; subjectivity required for identifying, 91; tacit knowledge in acquiring, 90; training computers to recognize, 201n6

aesthetic democracy, 17, 18, 21

aesthetic education: academic institutions as shelters for, 66; academic literary criticism as vehicle of, 95; Adorno and, 193n14; for aesthetic concepts, 91; aesthetic judgment and, 9, 17, 18, 183; aesthetic sense as product of, 18; in art market, 53; better forms of life discovered through, 63; capitalism and, 14, 199n55; commitment to hierarchy required for, 26; consensus of experts in, 22; counterexamples in, 99; creative writing programs, 94, 185, 209n34; criticism

ties, 32–33; Marx as interpreted in, 37, 38; as neutral about individual desires, 60–61; paternalism in, 43; right-liberal attacks on elitism, 23, 25; on values and markets, 32. *See also* neoliberalism

Lichtenberg, Georg Christoph, 114

Literary Criticism (North), 22, 24, 25, 93, 200n2

literary studies: aesthetic dimension of, 94; aesthetic judgment in, 73, 183; antipathy toward aesthetic education in, 23; as "bizarro world," 78, 185; Bloom on, 213n3; capacity for extraliterary knowledge, 104; close reading, 22, 74, 75–76, 84, 200n11; computational, 78, 186; consensus in, 95; conservative approach to method in, 74; creative writing and composition and, 185; divorcing skills from content in, 68; foundational move in, 103; Hume's principles for, 66; as institution of aesthetic education, 2; "interest" and, 28; Kant's influence in, 202n30; at level of appreciation, 167; literary expertise, 1, 75, 76, 84–87, 91; as moral education, 186–87; neuropsychological research in, 195n37; noticing in, 102, 104; status of professional writing in, 92–96; suspicion of expertise in, 77–83; this model as descriptive of current practices in, 183–84; what constitutes literature for, 203n38. *See also* criticism

literature: entering into and looking out from works of, 69; history's relation to, 170; how and what does it know, 111; judgment in syllabus of, 184; preference for great, 185; value of studying, 181, 182. *See also* authorship; canon, the; first-person narration; literary studies; minority literatures; readers

Long, J. J., 208n29

Longfellow, Henry Wadsworth, 192n3

Lorentzen, Christian, 49, 50, 51, 53, 54, 198n42

Loser, The (Bernhard), 207n10

Lovecraft, H. P., 51, 202n29

Love Three (Kunin), 95

low culture. *See* popular (low) culture

Lowney, John, 213n33

Madame Bovary (Flaubert), 11

Maguire, Matthew, 34, 35

Malone Dies (Beckett), 148

mapping, 173, 174, 175, 177, 178

Marcus, Eric, 197n39, 201n27

marginal utility, 40, 41

markets: all values coordinated by, 2; art and, 10–12, 13, 22, 32, 53, 54, 197n40; capacity to respond effectively to consumer judgment, 51–55; coevolution of liberal democracy and, 65; correcting inequities of, 33; cultural institutions fostered by, 56; egalitarianism of, 39, 44, 47, 49, 50, 56–57, 65, 66, 77, 198n42; everything is available on, 47; human flourishing limited by, 43; liberals attempt to limit scope of, 44; Marx on development of, 44; neoliberal hegemony of, 9; neutralize any value not derived from consumer preferences, 47; preferences of, 46, 64; rationality attributed to, 43; seen as self-organizing, 42; as sole space for formation of aesthetic values, 54; sources of judgment organic to, 48; unrestricted control over society of, 39–44. *See also* market values

market values: aesthetic expertise conflicts with, 77; aesthetic values vs., 12–14, 32, 33; in classical liberalism, 32; elimination of aesthetic judgments and, 9; equalization process in, 36, 37, 39; liberalism on market inequities, 32–33; literature shaped by, 35; in neoclassical economics, 39–44; refusal of, 9; values beyond market determination, 3–4, 34, 35, 37, 48, 63, 66, 76, 199n55